GEORGE R MITCHELL was born in Aberdeen and currently writes narrative travel columns for DC Thomson publishers. He doesn't do tourism – he travels what he calls 'off-grid', getting under the skin of a country, its culture and its people. To date he has travelled extensively in around 80 countries. His most annoyingly wonderful, frustrating and fascinating country to be in, is Russia.

Mankind's Great Divides is his first non-fiction book.

Mankind's Great Divides

GEORGE R MITCHELL

Luath Press Limited

EDINBURGH

www.luath.co.uk

First published 2017

ISBN: 978-1-910745-77-9

The paper used in this book is recyclable. It is made from low chlorine pulps
produced in a low energy, low emissions manner from renewable forests.

Printed and bound by
Bell & Bain Ltd., Glasgow

Typeset in 11 point Sabon by
3btype.com

The author's right to be identified as author of this work under the Copyright,
Designs and Patents Acts 1988 has been asserted.

*I dedicate this book to the brave
East German citizens who tried to escape
to freedom, but who were shot dead –
by their own side – in cold blood.*

Nothing would be done at all if one waited until one could do it so well that no one could find fault with it.

JOHN HENRY NEWMAN

Contents

Acknowledgements

I wish to thank the following people who have helped me in their own unique ways.

Vicki Murray, Florian Felten, Buddy, Alastair Beattie, Andrew Cook, Tony Burgess of Just Defence Law Practice, Aberdeen.

To all my Russian friends – thank you for answering the countless questions I have bombarded you with over the years. But mostly, thank you for your hospitality and the kindness you have always shown me. I hope that continues after you read this book...

From the *Press & Journal* – Sonja Cox, Damian Bates, David Dalziel.

From DC Thomson – Gillian Grierson, Craig Houston.

To all at Luath Press, for their constructive criticism and honesty. They have helped me make this book so much better than it was.

I thank my family for their unwavering support. I am sorry about the worry I caused you whilst off researching chapters of this book.

Most importantly, I wish to thank all the people I met whilst researching this book. To people on both sides of the divide. To the friendly ones, to the ones who I agreed with, to those who I most certainly did not agree with and even the suspicious, wary and not so friendly ones. I thank you. You all taught me something new and made me see sides to an argument I had never previously considered.

To all peoples who find themselves stuck behind one of mankind's great divides, I would like to say the following: I hope that one day, you will all experience the freedom that I, through birth in the UK, am lucky enough to enjoy and hold so dearly.

Introduction

They came from nowhere. Suddenly in English, I heard someone shout my name.

I looked up – directly in front of me stood four men. Two police officers and two men in plain clothes: black leather jackets and shades.

'Eh yes?' I said.

'Stand up.'

Taken aback, I actually asked, 'Why?'

'Stand up!' he barked. I stood.

They moved with lightning speed. My laptop was snatched, my camera, my day bag, my passport. With a firm grip on each arm, they then walked me down from the statue to a waiting unmarked car. One of them asked me if I was a Muslim. 'No,' I said, not sure where this was going. Now shouting at me, he accused me of spying on behalf of Azerbaijan. I knew this was ridiculous, but I also knew I was in serious trouble and I am not ashamed to admit, at that point, I was terrified.

'Who do you work for?'

'I told you, I'm a travel writer, working on a book.' I produced my press card but he was not interested.

He shook his head. 'You are a spy.'

Armed with my written notes, the Quran and goodness knows what else, they bundled me into the waiting car. I was in a country unrecognised by the world and these people were accountable to no one. This wasn't good.

This is a real life incident, something that happened to me whilst researching this book. I knew it would not be easy, knew that some countries I visited could prove problematic, but I certainly had not expected that to happen.

* * *

SHE LOOKED AT ME with bewilderment and said, 'Why can't you ever go somewhere nice?' That was the reaction of my good friend Gwen when I told her where I would be going to research this book. I laughed, but have to admit, she had a point. Sensible people go to chill on a beach in

Spain, whilst I head off to places such as the West Bank in Palestine or eastern Ukraine.

My fascination with off-the-beaten-track countries started back in the early 1990s. Up until then, I had only seen the world's usual tourist spots. However, that soon changed when I took part in a dance exchange to Russia and was introduced to a world I never knew existed. Just to help paint the picture, I am an ex-tap dance teacher and choreographer. That first trip to Russia was a life changing moment for me, and seven months after returning to the UK, I had saved up enough money to go back and then travel for six months, desperate to explore and learn. With a growing fascination about the crumbling Soviet bloc and its politics, off I headed on a trip through Russia – against the advice of my worried Russian friends – and on the longest train journey in the world, the Trans-Siberian Express. I made it as far east as China, Mongolia, Hong Kong (which was still under British rule) and as far south as Singapore. This was all achieved in the days of yore before internet and mobile phones. What made these first set of travels so special was the fact that I was out there, on my own, with no instant contact with 'civilisation'.

In the early 1990s, Russia was only just opening up to the outside world and I visited every year, often for several weeks and up to three months at a time. I was teaching and performing dance, and even teaching English at one point. More importantly, I was meeting everyday people who had lived lives completely different to ours. I knew I wanted to learn more about their world and very soon, I was hooked. It was as if a drug had entered my veins, and it felt so good. Like a real drug, I was addicted and wanted more. I explored as much of Russia as I could, from Moscow to as far east as Lake Baikal in Siberia and as far south as Volgograd. The highlight being of course when in 1994 I rode the Trans-Siberian Express from Moscow to Beijing. I always travelled alone and mostly by train.

I also spent much time getting under the skin of the former communist states of East Germany, Hungary, Romania, Ukraine and Slovakia where borders had recently come tumbling down. This led me on to former Soviet states in the Caucasus and then into what I call the 'Stans': Uzbekistan, Kazakhstan and Kyrgyzstan.

I have never had a proper nine to five job and never lived in one place. Granted, it has not been an orthodox way of life, but it seemed right for me. It also felt natural for me to, in-between working, spend the past 20-odd years travelling deeper and deeper 'off-grid'.

To be honest, sometimes I have sickened myself with the drug that is travel. I went on the wagon and said to friends, 'I'm never doing this again, I'm done with it.' Nevertheless, like any junkie, I kept coming back to it, and in fact, my travelling has only increased in intensity over the years. I have to admit though; it is getting harder as I get older.

In the past five years or so, my interest has turned to borders that were not crumbling but growing. In many parts of the world, millions of people are not living free as we are here in the West. Walls and razor wire not only still exist, but also are being built at an alarming rate. I just knew there was a book in there somewhere.

Since 2013, I have written a weekly column for the Scottish newspaper *The Press & Journal*. My column is called 'Never A Dull Moment', and highlights my experiences in places such as Ukraine, Russia and the Middle East. However, this book is not a book about my travels, it's about the people behind the headlines, the ordinary people who live every day in and around divided lands in the Middle East, the Caucasus, Northern Ireland, East Europe and North Africa.

For my own interest, I had already travelled through some of the places I would be writing about in this book, Kosovo, Armenia, Georgia and Moldova, so my appetite had been whetted in advance. I had seen contentious border areas, but that was it. Now, I wanted to go back, with a mission to learn.

We live in a world of 24/7 breaking news and, sadly, every other day there seems to be a terrorist attack or break-out of violence that is worse than the one reported elsewhere a week previously. We are bombarded by powerful images and we are shocked when an atrocity happens, but as the reporters move on to the next big event, we quickly forget about what we just saw. I wanted to delve deep, to spend time in these places and find what it is like for those who live there once the cameras move on to the next big thing and the world forgets about them.

I am by nature an opinionated person. Sometimes that is good, sometimes not. Therefore, I have tried immensely hard not to take sides. For example, if I think the Armenians have been wronged by Azerbaijan, I say so. If I then feel the Azerbaijanis have been wronged by Armenia, I say so. I have tried to do this in each chapter. I did initially plan to give my own opinion at the end of each chapter and say which side I 'backed', but I came to realise that that was not important. I know from talking with various people that many will criticise me for not taking sides. For example, pro-Greeks will want me to support them over Cyprus, and Turks will want me to support their side. Each side has their own story to tell, often horrific.

Possibly the most explosive and well-known divide I have written about is Palestine. Recently, I found myself talking with a pro-Palestinian group in the UK. They were delighted to chat with me after I said I had spent much time there and had written about the situation. However, when I said I took no sides, they were horrified I would not totally back Palestine over Israel. I explained I am not pro-Israeli either and condemn all violence, but it did no good. Only 100 per cent support for 'their side' will be acceptable to many who read this book. I understand that.

Russia is not divided, but nonetheless, Russia gets an entire chapter all to itself. Why? Well, Russia, due to past connections, is 'involved' or has influence in many divides; it is an important country that holds much influence these days. After 23 years of travelling, working and often living in Russia, I have learned much from ordinary Russians and how they see their society. Therefore, I make no excuses for giving my opinion in the chapter about today's Russia and the path down which it is heading.

The open borders idea of Schengen is in itself a unique 'divide'. One outer ring border for an entire continent that is holding back a growing tide of immigration and the threat of terrorism. In this chapter, I unashamedly give my opinion on why I think it is well past its sell by date.

In my initial planning, I decided I did not want this book to be a long-winded factual read like an essay for an undergraduate paper. I have tried to find a balance between factual reporting and creativity. Some of my interviews had been prearranged in advance through people who knew people who knew people. The majority of my interviews though were conducted with individuals I met by chance, on the street or in a café. Real people, talking openly about their lives.

Real people they certainly are, but as per individual request, many names have been changed in order to protect identities.

With regard to the actual content of this book, you may agree with what I say, or you may not. *I am only reporting on what I saw, was told and experienced whilst there on the ground.* This book is not a political or personal endorsement of claims made by people or governments on either side of each divide.

I have travelled in roughly 80 countries over the years, but working on this book has been the most challenging project I have ever undertaken. It really is an accumulation of years of fascination and a desire to learn. After coming up with the idea in late 2013, I spent Christmas mulling over how I was going to do it. Where to start, what format it should take, and most importantly how to pull my cash together to fund it all, for I had no book deal, no backer, no advance.

It was just me, with semi decent camera, cheap laptop, Poundland notebook and a dozen biros. After six months of initial research, I hit the road in July 2014 and did around two months on the road at a time, then spent two months writing, before heading back out again. I finally completed the travelling/researching/interviewing in June 2016. Then of course followed the inevitable numerous and seemingly never ending rewrites and edits. What a learning curve that was.

I wrote screeds of notes while on the road, and because I was out every day, I wrote almost everything initially in notebooks. After you have experienced Friday Prayers in Jerusalem, there is only one way to spend the evening – sat out at a café with a cold beer and a pad of paper and pen. I far prefer that to sitting in front of a computer screen.

There is one immense divide that I would love to have written about: North and South Korea. It has been my wish to go to North Korea for more than 20 years. In 1994, I was in China and tried to get a visa, but Kim Il-Sung had just died and no one was getting in. The North Korean regime has to be one of the most undemocratic entities on our planet today. As a dictatorship, millions of its citizens live in abject misery. The stories from the growing number of people who have managed to flee this sickening regime reveal a horrific picture: a real-life Orwellian 1984. I would also like one day to visit and write about Kashmir, the highly contentious and dangerous divide between India and Pakistan. Maybe there is a need for a second volume of this book? We shall see...

To keep this book as up to date and as relevant as possible, in March 2017, I added in a small update paragraph at the end of each chapter, because much can change in time. Then again, when it comes to division and hatred, not much really changes.

George R Mitchell

1

Israel/Palestine

The mother of all divides

Official name	State of Israel (which defines itself as a Jewish and democratic state)
Capital	Jerusalem (disputed)
Population	Approximately 8.5 million
Currency	Shekel

Introduction

THE HOLY LAND. There is not another place like it on earth. The birth-place of the three main Abrahamic religions, Judaism, Christianity and Islam. A land that seems more divided today than it has ever been. In fact, I would say that the divisions here run deeper than any other I'd experienced whilst researching this book.

The 2014 war between Israel and Hamas is still very fresh in people's minds, including my own. The whole world watched with horror in the summer of 2014 as Hamas pummelled Israel with rockets and Israel bombarded Gaza. Many innocents, especially in Gaza, suffered and died.

I was very aware that I was about to research and interview people in a highly sensitive part of the world. In fact, it seemed to me that this part of the world is permanently at war, with ongoing stabbings, killings and shootings, especially in and around Jerusalem.

The What, Where and Why

Complicated is not the word. I am not going back to biblical times or the Birth of Jesus, or Muhammad ascending to heaven. It is for each person to decide what he or she believes. I will start with the British era that kicked off the lay of the current-day land.

Britain seized Palestine from the Ottomans in 1917, and through the Balfour Declaration, gave support for a national home for the Jewish people.

When Britain ended its Palestinian mandate in 1947, the UN recommended the partition of Palestine into two separate states, one Arabic and the other Jewish. The state of Israel was thus born in 1948, with the Arab High Committee rejecting the partition.

To bolster its population and new country, Israel took in Jewish immigrants from Europe, the Middle East and North America. Much later, it also took in immigrants from the USSR and Ethiopia, amongst others.

This resulted in the displacement of hundreds of thousands of Palestinians. Finally, in 1959, Yasser Arafat formed the fighting group Fatah, in Egypt. Its job: to carry out raids into Israel.

Israel has fought several wars with its neighbours, most notably the 1967 Six Day War. In 1967, Israel launched pre-emptive strikes against

Egypt and Syria, while Iraq and Jordan responded by attacking Israel. To the surprise of many, Israel defeated Egypt and took control of the Gaza Strip and Sinai. Israel also took the Golan Heights by defeating Syria.

Following the 1967 war, Israel faced attacks from all sides, especially from the PLO (Palestinian Liberation Organisation) which had committed itself to armed conflict.

In 1973, as Israel was observing Yom Kippur (the most important Jewish holy day) it suffered a surprise attack by Syria in the Golan Heights and by Egypt in the Sinai. Israel held on, but suffered heavy troop losses. The short but brutal war left many thousands dead on all sides.

There have been countless attempts at peace in this region and whilst some would say that progress has been made, peace is a long way off. Many call for a two state solution. Many call for Israeli withdrawal from the land it has 'occupied'. Others say Israel has a right to exist and should not retreat. Total stalemate.

The very existence of the State of Israel is somewhat controversial. Taking land that Palestinians say is theirs and repopulating it with Jewish settlers is even more controversial. It is worth noting, that the State of Israel is the only country in the world with a majority Jewish population.

Each divide in this book is complicated, and each one seems even more complicated than the one I had visited previously. However, Israel/Palestine really is the mother of all divides.

Bethlehem

If your idea of Bethlehem is all cuddly and sweet with images of stables and baby Jesus, or Frank Sinatra crooning the delightful carol 'Oh Little Town of Bethlehem', I am afraid you are going to be bitterly disappointed. It is none of the above.

Although Bethlehem stands in Muslim-dominated Palestine, Manger Square and the Church of the Nativity are in the middle of the old town. It is an important place for Christians because they believe that this is where Christ was born.

In the same square, just a stone's throw from the supposed birth spot, stands the Mosque of Omar. With religion and killing at the forefront of the problems in the Middle East, I had to visit Manger Square. I do not mean to offend any believer, but Manger Square did absolutely nothing for me. I found it tacky, full of touts and lacking in spirituality. I felt rather despondent.

I am reminded of a new church in central Moscow, the Church of the Saviour. Ironically, it was built under Putin's regime that is stuffed full of the old school and ex-KGB members, a regime that treated the Church and its worshippers with disdain at best and brutality at worst during Soviet times. Many Russians sarcastically refer to this new church as the 'Ministry of Religion'.

In Bethlehem, I queued with the pilgrims to enter the Church of the Nativity. Many were female Westerners, dressed in old-fashioned frocks and headscarves. They clutched their Bibles, eyes wide open in anticipation. After queuing for over two hours, I found myself down in the crypt, standing in front of the sacred place. But forget all about stables. If it all happened like it is said to have happened, and even if it happened here on the spot, it *did not* happen in a stable, it was inside a cave. The actual spot where Jesus is supposed to have been born is marked with a star. I filed past, yet was more interested in the people around me. Grown women and men stood beside me and wept openly, clutching their Bibles, some in a trance-like state.

Jews also revere Bethlehem as the birthplace of David, the King of Israel. Then throw in Rachel's Tomb, which is the burial place of the matriarchal Rachel, mentioned not only in Jewish and Christian old testaments but also in Muslim literature – you can begin to see how it all gets rather complicated.

Bethlehem is under Palestinian Authority control. It is normally tourist friendly, as pilgrims coming to Manger Square have long been its chief source of income. However, after the 2014 war between Hamas and Israel, many tourists were frightened off and the town has suffered immensely from lack of revenue. Some tourists have returned, but now they face another dilemma. The tragic ongoing war, terrorist attacks and the bombings by various countries in nearby Syria and Iraq, not to mention the increasing violent attacks and stabbings by Palestinians against Israeli forces – these incidents are currently scaring off many foreigners from coming to the Holy Land.

From day one of my first visit, I became friendly with a souvenir shop owner called Adel, a genuinely kind man who speaks good English. Adel's trade has been hugely affected not just by the recent war and attacks in other parts of Palestine, but also he claims that tourists are frightened off by war and IS in nearby Syria. The truth is, Bethlehem is not only a safe city, but also a very friendly one.

I have learned much from Adel over the past two years. His favourite line, which he never said lightly, was, 'There will never be peace in the land of peace'.

I have never seen Adel angry, stressed or unhappy. He has a wonderful smile and always seems at ease. He takes the complicated life of Palestine all in his stride. He rather reminds me of a spiritual wise man. I have lost count of the number of times I've sat out with him and talked about the problems in this fascinating land. He has taught me much about Palestine.

When you watch the news about Israel/Palestine, what do you see? You see many violent young men attacking Israelis at checkpoints. Yes, that does happen and sadly is increasing. Nevertheless, it is very wrong to assume that all Palestinians are violent. The West Bank, which includes Bethlehem, Ramallah, Hebron and Jericho, is not Gaza. People in the West Bank, most of them anyway, have no truck with the violence of Hamas in the Gaza Strip.

I have made numerous friends in the West Bank, ordinary working Palestinians, both Christian and Muslim. Everyone from small shopkeepers to families, taxi drivers and even a dentist. I feel humbled by the kindness they have shown me. Nowhere else in the world on my travels have I been made so welcome by so many. I never felt alone in Bethlehem and always felt that somebody 'had my back'. Moreover, this felt special, in a land in the middle of ongoing division and violence.

Built by Israel, the 'West Bank Barrier', cuts right through the heart of this holy place. Simply staggering in size, it dwarfed any division I would see whilst working on this book. A multi-layered defence system, it is still being built and will be around 700 kilometres in length when finished. It features walls, razor wire, a 200-foot wide exclusion zone in the middle, tracking equipment, anti-vehicle ditches and, in order to deter snipers in residential areas such as Bethlehem, the concrete walls are 26 foot high.

Palestinians claim the wall is apartheid and an annexation of their land. Israel claims the wall is needed to protect its citizens. Before it was built, there were dozens of terrorist attacks and suicide bombings, killing many Israeli citizens. The wall has largely stopped this. Yet, this 'wall of division' is seen by most of the world as illegal.

Standing right up close, it towered over me. As I walked, photographing at will, I looked up. Looking back down at me were Israeli troops in paint-splattered and fire-damaged watchtowers. On the Palestinian side, where I was standing, the wall is covered in graffiti and political slogans, some peaceful, others not so.

A sign on the Israeli side near one of the checkpoints declares that it is forbidden for Israeli citizens to cross into Palestinian territory. As for Palestinians from the West Bank who want to come to Jerusalem in Israel, they need permission, which I am told can often take months. I was free to cross through the divide as I pleased, but of course, the security was intense.

Away from the wall, the atmosphere in Bethlehem was relaxed. However, the next day on crossing through the wall and heading to Jerusalem for Friday Prayers, it was a different ball game altogether. Adel had already warned me. 'Remember, tomorrow is Friday Prayers. Be careful when walking round by the checkpoint. There has been many demonstrations on the Palestinian side after midday prayers. People throw stones and other things; you will see the new paint damage high up. It gets violent and the Israelis respond with tear gas. Jerusalem is also very tense now. Be very careful.'

Friday Prayers in Jerusalem

It was Friday, a very holy day indeed. Midday is Friday Prayers for Muslims, and then when the sun sets in the evening, the Sabbath begins for the Jewish people. Holy it may be, yet violent attacks are ongoing.

In recent years, dozens of Israelis have died and hundreds wounded in shootings, stabbings and car attacks carried out by Palestinians. Meanwhile, Israeli security has shot and killed approximately 200 Palestinians. I take no sides.

By 7.00am, I was standing in a queue of Muslim worshippers on the Palestinian side of the West Bank Barrier in Bethlehem. Friday is also one of the few days that Palestinians from the West Bank are allowed to cross into Jerusalem, but only with advance permission. Dozens were queuing; it took almost two hours to get through. No Muslim men under the age of 50 were allowed, I was told, as they are seen as the most likely to be involved in terrorism, so it was just me, women and lots of old men. We passed through metal cages, one at a time, past various checks and CCTV, into the military buffer zone. My bag was scanned and my passport checked by border guards behind thick bulletproof glass. Four soldiers carrying machine guns stood nearby watching every move intently. The Palestinians beside me were electronically fingerprinted, I was not. I received a smile, was wished a good day and was told I could proceed. A sign in English, Hebrew and Arabic read, 'Welcome to Israel. May you go in peace and return in peace'.

After 20 minutes in an old minibus, we arrived in Jerusalem and I was dropped off close to the walls of the old city. Jerusalem, although under Israeli control, is itself divided. The Western part of the city is Jewish-dominated and East Jerusalem is mainly Palestinian. Palestinians see Jerusalem as the capital of Palestine, this particular land having been taken by Israel from Jordan in the 1967 war. In the centre of it all is the old city itself. It is a tiny ancient city that is holy to the three main Abrahamic religions, Judaism, Christianity and Islam. In a city already divided between east and west, the old city is again divided, into four quarters.

The Dome of the Rock, located on the Temple Mount in the old city of Jerusalem, is one of the holiest religious sites in the world. It is truly magnificent and marks the spot where some Muslims believe the Prophet Muhammad ascended to heaven. Some believe differently and say that the Prophet ascended from the al-Aqsa Mosque. The area of the 'Temple Mount' (English name) is also revered by Jews, many believing that this is where god gathered together the dust to create the first human, Adam.

Close to the ancient walls of the old city, I sat down outside the famous Damascus Gate. The security was, as always these days, intense. Groups of Israeli police and army, watching for anything suspicious, were not only armed with machine guns, but some also held personal tear gas launchers. These people are ready for anything and I had no wish to get on the wrong side of them.

Suddenly a young man wearing a padded jacket walked our way; I just knew he was going to be searched. He was taken aside, one soldier did a full body search with intricate detail as the other stood looking out with his gun at the ready to deter anyone from coming over and challenging the search. Tensions here are the highest they have been for years. There is no trust, only suspicion and much fear. I could feel their fear. This city is walking on eggshells.

Jews are being stabbed in Israel and the West Bank on a regular basis. There is a very disturbing clip on YouTube taken from Israeli CCTV. At a

West Bank checkpoint, a Palestinian woman in a black hijab approaches. She has a handbag over her shoulder. She hands over what I guess may be her ID to the Israeli official and they start to talk. She is calm, he is distracted and drops his guard. Suddenly from her handbag, she pulls out a huge kitchen knife and lunges at him. Horrific. Even if you, the reader, feel sympathy for individual Palestinians as I do, an attack on any human being is wrong and cannot be acceptable, can it? After all, this soldier is also someone's father, brother, son. Thankfully, the man survived. The woman sadly was shot dead.

Nearby, an elderly Arab who was also being body-searched called over to me in English. 'Look at the way the Israelis treat us!' The soldier quietly ignored him, finished his search and let the man pass. I found it unnerving to see the mix of Muslims, Orthodox Jews and Israeli security all in close proximity, yet hardly even looking at each other.

It would soon be midday and prayer time for Muslims. Groups of Israeli security forces were getting ready for whatever lay ahead. I tried to communicate with various members of the Israeli security forces but none of them would talk with me. Many female Israelis held guns. They looked so young. I was later told that some are as young as 16 and doing their compulsory national service. I found their age very disturbing.

Roughly 200 metres away, barriers were being erected as the security forces attempted to stop those without permission from making it to their place of worship. Blocking Muslims from their holy place on their holy day – can you imagine the tension in the air? Both sides took their positions in the middle of the road. Muslims on one side, thick lines of heavily armed Israeli security on the other. Dozens of men put down their prayer mats, then taking their cue from the Imam, as one, were down on their knees in the prayer position. They prayed in the middle of the road, on the tarmac. It was a remarkable sight. The Israeli forces stood in silence inches in front. The word 'tense' does not even come close to describing this scene. I was right behind the Israeli line and, much to my surprise, was allowed to wander and photograph as I pleased.

After prayers, small scuffles broke out as some tried to get through the lines. Thankfully, unlike other Fridays when knife and gun attacks occur on a regular basis, nothing serious happened. The following week, while I was elsewhere, a Palestinian driver deliberately mounted the pavement in his car and killed a young Jewish child. Hamas called it 'an act of heroism'.

I slowly meandered the tiny cobbled streets of the Muslim, Armenian and Christian quarters of the old town. I made it as far as I could before being stopped by three Israeli soldiers. They were firm yet polite as they made it clear I could go no further. I tried without success to enter the area of the Dome of the Rock, but lines of Israeli security had every narrow street blocked off. Muslims with permission were allowed, but not me. Instead, I ducked into a tiny coffee shop for a delectable Arabic coffee, and took the opportunity to write up some notes. Feeling refreshed, I then decided to cross over into the Jewish Quarter.

Within minutes of walking, I came to a checkpoint. I placed my small daysack and camera on the conveyer belt before walking through the metal detector. I beeped. Ah, that must be the coins in my pocket. I took them out, placed them on a tray and tried again. I still beeped and it was obvious I was going to get a body search. Hand held metal detectors scanned me and I beeped like crazy as they ran over a side pocket in my combat shorts. It slowly dawned on me. How could I have been so damn stupid? For in that pocket was my Swiss army knife. I carry it most places; it is useful for 101 everyday things. But here, in Jerusalem on a Friday... Oh this did not look good. Directly in front of me, two armed Israeli officials.

'What's in your pocket?'

I held up both hands. 'It's my Swiss Army knife. I forgot about it. I genuinely didn't know it was in my pocket today. I'm really sorry.'

The small yet very sharp knife was taken from my pocket, then what followed was an awkward moment of silence between the one who was now holding my knife and his comrade. They looked at each other, seemingly unsure how to handle this.

I actually expected to be taken away for some serious questioning, and to be fair, I could not have blamed them. However, after looking through my documents and a few questions as to why I was here and what I was doing, I was told, 'You are free to continue, but you must leave this thing here. You cannot go into the Jewish Quarter with a knife. You can collect it later.'

Relived, I thanked him, apologised again and walked into the Jewish Quarter. Having my knife in my pocket that day had been a genuine mistake, but a voice in my head chided, 'you idiot'.

That said, even when you do not make a mistake you can still land in trouble in Israel. Tel Aviv airport for example has security I have never experienced anywhere on the planet. On entering, it does not seem so bad, well not in my experience anyway, but leaving seems to be a different matter. I have been taken aside, and asked about the West Bank. Did I go there? Do I know anyone? Whom did I speak with and about what? Stamps in my passport to countries such as Uzbekistan and Kyrgyzstan all made for more intricate questioning. Whilst bag searches are standard, Israeli security are now increasingly making travellers open their laptops and even log into their emails. You have no choice, you must do it, if you have any desire to leave the airport that is. If you do not comply, you are going nowhere. Personally, I think being forced to log into your emails so they can troll through them is a serious breach of your rights, but the Israelis make no excuses for intense security. They claim that if you want a hassle free airport experience then go on holiday to Spain. I personally have never had my emails checked, but have made sure my laptop is clean, by deleting links to documentaries I have recently watched. The last thing you want an Israeli official to see is a link to a BBC documentary about Hamas.

I was now face-to-face with the famous Western Wall where many Jewish worshippers were getting ready for the Sabbath. I stood a respect-ful distance and watched as men prayed, faces right up to the Wall. As is custom, many placed tiny pieces of paper – personal handwritten notes to God – into crevices in the wall. A poignant sight. An old man sat nearby in a chair reading religious text from a scroll. I discreetly managed to get a photo without disturbing him.

On returning to the checkpoint, my Swiss Army knife was duly returned to me with a friendly warning that I should never again carry this item whilst walking around Jerusalem or indeed any other check-point. 'Good advice,' I thought and apologised again.

Days later, whilst I was in Ramallah, Hamas supporters blew up a bus in Jerusalem. No wonder this city is full of fear and suspicion.

Jerusalem may be one of the holiest places in the world and whilst it fascinated me, it did not make me feel positive about the human race. Fear, hatred and suspicion rule here. At night, as I made the long trip back through the checkpoints to Bethlehem, I was reminded of a slogan I had seen on the wall the previous day. 'We all bleed the same colour'. That has to be one of the most powerful slogans I have ever seen in my life.

Hebron

Hebron, a city in the southern West Bank, is divided into two sectors. H1 is the largest sector and is controlled by the Palestinian Authorities. The Israelis run H2. Astonishingly, around 30,000 Palestinians live in the Israeli controlled sector, yet only a tiny settlement of up to 800 Jews. Subsequently there are curfews and restrictions placed on the movement of Palestinians.

Hebron is famous for containing the tomb of the Patriarchs, built mainly by Herod in the first century BC. It is the second holiest site in Judaism and is the burial site for Abraham, Isaac, Jacob and their wives. It is also a sacred site for Muslims and like everything else here, it is divided. One section for Muslims, one for Jews.

Hebron's history is tragically soaked in blood and there are dozens of examples of brutality. I will give you two. In 1991, a Palestinian sniper shot dead a ten-month old Jewish baby in its pram. In February 1994, Baruch Goldstein, a Jewish man, opened fire on unarmed Muslims praying in the Ibrahim Mosque. He killed 29 of them. Utterly sickening, all of it, yet violence is ongoing in Hebron.

I took the early morning bus from Bethlehem and was dropped off in Hebron's chaotic and polluted city centre, on the Palestinian side. Sticking out like a sore thumb, I began to wander. I met friendly locals; many were market traders, desperate to communicate with me. I even shared coffee with a Palestinian police officer, in his actual home. I met him in a shop when he was off duty, and I explained why I was in Hebron. He asked me if I would like to get a good view of the divide. Not sure what he was getting at, we entered a small door and climbed the stairs to his apartment. Once inside, he led me to his rooftop courtyard, where I looked down over the divide to the Israeli side. I could not waste this opportunity, so started to take photographs, but my new friend warned me to be careful, as the Israelis would be watching. I spent an hour in this kind man's company and we talked about his life and the struggles of his people. His kids joined us and his charming wife made Arabic coffee.

Deep in the old town, I wandered the dry dusty streets. It was poor and run down, yet people again were friendly. Many called out to me wanting just to say hello or to shake my hand. They all seemed intrigued by my presence. As I continued walking down an empty side street, I saw close up the reality of this divide. In between two buildings, there was a fence with razor wire, then some metres – after that, a wall. Behind that was the Israeli sector. I stood there, trying to make sense of it all, when suddenly someone called out from behind. I turned and saw an old man waving, beckoning me over to what can only be described as a shack.

The old timer wore the traditional headscarf often associated with Arafat. I approached tentatively. He beckoned me in, smiled and shook my hand. Inside, the shack was a clutter of junk, but he cleared some space and proceeded to make tea. He spoke only a few words of English. Tea and Turkish Delight were soon on the table, not the ghastly fake stuff covered in cheap milk chocolate you get in the UK, the real stuff that melts in the mouth. One of his teenage children who spoke English joined us to help translate. This used to be his shop, I was told, but the Israelis closed almost half the shops in 1994, decimating the business trade and livelihoods of many Palestinians. They also banned Palestinians from using the main thoroughfare, Shuhada Street. According to Israel, this was done to protect the Jewish settlers.

An old TV sat in the corner of the shack. It was switched on and what I saw was very disturbing indeed. I can only describe it as *Jihad TV*, programmes glorifying terrorism, military training and killing. As he proceeded to pour the tea, I sat and watched the screen feeling very uncomfortable.

He is 72, has three wives and believe it or not, 22 children. With his shop gone, his children support him with money, his wives look after him, and neighbours sometimes bring food.

With intricate care, he peeled a photo off the wall and with immense pride showed it to me. His eyes were sparkling. It was a photo of him with the very man himself, Yasser Arafat. He told me that Arafat was a hero to all. I wanted to challenge him, but considering where I was, decided against it.

Was this a one-off meeting, or had he been officially involved with Arafat or even Hamas in some way? *Be very careful what you say, George.* I asked him what the future held for him. He told me that Israel would one day be defeated.

We then made small talk, him asking me about where I was from and about my book. After roughly 45 minutes, he wished me luck and to be safe. We shook hands, I thanked him for his hospitality and walked on. Ten minutes later, I passed through a military checkpoint and stood in the Israeli-held sector H2.

What to think? We are led to believe that Hebron is Palestinian and that Israel has taken parts of it illegally. Well, not according to signs that I saw in the Jewish sector. One sign claimed that this has been Jewish land since 1807. There really is no such thing as black and white here. There are numerous shades of grey and not two sides to the story, but half a dozen.

The Israeli sector was full of abandoned buildings. It was like wandering through a film set or a ghost town. The only people around that day was myself and groups of Israeli Defence Force (IDF) soldiers on foot patrol. They stopped me once and checked my documents, but there was no problem and I kept walking. Later, an Israeli armed vehicle came rumbling down the street, kicking up dust. It trundled on past, ignoring me. Israeli flags fluttered everywhere, road signs were painted with blue and white stripes (the colours of the Israeli flag) and from up high I spotted armed members of the IDF wearing shades. I waved at one of them. He smiled and waved back. Surreal.

Later, back through the Israeli checkpoint, I was once again stood in the Palestinian controlled sector H1, not quite believing that with walls and divides everywhere, I could come and go so easily.

Finally back in Bethlehem, I spent the evening talking with my friend Adel outside his shop. He told me once again, 'There will never be peace in the land of peace.'

Palestine – Muslims and Christians

Much of the news we see regarding Israel/Palestine focuses on the differences between Jews and Muslims. But what about the relationship and differences between Palestinians themselves, Muslims and Christians? By that I really mean, how are minority Christians treated by the Palestinian government? From the outside, it all seems harmonious, but after digging under the surface, it is not quite so.

I had an interview with John, a Palestinian Christian. He owns a small shop, selling everyday food items in Bethlehem. The shelves are not well stocked and the choice of goods on offer would depress a westerner.

John has also worked with Amnesty International for many years and takes a stand against corruption. This has not gone unnoticed by the Palestinian Authorities, and he claims he has been harassed for many years. When he has spoken out against corruption, the police came to his shop to arrest him on trumped-up charges. He has also had problems with local government who have told him the paperwork for his shop is 'not in order' and that they will take it from him. He has spent thousands of dollars on official paperwork to confirm he owns what he owns; all he needed was an official government stamp. He kept asking for it, they put him off and eventually told him they had lost his documents. The harassment he claims is ongoing because he keeps speaking out.

We started talking about the relationships between Muslims and Christians in the West Bank.

'People on the streets, we all get on well. No problem. But our Muslim dominated government do not treat us Christians as equals compared to our Muslim brothers. The result is that many have left, Christians are leaving all the time. They go far away, to forget. Half a million Christians from Palestine are now in Chile. They've had enough of the harassment and corruption. Do you know, until the dividing of this land by the British in 1948 and the creation of Israel, Bethlehem's population was 95 per cent Christian and only five per cent Muslim?'

'And today?'

'Today, Bethlehem is only 20 per cent Christian and 80 per cent Muslim. And in all Palestine, we are now only one per cent of the population.' He continued:

'Our government takes hundreds of millions of dollars from the international community. Palestine goes out with the begging bowl to the world and says, "Oh look how poor we are, it is all because of Israel, poor us. Give us money!" And they give, we get hundreds of millions. But where does it go? They don't build industry, we have water shortages and the roads are terrible. Look around, George, and tell me if you see millions being spent on the people? Where is it? Oh, I can tell you, gone, gone into the pockets of those in power. Corruption is endemic throughout Palestine. Recently the anti-corruption league did an investigation and produced many files on official corruption, but the Palestinian government did not allow the files to be opened.'

I mention to him recent journalist investigations into the billions of pounds the UK gives in foreign aid. To Palestine alone, we give around £72 million per year. Most of us would like to think it is being spent on roads, schools and hospitals. However, the in-depth reports claim widespread corruption/misuse and of UK aid being handed to the families of Palestinians convicted of killing Israelis. John replied, 'I believe it. The UK must be crazy to give this aid money to us. You shouldn't do it, because this aid is being stolen by our corrupt system. Do you want your tax money to pay for so-called "heroes", Palestinians who kill Israelis? Also, here is high unemployment and much poverty, yet a new palace costing £8 million has just been built for our President. Your taxes probably helped paid for it George.'

I must point out, that in response to the investigations, the British government says, 'No UK foreign aid is used for payments to Palestinian prisoners, or their families.'

We then moved onto the goods in his shop and John told me about a recent boycott of Israeli products.

'There were five major Israeli companies we dealt with that export goods. Good quality juice, salads, dairy etc. But that's all stopped. The word is that the son of our President was set up as an official distributor by our government, so he would be the middle man who buys from Israel and sells to us shopkeepers. Israel refused because of who he was. So, our government boycotted all these products. Now most of our goods come from Jordan and Turkey – but we pay a very high price for them, so when we sell them on to our customers we must keep the end price so small because many here are poor. Therefore, our profit margins are tiny.'

He gave me the following examples: on one of his shelves, he had a box of Kinder Bueno bars. He has to sell the entire box of 30 bars, just to make £1 profit. He also sells mobile phone top-up sim cards. When he could buy these from Israel, he had a 20 per cent profit margin on each one he sold. Now he can only sell Palestinian ones. His profit margin on these is a lowly four per cent.

'Our government blames all our problems on Israel, but that's not true. They are to blame for so much that's wrong here, it's certainly not all Israel's fault.'

Another Palestinian Christian went even further when he told me, 'I wish that in 2002 when Israel built this wall, they had built it on the other side of Bethlehem and taken the whole town into Israel. Israel takes care of its people, unlike our system. I dream to be a citizen of Israel; it's the only democracy in the Middle East.'

Palestinians not hating Israel, condemning their own side, and even wanting to be Israeli citizens? My head was spinning.

Ramallah

Ramallah is a city under Palestinian control in the West Bank. It is crowded, dirty, noisy and full of characters. I was there for one reason, to visit the tomb of Yasser Arafat. Once the charismatic Chairman of the PLO and leader of the paramilitary group Fatah, Arafat is a hero to many Muslims. To millions of others around the world, he is a terrorist and murderer.

It had been a 90-minute stunning but hair raising drive through desert landscape and I was convinced the driver was trying to kill us all. I felt rather queasy when the minibus finally arrived in Ramallah. Only one thing for it, a luscious cup of hot and sweet Arabic coffee, and what a café I found. Huge old fans hung from the ceiling and everyone was dressed looking rather like Arafat himself. Now I *really* felt I was in Palestine. My presence did not bother the locals and many of the old-timers nodded at me politely. Thick smoke hung in the air, not smelly cigarettes, but from the shisha pipes, it was gorgeous. If there were an Olympic games for smoking, these guys would win gold every time.

It was all very peaceful in the café – in fact it was an oasis of calm from the ramshackle and chaotic streets outside. Israeli forces enter the West Bank on a regular basis to arrest Palestinians they claim are involved in terrorism. At the time of writing, it had been reported that there were around 7,000 Palestinians held in Israeli jails due to such incursions and arrests. It is estimated that some 40 per cent of Palestinian men have been detained by Israel at some point in their lives.

After delectable Arabic coffee flavoured with cardamom pods, and a street map scribbled on the back of a napkin, I headed off in the direction of Arafat's Mausoleum.

With my shaved head and general appearance, I obviously was not a local, and the armed Palestinian soldiers at the main gate stiffened as I approached. One of them held up his hand, indicating I had gone far enough.

'May I go in?' I asked with my friendliest *I'm interested in your leader* smile.

'Yes,' but my small rucksack slung over my shoulder concerned them. It was searched before being taken from me. After a passport check, one of the armed soldiers escorted me to the gleaming mausoleum. With huge pride, my accompanying soldier told me how great a man Arafat was. I nodded my head politely.

Inside, I stood in front of the tomb containing the body of Arafat. Two soldiers stood behind it on permanent guard. I stayed respectfully silent, waited two minutes, then quietly left. I have now visited the tombs of Lenin, Mao and Arafat. Big names, big people.

Having soaked up the atmosphere in Ramallah, I then wanted to experience the polar opposite. A short taxi ride from central Ramallah took me to this section of the West Bank Barrier, whose checkpoint was even more intense than the section at Bethlehem. Out of my taxi, I stood taking photos of a nearby Israeli watch tower, which had recently been attacked with firebombs. I was literally standing in a war zone.

Once again, I proceeded through metal cages and numerous checks before crossing to the Israeli side. Another short bus ride later, I was back in Jerusalem. Starting from close to Damascus Gate, I then made the long walk to Mea She'arim.

Mea She'arim

Mea She'arim is a very old and small neighbourhood, populated by what we know as ultra-orthodox Jews, though they much prefer the name 'Haredi Jews'. Adel, my friendly shopkeeper from Bethlehem had already warned me not to go. 'They can attack you,' he said. 'You won't be welcome.' The first thing that greeted me on entering Mea She'arim was a sign dictating to outsiders how to dress and behave. I went in tentatively. Men were dressed in long frock coats and black hats, women in long sleeved garb and thick stockings. Had I just walked back into the 18th century? An old world enclave, these folks have completely cut themselves off from the outside world. I can only describe it as a self-imposed ghetto.

The residents seem to have totally rejected the outside world and their lives revolve around strict adherence to Jewish religious text and prayer. I had been warned that the residents do not like being photographed.

I walked the streets. I was quiet, dressed appropriately, did not have my camera on display. Not only did no one speak to me, but also as each resident walked towards me, they either looked away or down at the ground. Not one of them made eye contact with me – not once.

Unwelcoming, unfriendly and a general air of superiority hung in the air. I am sorry to say that, but that is what I experienced there. I wish it had been otherwise, I would have loved to talk with the members of the local population, but it wasn't to be.

I also have to say that I found the neighbourhood very dirty. Large piles of rubbish lay around most corners and many of the buildings were in poor condition. The actual pavements I walked on were grimy and slippery.

I spent a couple of hours there and *did* take photos very discreetly, although on one occasion a young man shook his fist at me as I snapped away at the buildings.

Respect goes both ways. But the residents of Mea She'arim showed none whatsoever to me. It was as if I was transparent; I did not exist. They simply do not want you there. I remember thinking that I would rather be back in Ramallah sitting with the friendly old locals in the coffee shop sharing a shisha pipe.

People have actually been attacked upon entering Mea She'arim, including police, government officials and some westerners. I learned of two young European women who wandered through wearing short skirts. OK, I accept this is very offensive to locals, but did they deserve to be stoned?

You read that correctly, they were attacked by male residents and stoned. I'm sorry, but I found it a very disturbing place. How can the world move on and try to achieve harmony between differing groups when people shut themselves off from society?

That evening, it was good to be back in Bethlehem surrounded by people who treated me like a fellow human being. Sitting outside his shop, my friend Adel asked me, 'So, how was your day?'

I shook my head before replying, 'Well, I was in Arafat's stronghold of Ramallah, then the ultra-orthodox Mea She'arim. It was one of the most mind-bending days I've ever had.'

After what you have just read about Mea She'arim, you have probably concluded that the ultra-orthodox Jews there are the real deal when it comes to being Israeli. Before I came here, that is what my lack of knowledge made me think. Wrong, wrong, wrong. What you are about to read, you may not believe, but *it is true*.

I have learned that Zionism and being Jewish are not necessarily the same thing. For sure, many Jews are pro-Israel, but certainly not all. Some believe that the Torah forbids the Jewish people a state of their own and that Zionism is irreligious by not adhering to the word of God (the Torah's commandments).

Judaism has been around for centuries; Zionism is roughly 100 years old. To some, Zionism is a political and military idea. Critics claim that

Zionism uses the Holocaust to bolster and ramp up the idea that the Jewish people should have their own independent state and all that that entails. Anyone who is against this is portrayed as being anti-Semitic. I've heard it said, somewhat controversially, that if it wasn't for the holocaust, Israel as a country, would not exist. Now that *really* made me think.

'Jews against Zionism' demand a peaceful dismantling of the Israeli state. They believe, according to the Torah, that they are a people in exile and therefore should have no claim to political power anywhere in the world. They also view the Palestinian people as victims of Zionism, but undoubtedly, their most controversial desire is that they, Jewish anti-Zionists, passionately believe that Palestine should have sovereignty over all the Holy Land.

One example of someone who holds these kinds of views is a man called Rabbi Yisroel Dovid Weiss, an international spokesperson for an organisation, 'Jews United against Zionism'.

The Rabbi tours all over the world, giving lectures, TV and radio interviews where he criticises Israel and speaks up for the Palestinian people. If you Google him, you will see him and many others holding up placards that say such things as, 'Israel does not represent the Jews'; 'Stop the holocaust in Gaza'; 'Free Palestine'.

I was fascinated when I learned all this. Many of us in the West equate ultra-orthodox Jews as the backbone of all that Israel stands for. How wrong we are to assume this. I wish the world's media would devote far more time to discussing this. It may make many people in the West think again about *who stands for what*. I now understand that to criticise some of the actions of Israel does *not* make you anti-Semitic.

I was transfixed the first time I watched an online interview with Rabbi Weiss as he criticised Israel. I could not take my eyes off the laminated documents he had attached to his jacket. A flag of Israel with a classic 'No' red symbol over it, while the following words are written underneath, 'The State of Israel must go!' Weiss also proudly wears the Palestinian flag and there are numerous photos online of him and many others like him, meeting with, shaking hands and actually embracing the ex-leader of Iran, the Israel-hating Mahmoud Ahmadinejad.

Confused? Don't worry, so was I.

People like Weiss, from what I can gather, class themselves as Palestinian Jews. They want rid of the State of Israel and to live in peace alongside their Muslim brothers.

However, if I were ever to get the honour of meeting Rabbi Weiss, I would ask him why the residents of Mea She'arim live in what to me seemed like a self-imposed ghetto. Not exactly conducive to living in peace and harmony with others is it?

In addition, why did they treat me as if I were invisible?

Gaza – Hell on earth?

The Gaza Strip is one of the most dangerous places on earth. An ongoing war zone in a small strip of land sandwiched between the edge of the Mediterranean Sea on one side and Israel to the other. Gaza, along with the West Bank, makes up what is known as the Palestinian Territories.

Under Israeli military occupation since 1967, Gaza gained various rights of self-governance under the Oslo Accords in 1994. Since 2007, Hamas, who won power by a democratic vote, but are seen by most of the world as a terrorist organisation, have governed Gaza.

Despite Israel withdrawing all its troops and Jewish settlers from Gaza in 2005, the UN still sees Gaza as 'occupied'. This is due to the ongoing blockade of Gaza by Israel. Since Hamas took over control of Gaza, Israel has done its utmost to block and control Gaza from outside. The Palestinian people, and many around the world, claim that Israel has turned Gaza into an open prison, while Israel insists that its blockade of Gaza is vital to stop Hamas arming itself and attacking Israel. One Muslim I met in Hebron who has friends in Gaza told me, 'Gaza is a living hell.'

I recently watched a superb documentary by the BBC's Lyse Doucet. Set in Gaza, it was about how young people have been affected by the 2014 war with Israel. It was harrowing to watch. She interviewed kids in Gaza who had lost family members and your heart could not but help go out to them. But I also felt despondent when some of the same children then said with steely determination that they would take revenge on Israel for the death of their family members (many who Israel say were Hamas terrorists). Israeli children were also interviewed and spoke of their terror of having to survive daily rocket attacks from Hamas.

I have seen footage of Hamas youth camps, where they parade children even under ten years of age in army fatigues. The kids get weapons training and are taught hatred. Documentaries like this can be seen on YouTube. But be warned, it is soul-destroying to watch.

No child is born to read or write. They are taught to read and write. Likewise, no child is born to hate. Hate is taught and bred into them by the system under which they live. I will make one further point: *all human beings are born atheists.*

2014 – Israel/Gaza conflict

The most recent bloody conflict lasted for 50 days in the summer of 2014. Israel claims it launched the offensive in Gaza (known as Operation Protective Edge) in order to stop the indiscriminate firing of rockets into Israel. A major part of their plan was to destroy tunnels used by Hamas and other militants to attack Israel.

There seems to have been two incidents that kicked this latest war off. Firstly, in May 2014, two Palestinian youths were killed by Israeli sniper fire in the West Bank. Then in June, three Israeli teenagers were abducted in the West Bank. Israel responded by launching 'Operation Brother's Keeper' and blamed Hamas for the kidnappings. Hamas denied involvement yet congratulated the abductors. Israel then made numerous incursions into the West Bank and arrested hundreds of suspected militants, claiming it was trying to secure the release of the kidnapped teenagers. Amnesty International and Human Rights Watch criticised the operation saying it was a form of collective punishment. The dead bodies of the three Israeli teenagers were found at the end of June 2014.

Israel then proceeded to launch air strikes against what they claimed was Hamas facilities in Gaza. Hamas replied with rocket and mortar fire, whilst we in the safety of the west watched it all unfold on our TV screens. Initial attempts at a ceasefire failed and the onslaught continued. A ground offensive then took place as Israel sent troops into Gaza City, with the aim of destroying Hamas tunnels. They managed to destroy 32. In early August, Israel pulled its troops out, but the war continued as a ceasefire failed. On 19 August, yet another ceasefire was violated in only 20 minutes after Hamas fired 29 rockets into Israel. By the end of the conflict, both sides claimed victory. Israel said that Hamas had been severely weakened and Hamas said that Israel had been repelled from Gaza.

So, what was achieved? After much thought and research, I have to say, from a neutral and humanitarian point of view, *nothing.* Just more hatred and more death that will probably help fuel the next war, which will come sooner or later.

As expected, casualty figures vary, depending on the source. The Gaza Health Ministry says that 2,310 Palestinians died, 693 of whom were militants, and 1,617 were civilians. The civilian figure also includes the deaths of 551 children. 551 children? I felt empty when I read that. Surely that can never be justified by Israel?

Israel, on the other hand, claims that it killed over 900 militants in Gaza, while suffering the loss of 66 IDF troops and five Israeli civilians.

Without taking sides or implying that one life is more important than another (which it is not), it is generally accepted that the death toll over the years on the Palestinian side is far higher. Some say a ratio of ten to one. Some say higher. Reliable exact stats are very hard to find.

More than a quarter of a million Palestinians were displaced in Gaza, with hospitals, schools, residential areas and dozens of mosques destroyed. The Israeli military claim that their targets were legitimate, as they targeted Hamas terrorists who often use residential areas and mosques for their own purposes. They say that mosques are used for weapons storage and that Hamas has even launched rockets from them. It has also been claimed that Hamas routinely uses Palestinian people as human shields. Hamas denies this.

When the long-awaited UN report came out in June 2015 it criticised both sides, saying that they 'both may have committed war crimes'. Israel responded by saying that the investigation into the 2014 conflict was 'politically motivated and morally flawed'. A Hamas spokesperson said the same investigation 'wrongly equated the victim and executioner'.

One of the most crowded places on earth, Gaza is only 139 square miles. In 1952, the UN claimed that the strip was too small to support its population of 300,000. Today, the population of Gaza stands at around 1.8 million. This, along with the 2014 war with Israel and the ongoing blockades, has resulted in tremendous hardship for the people living there.

There are Israeli checkpoints, walls and security all over the West Bank and every day many Palestinians find their movements severely restricted. As for me, I could come and go with ease. Getting into Ramallah or Hebron in the West Bank is one thing, but getting into the Gaza Strip is another ball game altogether. No one can just walk into the Gaza Strip. You either need a permit from the Israeli army or an official Israeli government press office card, and trying to get that was no picnic.

Permission must first be sought from the Israeli authorities. By that, I do not mean just turning up in Tel Aviv and asking a lowly official. It must be done weeks in advance and there is much officialdom to go through. I tried, believe me I tried. I tried with all my might but without luck. I jumped through every hoop they asked me to. I was in contact with an office in Tel Aviv and the Israeli Embassy in London. It took weeks and I had to keep producing more documents, personal details and was asked why I wanted to go, what I was writing about and whom I worked for. At the end of the day, I was denied entry. Why, I do not know. Most visitors to Gaza are either international aid agencies or various diplomats. TV camera crews and certain journalists who work for big organisations like the BBC get in, but not it seems little people like me. If I'd had the backing of an organisation like the BBC, I have no doubt that I would have gotten in. *C'est la vie.*

To be honest, even if I had gotten my official permission, I was never 100 per cent convinced I would have gone in. It is not safe at the best of times and with the near destruction of huge parts of it after summer 2014, I was extremely unsure. If the BBC go in, I presume they have local escorts and although it is still not totally safe, it would be safer than I walking in alone.

If I had been given permission, I had already decided that I would make my mind up on the very morning I planned to go. Once I had made the effort to get there and was standing near the heavily fortified border, if my gut said, 'No, don't do it', I would not have. I desperately wanted to see Gaza for myself, but at the end of the day, I do not chase trouble and I have no desire to be a hero.

When I did tell people I'd met that I'd tried to go into Gaza, be they Jew, Christian or Muslim, they all, bar none, replied, 'Gaza? Are you crazy?'

Not getting into Gaza did allow me to spend more time in Bethlehem, which secured me the following interview with a young man whose family live hemmed in and surrounded by the wall on three sides. Maybe me not getting into Gaza was a sign. Everything happens for a reason, they say.

Interview with a Bethlehem resident

Matthew is 20 years old. He and his family are Christians living in Palestine. A large painting of the Last Supper adorns their family living room wall.

The wall in Bethlehem is so close to Matthew's family home that it can block out the sun. The ground floor of the building hosts their family-run shop, a souvenir shop that I can only imagine is now struggling for business. In fact, I am surprised it is still open. Before this wall was built by Israel, the area in front of their house was a busy road that brought much business their way. It was the main road that linked Bethlehem in Palestine with Jerusalem in nearby Israel. As stated earlier, Israel says the wall is necessary for protection against suicide bombings, whilst Palestinians say the wall is apartheid and division of their land.

Inside the family home, directly above the shop, I interviewed Matthew.

'How old were you when this wall went up?'

'I was maybe six. The main road was not far in front of our house and Muslims, Jews and Christians all used it. Many would stop and it brought us good business for the shop, before the wall went up of course.'

I feel it is important to mention what took place immediately prior to the building of the wall. The siege of the Church of the Nativity in Bethlehem took place in 2002 and was part of the second intifada (the second Palestinian uprising against Israel). It all kicked off in Jerusalem when Israeli President Ariel Sharon made a very controversial visit to the Temple Mount in 2002. This angered Palestinians, rioting broke out in Jerusalem, and like much else here, the knock-on effect meant the situation escalated. In Bethlehem in 2002, the Church of the Nativity was under siege. Under the banner of 'Operation Defensive Shield,' the IDF entered Bethlehem to capture known or suspected Palestinian militants. Dozens of these suspects took refuge in the church and the standoff began. But it was this very house I was sat in which was of importance to me. I asked him what had happened in and around his family home.

'Well, remember the wall wasn't built yet, and we had Palestinian men inside our house.'

'Who were they? Why were they here?'

'I was young, I don't really know. But they were upstairs in our bedrooms. There was shooting going on between them and the Israeli soldiers just over there.'

Matthew then took me through to one of the front bedrooms, directly in front of the wall. The windows of this bedroom have bullet holes in the glass (all taped up now but still very visible)

I was standing inside a house that was caught up in the second intifada in 2002. Shots were fired from this bedroom window – or into this bedroom, I do not know which.

After Matthew admitted that there had been much bombing and

attacks on Israel at that time, I asked him if Israel had a right to defend itself. He took a moment or two to think then said, 'Yes, it does. But not with a wall like this. This is our land and they cut it in two.'

'What do you remember about the wall actually going up?'

'Because I was only five or six, of course, I didn't really understand what was happening. But they, the Israelis, were digging the road and surrounding area for two months. I saw them every day, dig, dig, dig. Then one day, I left for school in the morning and when I came back later that day, this section of the wall was going up. Once everything was in place, it was done very quickly.'

When you step outside their front door, the gigantic wall is about ten feet directly in front, and at more than 25 feet high, it towers over the entire area. But what Matthew told me next astonished me. He pointed to a spot not so far away from their front door and said, 'This is where they originally wanted to build the wall.'

Only two metres or so from their house. 'What made them stop?' I asked.

He smiled. 'When they were digging, they discovered under the ground the main sewage pipe system, and I guess they didn't want to go through all that. So the wall was built a few metres back.'

Thanks to sewage pipes, they have gained a few more metres, but standing outside their front door, it still feels like being inside a prison.

It seems that the West Bank Barrier is a form of collective punishment for all Palestinians, be they Muslim or Christian. Yes, there were suicide bombers, but this young man is not one of them. Nor is my friend Adel. Neither are the vast majority of people 'terrorists'. Many people are suffering in their daily lives due to numerous checkpoints and division in the West Bank. That said, it is also widely accepted that Israel has a right to defend itself against suicide bombers who kill with no mercy.

As already mentioned, I can come and go through the checkpoints at will. I feel guilty. I have a freedom that should never be taken for granted. I knew about Muslims needing permission for attending Friday Prayers in Jerusalem, but it had not occurred to me that Christians like Matthew would also need permission to visit Jerusalem. I asked him about the process.

'We can go up to three times per year, but most want to go at Christmas or Easter. We have to fill in paperwork and we apply through our Church, it must be weeks in advance. Sometimes you get permission, then you simply go to the checkpoint where you cross. But if they say "No you can't go", then you cannot and you get no explanation. I know many people who are refused.'

To get to this shop, you have to make a huge effort. It is far away from the centre of Bethlehem and the religious tourists who would buy their merchandise. You need to take a walk away from the centre, follow the wall, round a bend, down a nearly disused road (or what's left of the road) and then stuck in a cordoned off area stands the shop. It must be heart breaking for the family.

Matthew then took me outside again, this time into their small back garden. The wall towers over us on three sides. Various native plants and shrubs abound and vines hang on an overhead trellis. A tiny oasis of green and calm surrounded by walls and partition.

Suddenly Matthew turns to me and slightly alarmed says, 'George, do you smell that?'

I am puzzled.

'Listen. Smell.'

I hear shots going off somewhere nearby and start to smell a nasty acrid smell. I turn to Matthew to ask, but before I manage, he blurts out, 'The Israelis are firing tear gas, come on inside, quick.' He takes me by the arm and we go back into the building and up to the flat.

Back inside, Matthew explained to me that this often happens. There had probably been an incident somewhere along the wall, possibly Palestinians throwing missiles at the Israelis who responded with tear gas. As he is explaining all this, I start to taste the tear gas in the back of my throat.

'It's very bad. You don't want to be outside if the wind comes in your direction. It stings the throat and especially the eyes. But we are used to it. When we get the first smell, if we are outside, we always get inside and quick.'

What a way to live.

Interview with an off-duty member of the Israeli Defence Force

I met this man by chance in a coffee shop in Jerusalem. We shared a table due to there being no empty ones. We got talking and he asked me what

I was doing in Israel. I told him about my book... then he told me he was a member of the IDF (Israel Defence Force). Would he talk with me about his job?

I expected a firm 'no', but much to my surprise, he was willing to talk. No names and no photos, of course. I began by asking about the 2014 war with Hamas, and once he started talking, he did not hold back.

'Do you know, does anyone *really* understand this? Hamas have indiscriminately fired over 15,000 rockets into Israel. I ask you, what would you do if someone kept firing rockets into your country or at your house?'

I challenged him on Israel using excessive force. 'You respond to stone throwing teenagers by firing at them. Not just rubber bullets but also live ammunition. How can you justify shooting an unarmed teenager?'

He remained calm yet looked at me as if I were the naivest person in the world.

'Let me paint you a picture. First, forget all about politics, religion, and your own views on the situation. You, George, are a member of the IDF on patrol in, say, Hebron. Dozens of people are throwing stones and other missiles at you, eventually you reply with tear gas, and then suddenly a teenage boy comes walking directly towards you. He is now 50 metres away, he is wearing a jacket, zipped up. He walks directly down the middle of the road. Is he wearing a suicide belt? Am I going to die today? You shout at him, in Arabic, pleading with him to stop! He keeps coming, you try again, telling him if he doesn't stop, you will shoot. You are terrified, he keeps coming, time is running out for you George, you know that if he comes any further, you may be dead. You shout one last time, he keeps coming, and he's now smiling with his hand inside his jacket. We shoot him.'

He then leaned across the small coffee table, looked me directly in the eye and said in a deftly calm voice: 'So, what would you do, George? Would you take him out or let yourself and many others be blown to pieces?'

In the months that have passed since I was asked this question, I have asked myself the same question many times from the safety of the UK. When you take yourself out of the picture and away from those directly involved, it is so very easy to go for the obvious, 'Oh, I wouldn't shoot anyone!' However, the reality is that nothing in this troubled land is simply black or white.

I am eternally grateful that I do not have to make a split second decision such as that.

Female taxi driver from Tel Aviv

'The war in the summer of 2014 was terrible. We Israelis feel genuine sadness at deaths of Palestinian women and children, it's true. But you must realise this, after Hamas fired rockets into Israel and before we bombed Gaza, a huge effort was made by Israel to warn the locals to get out. Thousands of leaflets were dropped, text messages sent, phone calls made, all to families telling them the area would be bombed, so get out ASAP. Now, listen to this, Hamas forced people to stay, even gave them money to stay. They also deliberately hid weapons and ammunition in and around schools and hospitals. So, when Israel attacks what it thinks is a weapons dump, it hits a school and Hamas claim a political victory. It's disgusting. Hamas use their own people for their own purposes and then we are seen in the eyes of the world as child killers.'

Bethlehem shopkeeper, Adel

'Most people from all sides want peace, but *not* the authorities. They have their vested interests, politics and organised religion all benefit from these divides.'

I knew the answer, but had to ask the question one last time. 'Do you think the walls around Bethlehem will ever come down?'

'No, never. There will never be peace in the land of peace.'

An old Palestinian in the West Bank who lost his land when the wall went up

'They took my land. They destroyed my olive trees, my goats are gone. This farm had been in my family for generations. They took it, as they took from many. They bulldozed everything and now build their houses on our land. They've killed many of our people. Israel treats us like animals. What did I ever do to them? Nothing. But we will triumph in the end, Inshallah (God willing).'

Summing up

It is so very easy to sit from the comfort and safety of an armchair in the UK and have an opinion. Very easy to watch selective news and decide you are anti-Israel or pro-Israel. So easy to be disgusted by Islamic extremists and then tar all believers with the same brush.

After spending time in the Holy Land and especially after meeting people from all sides of the divide, I can only conclude that it is nowhere near as simple as that. In addition, I accept that in this chapter, I probably have not even scratched the surface. I could write an entire book just on this divide.

Admittedly, I did spend more time in Palestine-controlled areas than Jewish ones, but there was a reason for that. After all, it is the Palestinian people who find themselves locked up behind walls and cut off.

I accept that some Palestinians commit vicious crimes by stabbing and killing soldiers, but they are in the minority. I never once in all my conversations with Palestinians heard any of them say they hate Jews or that they wanted to kill them. However, stabbings of not just soldiers but innocent Jewish civilians happens on a regular basis. That is wrong and can never be excused. But of course there is also much brutality dished out against ordinary Palestinians and that is also totally wrong.

Who was here first? *Whose* land is it? I mean, how far back do you go? On what principles should land be divided up and countries created?

Are walls built to protect or separate? Palestinians say they are built to separate and divide. Israel says they are built to protect. Who is right? Possibly they both are.

As much as I am intrigued by the growing groups of ultra-orthodox Jews who believe in the dismantling of Israel, I, as of yet, do not know anywhere near enough to say whether I agree with this or not.

It's heart breaking to learn of the many innocents killed in Gaza in 2014, especially school children, yet I am also acutely aware of the thousands of rockets that Hamas fires totally indiscriminately into Israel. Some say Israel's response is like using a giant boulder to crush an ant. However, if someone, even if they felt totally justified in doing so, fired rockets indiscriminately into your back garden, how would you respond? That said, many say it's not Israel's back garden in the first place.

The bottom line is this, the State of Israel, backed by the USA, is not going anywhere. Whether we agree with its legitimacy or not, I think we can all accept that. Will there be a two state solution? It has been talked about for years, but it seems highly unlikely from what I have seen.

There is right and wrong on all sides. There are good people on all sides and there are despicable killings on all sides. So, how to solve the problems of the Holy Land? Is it contradictory to say that Israel should retreat to its 1967 line yet at the same time say Israel has a right to defend itself? I genuinely do not know.

Retaliation is also most definitely *not* the answer. It takes the bigger man to walk away. A Muslim kills a Jew, people are devastated. Then someone retaliates and kills a Muslim, now others are in turn devastated, so they go kill someone else, and so on, and so on, and so on...

On a separate point, and this really scares the hell out of me, I recently spent a few weeks travelling through Jordan. It has a border with the West Bank on one side and Iraq and Syria on the other. If IS ever get into Jordan and then make it into Palestine, I cannot even begin to imagine the horror they would unleash. Thankfully, Jordan is strong and takes its security very seriously indeed. Long may that continue.

The worst aspect for me, when it comes to blind hatred, has to be the brainwashing and indoctrination of children. I watched a clip from a children's TV show where the kids were encouraged by the presenter (who was dressed up as a cartoon character) to attack Jews. I am not making this up. One little girl of around seven was asked what she would do when she grew up. She replied, 'I will shoot the Jews. All of them.'

I believe that the man or woman who manages to bring peace to this most troubled of lands may well go down in history as the saviour of all humankind. But what a task.

The way people treat each other makes me conclude that humankind is very much in the infancy of its evolution. We still have a long way to go before we become truly civilised.

Update March 2017

I was last in Israel/Palestine in April 2016. The word on the street is that a third intifada (uprising) is inevitable. I am saddened to say it, but I feel the Holy Land is a powder keg, just waiting to blow.

At the end of July 2016, Palestinian officials announced that they are planning to sue Britain over the 1917 Balfour Declaration. They say the declaration led to mass Jewish immigration into Palestine to the detriment of Palestinians and then the creation of the State of Israel. The Palestinian Foreign Minister also claimed that Britain was responsible for all Israeli 'crimes' since 1948.

The 28th Arab League Summit took place in March 2017. Arab leaders gave their support for a two-state solution, whilst US president Trump seemed to indicate that he does not support this. Palestinian leader Abbas continues to proclaim that Britain should apologise for the now 100 year old Balfour Declaration.

The British Foreign & Commonwealth Office (FCO) travel advice on Israel/Palestine changes constantly along with the situation on the ground. One day, parts of Jerusalem may have no travel warning, the next day that can change. Gaza is always flagged as red, meaning **'against all travel'**.

2

The Caucasus

A melting pot of ethnic division

Abkhazia

Status	Abkhazia. A presidential Republic, governed as the Republic of Abkhazia. Only recognised by three UN member states
Capital	Sukhumi
Currency	Russian Rouble
Population	Estimated at roughly 250,000
Language	Abkhaz and Russian

Introduction

A MELTING POT INDEED. Much has been written about Russia's war in Chechnya and its problems in areas such as Dagestan and Ossetia. So for this chapter I wanted to focus on the divide between Georgia and Russia over Abkhazia, and between Armenian and Azerbaijan over Nagorno-Karabakh. First up, Abkhazia.

Does Abkhazia belong to Georgia or Russia? This tiny 'state' is now back under Russian control, and it takes much effort to get permission to enter. With paperwork in order, off I headed, but as you will read, things did not exactly work out as planned in my trips to either of these divided lands.

The What, Where and Why

Part of the Georgian dominated kingdom of Colchis from the ninth century, the Russian Empire annexed Abkhazia in 1864. After the Bolshevik Revolution, Stalin incorporated Abkhazia into the Soviet republic of Georgia in the 1930s. The culture of the Abkhazian people differs from the Georgians, so under the USSR they lost much of their culture as the Georgian way of life spread more throughout the land. Always feeling closer to Moscow than Tbilisi, Abkhazia was fearful when Georgia finally split from the USSR in 1991.

By 1992, Abkhazia decided to break away from now independent Georgia and form closer ties with Mother Russia. Desperate to hold onto part its new found territory, war broke out between ethnic Georgians backed by the Georgian Army and on the other side – Abkhazians backed by numerous groups such as Cossacks, Armenians and some say the Russian Army.

In a 13-month brutal war, the Abkhazians were the victors (but are there ever victors in such wars?) and the Georgian Army were forced out along with thousands of ethnic Georgians, who fled leaving behind their homes and possessions. Casualty figures for these parts of the world as always are difficult to quote accurately, but it seems that round figures of at least a couple of thousand soldiers died on both sides, with count-less thousands more wounded. Civilian casualties seem to be in the tens of thousands and possibly, up to a quarter-of-a-million Georgians were displaced.

In 1994, a ceasefire was agreed and Russian 'peacekeepers' moved in to patrol a buffer zone between the two sides, much to Georgia's concern. However, it was not until 1999 that Abkhazia declared its independence. At this point, Russia had not yet formally recognised the Abkhazian act of independence. Nevertheless, Russia continued to back Abkhazia which, by now, was under international economic embargoes and highly dependent on Russia for nearly everything.

In 2004, the new Georgian President, Saakashvili, vowed to take Abkhazia back under Georgian control. In 2008, tiny Georgia fought a short war with Russia over another breakaway region, Ossetia. It was during this conflict that Russian troops and tanks crossed from Abkhazia and rumbled onto Georgian territory. The Georgians eventually backed off, simply no match for the might of Russia. Moscow pulled its troops out of Georgia, back across the line into Abkhazia and there they have remained, just inside the breakaway republic. Are they planning ahead? Is Moscow concerned that tiny Georgia might soon join NATO? It would not surprise me; the Russians are not fools.

In 2008, the only part of Abkhazia that still lay under Georgian control was the Kodori Gorge, but that did not last long as Abkhaz forces triumphed there and drove the Georgian Army out. By the end of 2008, all Abkhazia now lay under Abkhazian (and Russian) control. There was no going back after this and Russia stepped up to the mark to officially recognise Abkhazia as an independent state. At time of writing, the only other two countries in the world that officially recognise Abkhazia are Nicaragua and Venezuela. There are many internal political reasons why certain countries recognise or do not recognise each other. I will comment on this later in the chapter.

Abkhazia is now a Russian protectorate where the Kremlin's influence is nearly absolute. Abkhazia may well have its own government, but I would guess that Moscow ultimately pulls the strings here.

After a very long day of getting from Israel to Tbilisi, Georgia, I was on a nine-hour sleeper train north, attempting to get into Abkhazia. I have had numerous delightful journeys on sleeper trains all over Eastern Europe and Russia, but that night train from Tbilisi was not one of them. The train was decades old and it clunked and clacked all through the night. It did not feel safe and in fact, I thought at one point we were coming off the tracks. I fell out of bed twice and it was so cold under my thin sheet that I ended up putting my fleece and hat on before climbing back in. It did not make for a pleasant night and when I arrived in Zugdidi at 6.00am, it was pitch black and there was no coffee to drink. Nevertheless, it would all soon be worth it, for I was about to enter a place very few Westerners ever have.

Zugdidi may be the end of the line in north Georgia, but it is still not at the actual border, which is another 15-minute drive away. Taxi was the only option. After the usual bartering, we agreed a price and off we headed in a ramshackle old Lada. After a short drive through bleak countryside, I arrived at the Georgian side of the border. A seriously run down area with absolutely nothing around apart from a horse and cart covered in a wrap that made it look like something out of *Little House on the Prairie*.

At the side of the road stood a small office and the reluctant Georgian border. Georgia still passionately claims Abkhazia as part of its territory so they are very unwilling to have a border here. Yet with Russian troops just across the bridge, tiny Georgia has no choice but to comply.

After leaving Georgia, the only thing between me and the unrecognised state of Abkhazia was a walk over the abandoned Enguri Bridge. Apart from a couple of very poor looking locals, there was no one else around. It took 15 minutes to walk over and I felt like I was in a scene from a classic Cold War spy novel. At the end of the bridge, I came to the first checkpoint. Razor wire, military, and a sign in English declaring the 'Republic of Abkhazia'.

A small hut stood at the side of a barrier, then 100 metres or so behind that, the so-called border itself. I handed my passport under the glass to the gruff looking official. He grunted at me in Russian as he flicked through it. Then in English, 'Permission, papers!' I handed him my printed document with the Abkhazia official stamp on it and smiled politely. All I wanted to do was get across the border, jump on a bus to the capital Sukhumi, check into my hotel and get some sleep.

After studying my passport in detail and reading the official permission document from his own Foreign Ministry, he then picked up the phone and spoke for around a minute. After ending the call, he came out of his hut, handed me back my documents and said in English, 'No, sorry. Closed. No entry.'

'Pardon?' I said.

'Border closed for you. No entry, you come back, maybe ten days.'

I was totally caught off guard but managed to keep my head. No point in upsetting these people. I tried to get an explanation but got nowhere with him so asked to speak to his boss. Various armed officials then appeared and I tried again with them, but to no avail. Even with my official permission, I was not getting in and they gave me no explanation as to why. It made no sense whatsoever. Nothing would budge them, not even the mention of a possible 'contribution'.

An hour later, I gave up, my head scrambled and my plans shot to bits. Reluctantly, I dragged my luggage back over the same bridge towards the Georgian border, feeling very dejected, cold and tired. I had come all the way from Israel for this, had just lost a week of my planned work, a week's hotel had been paid for and I had endured last night's terrible train ride, not to mention the cost of my flight from Israel. I started to count the pennies, but that was not a good idea. I kept walking and it started to rain. The air turned blue, but it was certainly not because of the weather. The photos of inside Abkhazia, I got courtesy of my German friend Florian, who did manage to get into Abkhazia, on his second attempt.

I was bitterly disappointed about not getting into Abkhazia and that is putting it mildly. However, there is nothing I could have done and considering the places I visited for this book, I thankfully had few bad experiences. Shit happens, they say. True. But then again, things happen for a reason also they say, well maybe... for despite my not getting into Abkhazia, it did push me into securing a remarkable interview in Tbilisi.

After the Abkhaz border fiasco, I spent a week exploring rural Georgia. Not part of this book – not my plan – but that's the situation I found myself in. I visited Borjomi, a once thriving Soviet holiday resort but now depressing and well past its best. I also spent an uncomfortable day in Gori, the birthplace of Stalin, where I visited the museum that is dedicated to this despicable man.

Finally, I made my way back to Tbilisi, where, through contacts, I had managed to arrange an interview with a prominent blogger. He is Georgian and from Sukhumi, which to him is simply a town in Georgia. Sukhumi though is now the capital of the breakaway Russian-backed Republic of Abkhazia. He has not been to Sukhumi since 1993, and fears he will never be able to return.

Just to confuse matters, his name is George. Therefore, George from

Georgia sat down to be interviewed by George in Georgia. He is a very outspoken critic of the Kremlin's policies and activities in the Caucasus. This of course does not go unnoticed by big brother and he claims that he was cyber-attacked by the Kremlin for his views on Russia and Abkhazia. This incident was huge news all over the world.

Just to put a line under the border debacle, I did contact the Abkhazia Foreign Ministry, the same people who happily gave me permission to go there in the first place. I explained what happened and complained about being turned away at the border, the inconvenience and huge cost to myself in getting there. Why was I refused entry? I emailed them three times. No reply.

George and I met in a traditional restaurant, away from the city centre in Tbilisi.

'I was born in Abkhazia, city of Sukhumi. I class myself as Georgian.'

'How old were you when the war happened in 1992?'

'I was 17. War raged for over one year. Many died, many refugees. Terrible time in the '90s in Abkhazia and all Georgia. No one thought the USSR could destruct, but when it did, no one knew who was in charge.'

'You were in Sukhumi during the entire war? Tell me about this time.'

'Georgia had recently taken independence from Russia, and was very anti-Moscow. Then Abkhazia, which was part of Georgia but always pro-Russian, wanted independence, so war broke out.'

'Was Russia involved in the war?'

'Not really, not at the start, but they gave weapons and tanks to Abkhazia. It was mostly between Abkhazia troops and the Georgian army.'

'I've read that other nationalities got involved. Is this true?'

'Sure. Chechens, Armenians, fighters from Dagestan were all involved. Very tribal. There were wars all over the Caucasus at this time, it was a terrible time. Many days we had no food, not even water. Many people died, many civilians on both sides.'

'What was the population of Abkhazia back then?'

'Last census under Gorbachev said 538,000 people. Now in Abkhazia it is only 224,000. Half of the population has fled. After the war, we knew that if we stayed we could be killed as many Georgians had been killed already. So in September 1993 my family and many others fled to Tbilisi, via the mountains. It was very cold there and many people died on the way.'

'Where did you stay in Tbilisi when you arrived?'

'Hotels in Tbilisi took us refugees in and we stayed there until we got back on our feet.'

'Back in Abkhazia, what happened to your house?'

'Everything was just left. Our house was taken over by a military man.'

This was obviously painful for him, but he then gave a sarcastic laugh, shook his head and told me something remarkable.

'You know, my father is a professor and he left many books behind. Once we were in Tbilisi, this military or police man wrote to us saying he now stayed in our house and was willing to send on my father's books, but he demanded 5,000 US dollars to do it.'

That is a lot of money. I was astonished. 'Five thousand US dollars, 20 years ago?'

'Yes. It was impossible for us. Some years later, he contacted us again saying the price had now dropped to one thousand, but we can't even pay this, so my father's books remain there.'

'I want to ask you about the war between Georgia and Russia in 2008. My Russian friends tell me that Georgia started it, by firing first into Ossetia. Is this true?'

'No, it's not true. The Russian army were in Ossetia and then entered Georgian territory. They started it.'

George then talked at length about the 2008 spat with Moscow, and it soon became obvious to me that I would never get to the bottom of this. Israel and Palestine are very complicated, but at least I understand them. Abkhazia is a melting pot of ethnicity and when fighters from places such as Chechnya and Dagestan all get involved on various sides, with big brother from Moscow watching over, well, it's like tactical voting at a UK general election. No one really knows who is backing whom and for what reason.

'If Georgia can break away from the USSR, then why can't Abkhazia breakaway from Georgia?' I asked.

'Ok, listen, who can say if a territory is independent? Only the people. But many of us were forced to leave after the war. *All* the people who would have said *no* to Abkhazia leaving Georgia are gone and have no say. So, it's now easy for Russia and Abkhazia to say their people want to be independent and close to Russia. It's ethnic cleansing. Almost half the population in Abkhazia were Georgians and the rest split between Russians Armenians and local Abkhazians. Now, we are all gone.'

This makes me think that it is only a matter of time before Abkhazia will have a Crimea-style referendum to join the Russian Federation.

'Tell me about your blog.'

'After the 2008 war with Russia, I was constantly openly criticising the Kremlin and one day there was big virus attack to my blogs. Hundreds of thousands of spam emails, supposed to be from me, were sent all over the world, inviting people to my blog. Many people out of interest did so and my blogs crashed. The attack was massive and affected hundreds of millions of accounts worldwide with sites such as Live Journal, Facebook and Twitter. A cyber-attack on this scale could only have come from an organisation with huge resources. I believe the order came from the Russian government, and you know in recent years organised online attacks on freedom of speech coming from Russia have grown very big.'

'I read somewhere that what happened to you is officially one of the ten biggest online attacks of all time. Is this true?'

'Yes.' He enjoyed a little laugh, before continuing.

'You know, I wrote open letter to then Russian President Medvedev. I asked him why his government is doing this to me. The UK newspaper *The Guardian* picked it up and published my letter and story went all over world. CNN, BBC, many called me and interviewed me. Very soon after that, all my systems and blogs were working again.'

'You've never been back to your homeland have you?'

'No, it's impossible for us.'

'In your heart do you still think of Abkhazia as part of Georgia?'

'Of course.'

'Do you want Georgia to join NATO?' His face lit up.

'Oh yes, definitely. It will be an umbrella, a good protection against Russia taking more of Georgia.'

I understand the Georgian desire to join NATO for protection, but I could not help thinking the worst. One can only imagine the uproar from the Kremlin if Georgia was ever to gain entry into NATO.

While George is certainly critical of the Kremlin, he was surprisingly not without praise for Vladimir Putin's early days.

'The early Putin years were good for Russia. Post-Yeltsin, Russia was a mess, big mafia and crime. Putin took control and made many things better. But then he went onto looking outside Russia and wanting to take back old Soviet lands. He is a dangerous man for many of us small nations, like the Baltics. Democracy is becoming less and less in Europe. Also, NATO is strong but doesn't show it. The USA and UK don't show their strength, but Putin does.'

'Do you have Russian friends?'

'Of course, Russian and Georgian people are close, despite everything. I have friends in Russia, we communicate well. There are good and bad people in all countries, but the Russian government has always been bad for many nations, including Russia.'

'Do you think that one day Abkhazia will again be part of Georgia?'

'No, it is almost impossible. Russia is just too powerful now.'

Summing up

Every Georgian I met, when being honest, accepted that they have precious little chance of getting Abkhazia back. Russia is simply too powerful. The bigger issue though is more than just Abkhazia belonging to Russia or Georgia, for there are so many conflicts in this part of the world with differing groups vying for support and recognition. Just look at what we have learned: people from Dagestan, Armenia, Chechnya and goodness only knows where else took sides during the '90s war.

Russian investment has poured into Abkhazia since the short 2008 war with Georgia, and in 2014, they announced millions of dollars more would be invested into industry and defence. Is Russia going to pull out and hand back Abkhazia to Georgia? Absolutely not. What can Georgia do about it? Absolutely nothing.

Georgia may be minuscule in comparison to mighty Russia and no match for it militarily, but it is the most Western leaning nation in the Caucasus and Central Asia. It has expressed a desire to join the EU (and much to Moscow's disapproval) has recently signed a trade agreement. It also wants to join NATO, which would infuriate Moscow. Personally, I do not think Russia would even allow Georgia to join NATO. How can Russia 'disallow' another country in its desire to join NATO, you may ask? All I would say is this – *never* underestimate what today's Russia is capable of.

Does NATO have the balls to let Georgia join its ranks? I do not know. Moscow could crush Georgia in a matter of days, but if it did so *after* Georgia joined NATO, Article 5 of the NATO constitution states that 'an attack on one is an attack on us all'. That does not bear thinking about.

With Georgia wanting to move towards the West and growing tensions in Nagorno-Karabakh, true peace in the Caucasus is still a long way off. One only has to look at the history of just the past 25 years to realise that if it *did* all kick off here, it would be a bloodbath.

Update March 2017

Russian troops remain in Abkhazia and millions of roubles keep pouring in from Moscow. Two out of three crossing points between Abkhazia and Georgia are now closed.

Apart from Russia, Nicaragua, Venezuela and Nauru, the countries of the UN reject Abkhazia as an independent country.

The British Foreign & Commonwealth Office (FCO) flags Abkhazia as red, meaning they advise **'against all travel'**.

Nagorno-Karabakh

Official title	The Nagorno-Karabakh Republic (unrecognised)
Capital	Stepanakert (population 53,500)
Population	Approximately 145,000
Language	Armenian
Religion	Christianity
Currency	Armenian Dram

Introduction

A SMALL STATE DEEP in the Caucasus – cut off from the world – Nagorno-Karabakh is the most isolated 'country' I have ever visited. Formerly part of Azerbaijan, since 1994 it has been under Armenian control. Today's Nagorno-Karabakh is unrecognised by every member of the UN and remains a frozen Cold War conflict zone.

The What, Where and Why

Nagorno-Karabakh is contested by two countries, Christian Armenia and Muslim Azerbaijan. It was once a region of the Azerbaijan Soviet Socialist Republic, but with a population that was predominantly Armenian. Held together by Moscow for decades, it started to unravel in the late '80s and soon all hell broke loose. Tens of thousands have died in brutal wars over this region.

The 1994 ceasefire officially holds, but with no peacekeeping force between the two sides, sniper fire and attacks can happen on a regular basis. Officially, most of the world sees Nagorno-Karabakh as part of Azerbaijan, so in its current state, it remains an unrecognised entity. There are no embassies in Nagorno-Karabakh to help you, should you go there and find yourself in trouble with the authorities.

Just getting there – an effort in itself

My starting point for this chapter was from the Armenian capital of Yerevan. I had arrived the previous day on a bus from Tbilisi, Georgia. But even from Yerevan, which is the only real way to get to the Republic of Nagorno-Karabakh, it was no easy task.

At 9.30am – as soon as it opened – I entered the British Embassy in Yerevan. Inside, I had a fascinating chat with one of the staff who reminded me that the official advice is *not* to go. She informed me that embassy staff are not allowed to go, yet then admitted that she'd read up about Nagorno-Karabakh and was jealous I was going.

What was the reason for the fascination? It's probably one of the few remaining unique destinations left on the planet. Hidden away from the outside world, it's a place that takes monumental effort to get to. An explorer's dream.

At 10.30am, I was in the car with my driver, Aman. Once out of Yerevan, the first thing that catches your eye is Mount Ararat. It stands a colossal 16,946 feet and seems to be within touching distance. However, that is an illusion, for Ararat now stands on Turkish soil. A symbol of everything Armenian, Ararat is a breath-taking sight, yet for Armenians it is utterly heart breaking as it is located on enemy territory. So near, yet so far. According to the bible, Ararat is where Noah's ark came to rest.

On we drove and the modern world literally evaporated before my eyes as we entered an untouched and untamed world. Higher and higher we climbed as the temperature dropped. The scenery became more spectacular with each passing mile. However, this was not about a drive in beauty, for I once again had that unique feeling of heading to a place that very few Westerners have ever seen.

We passed through the odd hamlet, just a smattering of roadside houses, and stopped at a roadside shop. The coffee, made in true Armenian style, was heaven-sent. We took it back into the car and Aman produced a bag of buns his wife had baked that morning. We shared them and talked about life, me asking questions about his childhood in the USSR and he about my travels. Often though, I just sat in silence, staring out of the window at a world that very few know anything about.

After my Abkhazia experience, I have to admit that the closer we got to the border, the more concerned I became. This was an even bigger effort to get to than Abkhazia, surely they would not deny me entry, would they?

Through steep, jagged mountains, we turned a corner and just across the small road stood a hut and set of flags that indicated the border. I handed my passport to the official sat behind the glass, who to my surprise, was friendly. Two minutes later, he handed me a piece of paper that contained my personal details. I had to take this, without fail, in the morning to the Foreign Ministry in the capital, for only they could give me the actual visa.

We drove into Nagorno-Karabakh. It was just wilderness, nothing but mountains and one road. We continued on our journey, but now, the blue skies were giving way to thick fog and more snow. We came to an unmarked crossroads and Aman pointed out to me that we were only 70 miles from the Iranian border. 'Don't take the wrong road then,' I replied.

After spending most of the day climbing high then coasting along, it was time to come down the other side. It was snowing hard now and the roads resembled a helter-skelter with no crash barriers, the drop over the side was huge. I stopped looking as we went round hair bend after hair bend.

Eventually at around 8.00pm, we rolled down out of the mountains and into Stepanakert. With the population of the entire country at only around 145,000, the capital city Stepanakert is more like a town. Aman dropped me at my hotel and we agreed he would pick me up in one week's time. I paid him the agreed price of £60, which included his petrol and the fact that he had to drive the ten hours back to Armenia. What a guy. What a drive. Damn, it felt good to be alive.

Stepanakert

Based in the capital Stepanakert for an entire week and after the mammoth drive through the wilderness to get there, it was quite hard to imagine that anything remotely resembling civilisation could exist beyond these mountains. It had been pitch black when I arrived the night previous, so I had to wait until morning to actually see Stepanakert for myself. The centre of the capital city is very clean, civilised and somewhat charming. Considering its disputed status and the fact it was once part of the Azerbaijani Soviet Socialist Republic, there is surprisingly no communist hangover.

The locals who are of Armenian ethnicity are genuinely friendly. However, as citizens of Nagorno-Karabakh, they are near cut off from the outside world and therefore were cautious towards me at first. I saw no other foreign people during my time there, apart from one guy who I will explain about later. Many locals on the street had a good look at me, not aggressively, but it was something I had not experienced for many years. On my first day, I felt rather like Dorothy when she arrives in Munchkin Land and the locals look on in bewilderment at the strange foreigner.

The first task of the day was to get my visa, thus making myself legal in the country. This is one place you do not want to get on the wrong side of the authorities. I walked down through the town centre and quickly found the building of the Foreign Ministry. In the lobby, I was directed by a guard to a room and told to go in.

Inside sat an official in his late 20s, smartly dressed in a Western style suit. His English was near perfect, he took my passport, did the paperwork and within ten minutes I had a colourful Nagorno-Karabakh visa that cost £5.

The official was very friendly and delighted I had made the effort to come to Nagorno-Karabakh. He was also intrigued as to why I was there. Was it to walk in the glorious mountains, to experience the culture? 'Yes,' I said, saying nothing about writing or working on my book. This was the beginning of a series of mistakes I made.

Every day, out in the streets, I wandered with my camera taking photos of the buildings and surroundings. No one stopped me from photographing in the capital and despite plenty of various uniforms around, I was never once stopped for a document check. I was either just ignored by locals or they nodded their heads in acknowledgment. Plenty of kids and teenagers would come up and say in English, 'Hi, hello, where are you from, what's your name?'. Then they would giggle, laugh, wave and walk on. I was enjoying my time in this alien land and getting lots of research done. One morning, a man in his 60s who was walking towards me on the street, stopped and said in English, 'You are British.'

This was strange as very few speak conversational English here. 'Eh, yes,' I said, 'but how did you know?'

'Just a guess,' he said. His name, he told me, was Alexander (Sasha) and we talked about Nagorno-Karabakh, its history and politics. This was my second mistake. Later in the week, now in full flow with info gathering, I managed to get an interview about life in Nagorno-Karabakh with a hotel receptionist I had met one evening. That was my third mistake.

A short drive from Stepanakert is Agdam, a town that used to belong to Azerbaijan. Until 1993, it had a thriving population of 40,000. After brutal fighting, Agdam was captured from Azerbaijan and those who did not die, fled. Agdam is now part of Armenian backed Nagorno-Karabakh, but unlike other captured towns that have since been re-populated by Armenians, Agdam remains a ghost town, empty of all human life.

Agdam is out of bounds, a military zone, and being close to the Azerbaijan border, it sees frequent sniper fire. I did not know it at the time, but going to Agdam would turn out to be the biggest mistake of my life so far.

Agdam

Agdam is a tragedy, a black mark on mankind. This once prosperous town is now lying in ruin, a ghost town, empty of all human inhabitants.

Armenians are amongst the kindest people I have ever met. They passionately believe that Nagorno-Karabakh belongs to them and whilst admitting that people suffered on both sides, they do not (or are possibly unwilling to) understand what took place in Agdam was brutal to innocent men women and children, who were simply in the wrong place at the right time.

From what I have heard and seen for myself, it would really play on my conscience if I were asked to back Armenia over Agdam.

Foreigners are not permitted to visit Agdam. In fact, it states on my official visa registration, which declares that I am legal in the country 'WITH EXCEPTION TO THE FRONTLINE'.

I asked in my hotel about getting to Agdam. They were unsure what to say, and did not want to commit themselves. Understandable, as if I got into trouble, it may well come back on them. I asked various taxi drivers in the streets, money always talks with taxi drivers. Three said no. Two of them were an outright no and the other, although he had initially said no, eventually said he would, but wanted a lot of cash. On hailing a taxi back to my hotel one snowy late afternoon when I was too cold to walk anymore, I asked the driver in my poor Russian, how much to take me to Agdam, wait for me to take some photos and drive me back to Stepanakert. 'Twenty dollars,' he said.

'It's really possible to go there?' I asked.

'Yes. I know a way to avoid military. We enter, you take photo, and then quick, we go!'

The following morning my driver picked me up at my hotel in Stepanakert and 30 minutes later, we pulled off the road onto a dirt track. It was at this point that he started to get nervous, even though he knew exactly where he was taking me.

Ten minutes later, we approached the outskirts of the town and drove in slowly. Little wonder Agdam has been dubbed the 'Caucasian Hiroshima'.

Total devastation all around and Mother Nature has now taken over. As we ventured deeper into the town, my driver got more and more nervous; that 20 dollars he had been happy about getting was a distant memory.

Ironically, the only thing left standing in Agdam is the central Mosque, so I asked him to make his way there. He kept driving while repeating, 'No good my friend, no good.'

Fifty metres from the Mosque, he killed the engine and I got out. I saw no one around, there was only an eerie calm. I walked up to the Mosque, covered in bullet holes and pieces of it lying on the ground. I stepped inside where I encountered a distinct smell of animal manure. Totally derelict, its once stunning interior stripped of everything sacred.

I cannot imagine the heartache this must cause for people who once lived and worshipped there. I climbed the inner stairs, my every step making a loud crunching sound. From up high, I looked out over the deathly quiet ruined town. Nothing but devastation around.

Apparently, even the Armenian people are very uncomfortable about what happened here. The deaths of so many in Agdam is not something they are proud of and they do not like to talk about it. Even officially, Armenia does not harp on about 'victory' here, and I learned that they have indicated that if Azerbaijan would recognise Nagorno-Karabakh as an independent state, they would be willing to hand back what is left of Agdam to Azerbaijan. I cannot see any of that happening though.

I took photos, but did not stay long as my increasingly nervous driver pointed to his watch, indicating *that's enough, let's get out of here*. Back the same way, avoiding the craters in the roads, we soon arrived at the junction and the main road to Stepanakert. I felt numb, yet glad I had managed to see Agdam for myself.

With each mile that we sped away from Agdam, my driver visibly relaxed before my very eyes. I had been warned it was best not to mention in conversation with locals in Stepanakert that I had been to Agdam and most definitely not to discuss what happened there.

On the way back to Stepanakert, I convinced my driver to pull in at the only passenger airport in Nagorno Karabakh. The facts surrounding this building are truly fascinating. Originally built in the Soviet 1970s, this building has been lying idle since 1992. In 2008, it was re-built and stands just off the road. It is a brand new state-of-the-art airport in the shape of an eagle with open wings. It looks so out of place, and is currently only used by the military.

There was only ever going to be one destination you could fly to from here and of course that was to the Armenian capital Yerevan. Flights were supposed to commence on 9 May 2011, but have been delayed ever since.

'Technical reasons' have been offered but that makes no sense. Some say the real reason is that Azerbaijan reportedly said that it would shoot down any civilian planes that appear in Nagorno-Karabakh airspace, which they claim as their own. The Azerbaijan Foreign Ministry has denied this, but whatever was said or implied or even made up seems to have done the job, as passenger flights remain grounded indefinitely.

There are no trains to Nagorno-Karabakh, still no flights and the only way in is the monumental drive I did through the mountains. This is why I have referred to Nagorno-Karabakh as *hidden away from the outside world*. I took photos of the airport, another mistake, got back into the car and we returned to Stepanakert.

As I have already mentioned, going to Agdam would soon turn out to the biggest mistake of my life. I had been followed and photographed there. As I later found out, I had been followed all week. The very people I had talked with and asked questions, had in fact been asking *me* questions and reporting back.

However, the authorities did not make their move. Not yet anyway.

Interview with a receptionist

Olga is a 20-year-old student born in Stepanakert. When not studying, she works as a hotel receptionist and we met when I went in for a meal one night. Olga speaks excellent English and after I explained that I was writing a book about lands such as Nagorno-Karabakh and that I wanted to find out what it was like for a young person to live here, she agreed to be interviewed. She said it would give her the rare chance to speak English with a native Brit. We agreed to meet two days later and to make it all above board, we met in the hotel's dining area.

'Nagorno-Karabakh is a long way from anywhere. What it's like for a young adult to live here, knowing you are so far away from the rest of the world?'

'It's safe here. If we look at the TV and watch what is going on in Europe and Syria and other places, we are happy to live here. But many young people of course want to go out and discover something else.'

'Do you want to continue to live here?'

'Yes, I do. But there are not so many opportunities here.'

Olga is not a brainwashed everything-is-wonderful-in-my-country

75

person. She has her own mind, is highly intelligent, was not political and had no hatred towards Azerbaijan. She impressed me greatly.

'Now with the internet, you can look out into the world. Don't you feel a kind of prisoner here?'

'In some ways yes. The only country we can go freely to is Armenia. Anywhere else, only a few can do it.'

'You live in a country that is unrecognised by the world. How does that make you feel?'

'Of course we are not recognised, but we are here, we are living, this is a country. But we are frustrated. We always hope that other countries will recognise us, but it's not the most important thing.'

'You told me that you study English, well it's obvious to me because your English is so good. With all due respect though, surely you're not studying English for six years to work as a hotel receptionist?'

'No. I would love to maybe do some kind of journalism, maybe write stories, maybe an interpreter.'

'Would you like to travel?'

Her eyes lit up. 'Oh yes, I want to see Africa and maybe India.'

'Would you like to *live* abroad, say London or Paris?'

'No, I want to live here and have children here. But much later.'

We discussed the uniqueness that is Nagorno-Karabakh. Many might see the total lack of Western influence, Americanisation and capitalism as a bad thing, as if their country had been left behind, but not Olga, nor myself. I felt the same way I did in Transnistria, as if I was in a land that time had forgotten, or possibly even in a Brigadoon where much of the modern world had passed by like a dream.

Olga expressed her delight that there are no such companies as McDonald's, Pizza Hut or Starbucks in her tiny hidden away country. Globalisation has not yet reached Nagorno-Karabakh, and in some ways, long may that continue.

Of course, other young people in Stepanakert did not share her views and she admitted that many of her friends longed for the trappings of the West. With few opportunities, she told me that many young girls of 18 or 19 just get married, have babies and do not work. As for the boys, they want a beautiful wife who will be in the kitchen.

I asked Olga about her job at the hotel, she was very open and gave me the details of her hours and wages, which I later worked out in hard currency. I was shocked to discover her hourly wage, according to exchange rates on the day, was roughly 50 pence per hour. This, she told me, was one of the better jobs around. She is a hard-working young woman who studies hard and has a good head on her shoulders. I do hope she gets the chance to see more of the world.

At times, I felt that Olga contradicted herself by saying she wanted to live in Stepanakert and raise children, whilst at the same time admitting she was frustrated by the lack of opportunities for young, educated people like herself. She also claimed she was not bothered about the outside world not recognising Nagorno-Karabakh as a country, yet she knows that the only way the foreign people – with whom she craves to speak – will come here, is if the outside world recognises Nagorno-Karabakh.

I had a fascinating insight into what life is like for a young person living in Nagorno-Karabakh. But was my meeting with Olga the catalyst for what would soon happen to me? At the time, I could not have possibly imagined it, but in hindsight, it was certainly one of the main factors.

During our interview, Olga told me about her studies. She attends the only faculty in Stepanakert, which teaches various subjects. She studies English and told me there were 50 students in her class, but that they had little chance to chat with a native English speaker. I said I would love to visit and talk with them. She was delighted and said, 'we will go there tomorrow.'

She even agreed for me to meet with her father who would be able to talk about the war with Azerbaijan. 'Ok, with pleasure,' she said. There was also a possibility that I could get to meet her grandmother, who would be able to give me an older person's perspective on what it meant to live your whole life in Nagorno-Karabakh.

However, none of this happened, for it seems that after our meeting, Olga had been warned not to communicate with me again. By whom, I have no idea. In fact, after our meeting, Olga did not return any of my emails and I never saw nor heard from her again.

Shusha

The town of Shusha was part of Azerbaijan, but since the early '90s, it has been part of Armenian-backed Nagorno-Karabakh. For hundreds of years, there has been a mixed population of both Azeris and Armenians in Shusha, meaning that the history is anything but peaceful.

In 1920, Azerbaijan carried out a massacre in Shusha with support from Turkey. The Armenian half of the city was destroyed. Churches, schools and businesses were turned into infernos and almost 30,000 Armenians died.

Decades later, during the Nagorno-Karabakh war in 1992, Armenian backed forces 'liberated' Shusha, or 'captured' it according to Azerbaijan. Local Azerbaijanis fled their half of the city and, as of today, none have returned.

Florian is a young German I had met on my travels in Georgia. We had kept in touch and finally met up again when he arrived in Stepanakert, a few days after me. He is travelling the world for his own interest, and in many ways he reminded me of myself 20 years ago.

Taking a taxi from Stepanakert we drove the short distance to Shusha. In the centre it was nearly dead and I had the same thought I'd had in Borjomi Georgia; one could easily lose the will to live here. On foot, we headed off to explore, yet looked so out of place as we walked the run down town. There were a couple of cafés, but both were closed.

The locals mostly live in classic grey Soviet-style apartment blocks that look like they could fall down at any second. What an existence. We walked on and soon found a sight I have seen so many times over the years in places such as this: a recently renovated church. Housing may be in shocking condition, roads may be full of giant holes and the entire infrastructure may be crumbling, yet the government somehow finds money to restore churches.

A little further on, we came across a brand new four-star hotel, empty of tourists. If *we* stood out like a sore thumb, then so did this hotel. Why is it here? Who is it for? No idea. We sat outside on the extensive veranda and enjoyed freshly made Armenian coffee, both finding it all rather surreal.

In the old Azerbaijani quarter, the devastation from 1992 was right before our eyes. There were huge apartment blocks that looked like they had been bombed only yesterday. We approached one tentatively and went inside. Horrendous. It was completely gutted with gaping holes in the sides of the building that indicated direct hits by mortar or rocket fire.

This apartment block would have once housed hundreds of people, therefore the death toll must have been high. To me, this did not look like soldiers fighting soldiers on the battlefield.

Both feeling numb, we headed to the old Mosque lying derelict nearby. With bullet holes everywhere, a sad silence hung over it. Inside the once holy grounds, Mother Nature is again reclaiming her land.

Having seen enough, we took an old marshrutka back to Stepanakert and after I'd had a long hot shower and change of clothes, we met later at a charming little restaurant I'd found previously. We ate, drank local wine and talked openly and passionately about the politics of this region. Another mistake.

I had one full day left in Nagorno-Karabakh before my long drive back through the mountains to Armenia. I had done all my research and planned to relax, go for a stroll and write up some notes. I take no sides in the ongoing dispute over territory here. There have been terrible atrocities committed by both sides. I have only been in the Azerbaijan capital Baku once, and if truth be told, wasn't really taken with it. I have been in Armenia a few times over the years, love the culture, love Yerevan, and love the friendly people. I have also written very compassionately about the genocide of 1.5 million Armenians at the hands of the Turkish Ottoman Empire in 1915.

Therefore, you can only begin to imagine my shock, horror and fear, when on my last day in Armenian backed Nagorno-Karabakh, plain-clothes members of the security services forcibly took me off the streets. I was held, interrogated and accused of spying for Azerbaijan.

My last day in Stepanakert

I made my way out of Stepanakert to the statue that is the national symbol of the people. Situated atop a small hill, a few kilometres from the centre, I sat underneath it with my book and relaxed. Florian joined me later, and the two of us just chilled, enjoying a bit of late winter sun.

They came from nowhere. Suddenly in English, I heard someone shout my name.

I looked up – directly in front of me stood four men. Two police officers and two men in plain clothes: black leather jackets and shades.

'Eh yes?' I said.

'Stand up.'

Taken aback, I actually asked, 'Why?'

'Stand up!' he barked. I stood.

They moved with lightning speed. My laptop was snatched, my camera, my day bag, my passport. With a firm grip on each arm, they then walked me down from the statue to a waiting unmarked car.

'What's happening? Where are you taking me?' No reply.

Florian was taken off in another car, but it was not him they were interested in. Jammed into the back of a car, I was driven to my hotel and frog-marched through the foyer, past the once friendly staff who now looked at me as if I were scum.

Inside my room, a police officer stood with his back to the door, while one of the men started to rifle through my luggage. They turned the entire room over. They found my electronic cigarette and claimed the battery with the flashing light was a secret camera. I could not believe what I was hearing. The other man flicked through my passport and found the visa from a past trip to their hated enemy, Azerbaijan. He was disgusted.

'You went to Agdam.' It was a statement, not a question. I knew that they knew I had been there. *Don't lie to them George* a voice in my head said.

'Yes,' I said.

'It is forbidden!' he spat at me.

'Why did you interview that girl? What did you ask her?'

I explained that I was a travel writer and working on a book

They looked through my writing pads, notes and documents, they questioned everything and took what they wanted.

Then, when I thought it could not get any worse, in the bottom of my bag, they found Israeli money and worst of all, my copy of the Quran that I had been reading for months. Nothing illegal about these items, but it did not look good in their eyes.

He then asked me if I was a Muslim. 'No,' I said, not sure where this was going. Now shouting at me, he accused me of spying for Azerbaijan. I knew this was ridiculous, but I also knew I was in serious trouble and am not ashamed to admit that, at that point, I was terrified.

'Who do you work for?'

'I told you, I'm a travel writer, working on a book.' I produced my press card but he wasn't interested.

He shook his head. 'You are a spy.'

Armed with my written notes, the Quran and goodness knows what else, they bundled me back down the stairs to the waiting car. I was in a country unrecognised by the world and these people were accountable to no one.

'Where are we going?'

One laughed while the other held onto my arm and just smiled. They took me to the police station. Sat in the foyer, totally fine and free to go was Florian. I tried to speak with him but they directed me upstairs. I turned and called back, 'Don't you dare leave here!'

In a room upstairs, I was questioned, the language changing from Armenian to English when it suited them. My fear was that they would force me to sign something in a language I did not understand.

With one of them sat beside me, I was forced to delete many photos and several documents from my laptop, anything they did not like the look of. They thought they had deleted some of the photos you see here, but I had already emailed them to myself previously. They show more devastation inside the town of Shusha.

They continued speaking in Armenian, and I kept repeating that I wanted them to contact the British Embassy in Yerevan. I was told that that was not possible. Therefore, deciding I may only end up digging myself a deeper hole, I shut up and said no more.

Eventually, realising that their English was not good enough for me to understand everything, they said they would get an interpreter. Ten minutes later, the door opened and in walked the man who had given me my visa one week previous.

'How are you?' he asked me.

'How do you think?' I explained that I had been man-handled, shouted at in a language I didn't understand, my luggage ransacked, loads of info deleted on my laptop, some of it nothing to do with Agdam or Shusha.

'You have been asking questions all week. You interviewed a girl, you spoke with people on the streets. You went to Agdam, which is not allowed. You also did not declare to me your real reason for coming here, which is to write about us.' I was now feeling more confident, yet still nervous.

'So you accept I'm a writer? Oh and just because I have Israeli money and am reading the Quran, that does not make me a spy!' I asked him how he would feel, being hauled off the streets and questioned in a language he did not understand. Did he think this was acceptable?

To be fair, he actually looked concerned at that comment and talked rapidly with the plain-clothes men. They spoke for only a few minutes but to me it seemed like hours. He then turned back to me.

'I am here to help you, so don't complain about our people. If I leave, you are on your own with them.'

'Do they seriously think I am a spy?'

'No, not now.'

Relief flooded over me. 'What happens now?'

'You have two options. One, you decide to stick to your story of being treated badly by our officials and write about it, then we keep your laptop, your camera, all your devices, you will be driven to Armenia right now, put on a plane and deported.'

I did not find this option so bad – beats being thrown in jail without trial or representation. I was scared though what option two was going to be.

'Option two, you apologise for coming here under false pretences. You apologise for going to Agdam, you apologise to these men for everything you have done. Then you are free to go.'

An angry voice in my head said, *apologise for what*? *Writing about the killing of civilians*?

'What's the catch?' I asked him.

'No catch, just apologise and you can go.'

The same voice in my head now said, *just get yourself out of here*.

I apologised. I apologised for anything and everything they wanted to hear. Moments later, after photocopying my personal documents, they told me I had to leave Nagorno-Karabakh first thing in the morning. Then, they simply let me go.

Outside, I thanked Florian profusely for waiting for me. We walked in no particular direction, just to get away from the police station and half an hour later, ended up in a coffee shop. Bizarrely, who soon appeared? The Foreign Ministry guy who had helped me out. I was nervous as hell – was he following me?

I sat with him and thanked him once again. Would he talk, I wondered? Yes, he did. He reminded me once again just how dangerous a situation I'd put myself in. Again, I apologised for going to Agdam, but did tell him that I would be writing about the incident and the way I was treated.

'You really must leave here tomorrow,' he instructed me.

'Don't worry mate,' I said, 'I'm leaving.'

Later, back in my hotel room, my mind was going crazy, for I did not feel it was over, I did not feel safe. I expected them to come back in the middle of the night and haul me away for good. Using a VPN to hide my IP address and through Skype, I called a lawyer friend in Scotland and explained my situation. When I told him I'd been accused of spying he let out a long breath and said, 'Jesus, George.'

I told him that if I had not checked in with him by midday the following day, he should contact the nearest British Embassy, which was in Yerevan Armenia.

To add to my now racing mind, a black Mercedes with tinted windows sat outside my hotel room all night. It only left when, after a sleepless, paranoid night, I came outside.

As promised, Aman, my driver from the previous week, picked Florian and myself up. A couple of hours later, we crossed the border out of Nagorno-Karabakh. I felt huge relief, but knew I would not feel at total ease until I was finally out of this part of the world.

The drive back through the mountains meant nothing anymore and although taking most of the day, it passed in a blur. Florian and I discussed in detail the past few days, especially about the people we had both met. It became so obvious to us that I had not been the one interviewing people, *they* had been following *me* and asking *me* questions. Had the young woman I interviewed also reported back on me? I have no doubt that she did. The Stasi would have been proud.

Florian and I parted company at Yerevan's tiny airport. I cleared customs and was soon on a flight to Moscow. Spying? Ridiculous, but I really scared myself on the plane as I mulled over what *could* have happened if they had decided to hold me on spying charges. In hidden-away-from-the-world Nagorno-Karabakh, there's not a lot I could have done.

In the months since this scary incident, it has often crossed my mind... would it have turned out differently if Florian had not been there? If I had been totally on my own? They could have held for as long as they liked. No one would have had a clue as to my whereabouts. I would just have vanished...

Summing up

I wondered who backs who when it comes to Nagorno-Karabakh. When I delved into it, it certainly showed up some bewildering alliances.

Firstly, let us consider Russia. Currently, the Kremlin has cordial relations with both sides and often tries to mediate between the two. Russia has a military base in Armenia and many people I met in Armenia do not have a dislike and or distrust towards Moscow that other ex-Soviet states have. There are close links between Russia and Armenia, yet it would seem that Russia is leaning towards Azerbaijan, having recently supplied Baku with offensive military equipment worth around

USD five billion. For the life of me, I cannot say which 'side' Russia is on, if any.

The United Kingdom does not recognise Nagorno-Karabakh as an independent state, while the United States says it supports the territorial integrity of Azerbaijan.

Turkey, which is a major player in the region, backs its little brother Azerbaijan. Having much clout, Turkey could well be in a position to help solve the issue at hand, yet this is hampered due to its extremely poor relations with Armenia.

Iran, despite its obvious Muslim connection to Azerbaijan, has often, it seems, backed Christian Armenia (whilst continuing to give humanitarian aid to Azerbaijan). As for Israel, it backs Muslim Azerbaijan. Israel, by all accounts, has excellent diplomatic relations with the regime in Baku. Complicated and bewildering alliances indeed.

In my opinion, Armenia will never voluntarily hand over/give back Nagorno-Karabakh to Azerbaijan. It is simply not going to happen. Deep down I am sure Azerbaijan also knows this, and whilst not happy about it, accepts it as the true state of affairs. So what are Baku's options? Rather limited it would seem. In fact, I think they have but only two options.

Option one. Accept that Nagorno-Karabakh is lost to them forever. That is a big ask and one that I am sure would make the blood of every Azeri boil. That said, if we concede that Armenia will never hand it back, why not just accept it? If the goal is politics, power and strongmen, then of course do not accept it. If the goal is military strength, saving face, never letting anything go, then again, do not accept it.

However, what if the goal is *enough is enough*? What if it could be, 'Ok, we are not happy with the situation, but we want peace and no more killing'. It often takes a far bigger man to walk away from a fight then it does to retaliate. Lose face? Yes, in the short term. Aren't there enough killings in the world over land? Surely enough is enough.

Accepting would undoubtedly be a bitter pill to swallow for Azerbaijan, but no one can deny that it is an option, *if* people decide enough is enough. Will Azerbaijan do this? I am not kidding myself, I do not believe they will. Therefore, there may only be option two, and that is war.

Azerbaijan would need to use its full military might to invade and reclaim Nagorno-Karabakh. Would they win? On paper, the stats tell us that they probably would. But thousands would die, thousands on both sides, and it would make a volatile region even more volatile as it would undoubtedly draw in big players like Russia, Iran, and Turkey. Without wanting to disrespect *any* side, more mass killings and deaths are *not* worth a piece of land, as treasured as it may be to many.

All that said, I do not think that either of the two options I have given will happen. I certainly hope it is not the second one. Therefore, I feel the current state of affairs will continue as it is, with division, hatred, border shootings and violence. I feel this complicated divide will continue for many decades to come, and unfortunately only intensify.

Update March 2017

During the time since I was in Nagorno-Karabakh, the situation has gotten much worse. In April 2016, the worst fighting for 20 years between Nagorno-Karabakh and Azerbaijani forces took place. Dozens more have died on both sides. Just look at what I wrote in 2015. I said, 'I feel this complicated divide will continue for many decades to come, and unfortunately only intensify.'

Turkey's controversial president Erdogan has recently said he backs Azerbaijan to the end in its battle with Armenia over Nagorno-Karabakh.

I fear there is going to be an all-out war here. I hope I'm wrong.

The British Foreign & Commonwealth Office (FCO) advise **'against all travel'** to Nagorno-Karabakh.

3

Crimea

The new kid on the block

Status	Officially an autonomous part of Ukraine but under control of Russia after being annexed in February/March 2014
Population	Two million. 58% ethnic Russians, 24% Ukrainians, 12% Tatars (2001 census)
Languages	Russian, Ukrainian, Tatar
Religion	Mainly Russian and Ukrainian Orthodox

Introduction

EACH DIVIDE IN this book is different and in Crimea there are no dividing walls or razor wire. This divide is in reality an annexation, land 'taken' from Ukraine and now back under the control of Russia.

On 19 February 1954, while Ukraine was part of the USSR, Moscow gifted Crimea to the Ukrainians. Some say Crimea was given away; some say it was leant; some say it was given back. You will get a completely different answer from whomever you speak to, be it in Russia or Ukraine.

In 2014, after the revolution in Kiev and the horrendous civil war in Eastern Ukraine, Russia stepped in and took control of Crimea once again. Why is Crimea so important to Russia? Is it national pride? No, but that does come into it. It's about control of this vital piece of land that sticks out at the very bottom of Ukraine. If you control Crimea, you have huge influence on the strategically important Black Sea.

Passions run deep over Crimea. Ukraine claims it and wants it back. Russia claims it, *has it* and is *not* going to hand it back. Russia claims Crimea is now reunited with the motherland. But during my week there, I saw much internal division. I accept Russia is strong enough to hold onto Crimea, but the will of the people on the ground is nowhere near as pro-Russian as the Kremlin has made out. Russia claims that the vast majority voted to join Russia. This vote, as I learned, was anything but free and fair.

What is vital to point out here is the following: In 1994, Russia, the US and the UK signed what is known as the 'Budapest Memorandum'. It was clearly agreed that these powers would 'respect Ukraine's internal borders'.

So much for Crimea.

The What, Where and Why

Originally known as the Tauric Peninsula, Crimea was first annexed by Russia's Catherine the Great in 1783. From 1853 to 1856, the peninsula was at the heart of the Crimean War, a conflict between the Russian Empire and mainly Britain and France. The British, as history records, suffered big defeats and experienced the near suicidal 'Charge of the Light Brigade'.

After the Russian Revolution, Crimea came under the control of the

Red Army and became the Crimean Autonomous SSR, finally joining the USSR proper in 1922. During WWII, Crimea was under Nazi control between 1942 and 1944, but was then 'liberated' by the Red Army. It remained under Russian control until 1954 when Soviet leader Nikita Khrushchev gifted it to Ukraine. Of course, Ukraine was then part of the USSR, so Moscow still had ultimate control.

In 2014, after the revolution in Kiev's Maidan, Russia moved swiftly and the absorption of Crimea into the Russian Federation took place. This action is not recognised by Ukraine nor most of the international community.

Simferopol

With no flights into Crimea from mainland Ukraine, nor indeed anywhere else in the Western world, the only way for me to get there was via Moscow. Now a Russian visa is required to enter Crimea, which is becoming increasingly expensive and cumbersome to secure. On this occasion when I applied for my Russian visa in advance, using my usual agency in London, I asked them, 'Now that Crimea is Russian again, do I need a single entry or double entry visa?' They were unsure as the goalposts had now changed. I then called the Russian embassy and they clarified that a single entry visa would suffice.

After warnings from my Russian friends about going to Crimea, I headed to Moscow's Domodedovo airport. I noted that the flight to Crimea departed from the domestic terminal. Had I taken this route just months previously, my flight would have departed from the international terminal as Crimea then belonged to Ukraine. This was my first feeling of the change that had happened to this land in 2014.

After a two-hour flight, I landed at Crimea's Simferopol airport and what struck me first were the rows of empty and idle passport control booths. They were brand new, but lifeless. Again, in previous months, I would have had to go through passport control as I was landing in Ukraine. Now, coming here is classed as an internal Russian flight – so no passport control. It just did not feel right to me at all.

The area surrounding the airport is dated and run down. Hanging around were many middle-aged overweight men wearing 1980s style tracksuits. Everybody seemed to be smoking.

The following morning, I headed out of my apartment and stopped in front of a huge supermarket. These stores should have been full of produce from all over the EU, but now part of Russia, the Crimean people find themselves having to deal with Western sanctions that include many everyday items. They now, interestingly not unlike the old Soviet days, have to rely on inferior Russian goods. It was a brand new store, similar in style to a UK one, yet its shelves were nearly empty. Smaller stores were stocked with Russian goods, but many are struggling as supply lines with the outside world are severed.

All Ukrainian flags are gone in Simferopol. Parliament Square disturbed me. Lenin stands tall with the Russian tricolour all around. At another Lenin statue in a nearby park, I even saw three Hammer and Sickle flags fluttering behind him.

I was mindful of taking photos, but I was not stopped. I saw no other Westerners during my week in Simferopol. I had been warned by a contact to be careful: 'You will be followed and watched,' he said.

Gone is the Ukrainian currency, replaced by the Rouble. Gone are the Ukrainian police, replaced by Russian police. Even McDonald's pulled out in 2014.

In the centre, there are a few pretty European-style streets. Venture into a café, and try to order a *panini* for lunch, they can't supply it. No such products were available while I was there, due to Western sanctions. I shopped at local markets and cooked my own food.

Crimea should be bustling with life, but it's not. Cut off from the outside world, there was an air of uncertainty that hung over Simferopol. Overall, it was a depressing place.

Does a country belong to anyone? I don't know. But if Crimea does belong to anyone, the Tatar people, who are native to the Crimean Peninsula, surely have a claim to it. Through a contact in Tbilisi, I managed to arrange an interview with a member of the Tatar community. Widespread famine in the 1920s due to disastrous Soviet economic policies caused the deaths of tens of thousands of Tatars. Then in 1944, Stalin deported the entire Tatar population. They were only allowed to return to Crimea in the late 1980s.

The Tatar People

Ethnically Turkic, the Tatar people were by far the largest population in Crimea from the 15th to the mid-18th century.

In 1921, there was widespread famine due to failed Soviet economic policy, which resulted in the starvation of tens of thousands of people, while tens of thousands more fled to Turkey and Romania. It has been said that no other nationality suffered more under the USSR than the Tatar people.

In May 1944, on orders from Stalin, the entire Tatar population of 180,000 were deported *en masse* as a form of collective punishment for a small number of them siding with the Germans in WWII. The Tatar people were sent all over the USSR, some even to Siberian gulags, and untold thousands perished of cold and disease within months. This, in my opinion, is another example of genocide that is not recognised by the world.

In 1967, Soviet Russia removed the Nazi charges against the Tatars by decree, but they were not re-settled in their homeland. That would take another 20 agonising years, for the Tatars were only allowed to return to Crimea under Gorbachev's Perestroika in the mid-'80s. Since 1944, the Soviets had done everything possible to destroy the Tatar heritage. As early as 1920, Lenin commented: 'We will take them, divide them, subjugate them, digest them'.

The Tatars did return to Crimea, but the land they returned to was a very different place. Ethnic Russians had repopulated the land, and today the Tatars are now a minority of around 12 per cent in their native land.

Based for a week in the rather depressing and grey capital Simferopol, the evidence of the recent Russian annexation was very apparent. From my contact in Georgia, I had been put in touch with a Tatar male who lives in Simferopol. Only a first name and non-descript Gmail address was given. Definitely no phone numbers, as the security services could listen in.

Arranging my interview was very cloak and dagger and it did unnerve me. As we communicated, I was initially wary of *his* questions. He wanted to know much about me. I soon realised that he was probably worried that I was not who I said I was. I could have been working for Russia and once he opened up to me, I could report back on him.

I, on the other hand, was very wary of making the same mistakes I had done only two weeks previously in Nagorno-Karabakh. Was *he* working for the Russian security services and would he report back on me? I decided I would not meet on the street or in a café to discuss politics with anyone. I asked for the interview to be held in my apartment. He declined. He asked me to come to his apartment. I declined. His English was not great and I contacted my man in Georgia, passed on emails and asked him to confirm that this man was the person whom he claimed he was.

'It's him,' my Georgian said. 'He really wants to talk with you, but he's nervous and you will soon learn why.'

After a flurry of emails, I finally received the message: 'We meet Friday 1.00pm. Beside central market is a bus stop. I saw your picture on the internet. I will come to you. I am wearing jeans, leather jacket and black hat, I will be holding a newspaper.'

I went to bed that night, wondering if I was about to walk into a Nagorno-Karabakh mark two. The following day, after a breakfast of coffee and eggs, and a hot shower in my 1960s Soviet-style apartment, I headed out onto the streets. It was cold and bleak but dry. I gave myself two hours to walk and collect my thoughts. At 12.50pm, I was stood waiting.

Within minutes, a man walked towards me, dressed as the email said. He smiled and nervously shook my hand.

'I came alone,' I reassured him. 'I don't think anyone followed me.'

'They didn't.'

'How do you know?'

'We had our people follow you just to make sure no one from the security services was following you.'

I did not know what to make of that. 'What would you have done if you'd seen I'd been followed?'

'I would not have turned up.'

We walked; I had no idea where we were going. We made small talk and I realised I was as nervous as he was. I need not have worried though. The Tatar people I interviewed were amongst the kindest I have ever had the pleasure of meeting. The story of their history and what really happened around the 2014 vote in Crimea to rejoin Russia is nothing short of remarkable.

Tatar interview

The Crimean Tatars were largely happy to live in a Crimea that was part of Ukraine. However, against their own wishes, they have now found themselves back under Russian control.

We met in an undisclosed building in Simferopol. Present were four members of the Tatar community including our interpreter. I will use no names. We enjoyed tea and cakes as they asked about me and my background. Everyone soon became very relaxed and I started our interview.

I asked whether any Tatars had supported Nazi Germany in WWII.

'Yes, a very small group did, but the vast majority of the Tatar community was fiercely loyal to Russia. Even after Stalin had many Tatar intellectuals executed in the 1930s, our men fought and died for the Red Army. But the reward for their bravery and loyalty was to be deported. In fact, the entire Tatar community – men, women and children – was deported in 1944. We call it *Surgun*. It was only under Gorbachev that we were allowed to return. But by then, our land had been repopulated by Russians and we are now in the minority.'

'You are still living in the same city, but it is now not part of Ukraine. You now live in Russia and are subject to Western sanctions. What are your views on sanctions?' Their answers surprised me.

'We support them. My father recently said to me, more sanctions please, more! We want the West to squeeze the Kremlin so they back off. We are ready to suffer in the short term.'

They then went on to tell me how the Maidan protests in Kiev affected Crimea.

'In February 2014, Russia moved at quick speed, and they were organised. Troops flooded into Crimea, military equipment and trucks. It had obviously been planned long in advance. Anyone complaining was warned off or arrested. But even up to early March, they said they had no intention of annexing Crimea. But we *knew* it would happen.'

'The Kremlin says the troops were local self-defence volunteer groups.'

Their incredulous reply was, 'With guns, bombs and the best military equipment? This was not volunteers. It was Russian troops.'

My mind wanders to Eastern Ukraine.

'I want to talk about the vote on 16 March 2014. What is your first-hand experience of this time?'

'Oh, it was a total farce. At the vote and the counting, there were no international observers allowed to witness it. Western journalists were locked outside the buildings. One local reporter did an experiment. Using his passport, he managed to vote five times in five different polling stations. There are many examples of this. How can this be right? Also, not up to date registers were used. Even people who were dead voted. I mean someone who was alive voted in their place.'

'Are you saying that people used the documents of dead people and voted pro-Russian on their behalf?'

'Yes, it happened.'

Officially, the Kremlin says 97 per cent of voters voted for annexation, and that the turnout was 83 per cent. But, and this is truly fascinating, the Russian President's own so-called 'Human Rights Council' wrote that a mid-point estimate was that only 55 per cent of voters voted 'yes' with a turnout of 40 per cent. Therefore, only 22.5 per cent of the total Crimean population had actually voted in favour of joining Russia.

Our interpreter said: 'Here is the critical thing. There was nothing on the ballot paper asking "Do you want to remain part of Ukraine?". Can you believe it? We were given the choice of joining Russia or becoming a separate state. Nothing about remaining part of Ukraine. The whole thing was nonsense. I just wish Russian people would understand this.'

'Am I right in saying that the Tatar community boycotted the vote?'

'Yes. Less one per cent of our people voted.'

'What happened after the vote?'

'Parliament was immediately taken over by Russian soldiers. In the months since, signs and symbols of anything Ukrainian were destroyed. Books in Ukrainian have even been burned.'

Another voice at the table added: 'Tatar and Ukrainian children in schools are now forced to sing the Russian national anthem. And, I tell you this, a teenage daughter of my friend recently went on holiday to Kiev. When she returned to school, the Russian children in Crimea who knew she had been to Kiev called her a fascist, a Nazi.'

The discussion soon moved onto passports – and what a minefield that was. They showed me their brand new Russian passports, only months old. Yet they still have their Ukrainian passports. There is confusion, for me anyway, as to what is real, legitimate or internationally recognised. The new Russian passports actually looked and felt fake to me. Cheap, poor quality. The Tatar people have them because they now need them to get a job and open bank accounts. These new Russian passports are issued by the Federal Immigration Agency, although the rest of the world does not recognise them. If the Tatar people want to travel abroad, they use their old Ukrainian passports.

'Did everyone take a new Russian passport?' I asked.

'No, many refused out of principal. Instead they were given a document that basically treats them as a foreigner in their own country.'

Considering how difficult it was to set up this meeting and their initial concerns about who I was, I simply had to ask. 'Are your people being watched by the Russian security services?'

'Sure we are. Several friends have already been arrested according to phone calls they made. You know, many people who spoke out against the annexation have gone missing. My friend's brother is still missing.'

'So the authorities are listening in to phone conversations?'

'Definitely. There is no freedom of speech here, not if you speak out against Russia anyway. Journalists are being arrested by the FSB. We know one guy, only 20 years old, who held a one-person demo in Lenin Square. He simply stood there quietly with a sign that read 'Crimea is Ukrainian.'

'What happened to him?'

'He was beaten badly by the police.'

'You've said that you believe that the actions taken by Russia over Crimea were well-planned. How far in advance do you think?'

'I think we can go right back to 2004.'

'The Orange Revolution?'

'Exactly. Of course, nothing changed in Ukraine after 2004, because few people knew how to change things. Now though, ten years later, many young people have been to the West, understand democracy and these values. They don't want to belong to a Russian/Soviet-style corrupt country.'

'But what's this got to do with Russia having planned this for years?'

'The Kremlin is not stupid. It can control many people for a long time, but not everyone forever. They didn't like what happened in 2004 and of course then helped keep things the same in Ukraine, but they also knew that 2004 would come round again and they were prepared. We feel that they saw the demonstrations coming in Kiev and planned to retake Crimea years ago.'

We discussed *Stockholm syndrome* and large chunks of the Russian population. However, and this was the interesting thing, although it is my own personal opinion, which I will explain in detail later in this book, I did *not* bring it up at this point. The Tatar people brought it up as their opinion. *Finally, someone understands*, I thought.

The Tatars are of Muslim faith. I asked if they are free to worship.

'Officially yes, but the security services watch who attends the Mosques. There is also a list of Islamic books that are now banned under Russian law.'

'What's the future for the Tatar people?'

'Just to survive as families and a nation.'

The Tatar people I met were extremely friendly, intelligent, well read and open-minded. Despite their decades of repression by the USSR, I never once detected an ounce of hatred towards Russian people. I was proud to have been in their company.

To give you a completely different take on the problems between Ukraine and Russia over Crimea and eastern Ukraine, here are two interviews I conducted in Moscow the week *prior* to coming to Crimea. The first is with a pro-Russian family who fled Lugansk area in eastern Ukraine. They are currently staying in the Moscow region with the older man's brother (a family that I have known and been good friends with for more than 20 years).

Sat around the kitchen table were father and son, my interpreter and myself. The son used to live in Lugansk Ukraine (which has seen fierce fighting between government troops and separatist rebels) and is now called the 'Lugansk People's Republic.' The father lived in a small country house (a dacha) just across the border, 100 metres inside Russia. Along with their family, they fled this region in late 2014, fearing for the lives of their family and children. They say they were under attack from the Kiev government.

'What was it like to live in Lugansk and the surrounding areas in 2014?'

'It was terrible. After Maidan and then the attack on us by Kiev, we felt it, heard explosions all day and night. We've had no running water and no electricity. But thankfully we are still alive. But we had to get out, while we could.'

'How did you manage to get out?'

'There was a lull in the fighting and we decided we could leave then. It was not safe for our children there. Our house in Lugansk has no water, no electricity, from July 2014. Schools and hospitals are all affected. The airport is ruined, the roads are terrible, and there were snipers and shooting. We took cars and we drove the long drive up through Russia to Moscow region. Now we are here with my brother and are very grateful to him.'

'The Kremlin keeps saying that there are no Russian troops in eastern Ukraine. You lived there. Are there Russian troops in eastern Ukraine?'

'No, only volunteers.'

'For volunteers, they seem to extremely well organised and are armed with the best of equipment. Where does it all come from?' I asked.

They simply replied, 'We have never seen a regular army in eastern Ukraine, only volunteers.'

'In eastern Ukraine, we all speak Russian. It's our culture. But after Maidan, we had to start filling in documents in Ukrainian. They want to stop us speaking Russian. They want to take away our history.'

'And the Ukrainian army are bombing us, we are supposed to live in Ukraine, but they bomb us. Many civilians have died.'

Civilians dying on any side is wrong and never gets my support. Russians being forced to speak Ukrainian in eastern Ukraine is wrong and does not get my support. Oppression of the Tatars in Crimea, ordinary people arrested by the FSB and Ukrainian books being burned is wrong, and something that few Russians know anything about.

The problem is, as in all divides, most sides can only see their point of view. My interest (for this book) is the divide that is Crimea. This is not a chapter about the war in eastern Ukraine. However, I felt it important to point out that innocent pro-Russians in eastern Ukraine have also suffered immensely after being caught up in this highly fuelled political war. The son continued:

'Do you know that all the money produced in places like Donbass was taken by Kiev? They take our money. We are paying for the good roads in Kiev and other Western cities. Look at the roads in eastern Ukraine, not good. All the money goes to Kiev and Western Ukraine.'

'That is kind of what central governments do all over the world. So, I have to ask, what do you think of the government in Kiev?'

'It's not a real government, we didn't vote for it,' said the father. I then asked the son the same question.

'They take their orders from America.'

'What are your views on what happened in Maidan?'

'It was a planned action. All controlled by a third party.'

'And that third party was?' I asked.

'The Americans, the British and the EU of course.'

We then discussed *why* Maidan happened. The reasons for it. I said that the then pro-Russian Ukrainian leader Yanukovych had said he would sign the infamous EU trade deal. But after a trip to Moscow, Putin put pressure on him and Yanukovych did a complete U-turn and then said he would not sign it. The family sat in front of me, didn't actually dispute that, they simply commented, 'The actions in Maidan were planned by outside third parties. It was not spontaneous action by ordinary people. Who do you think paid for Maidan?'

I did not get a chance to answer – they answered their own question. 'It was paid for by less than ten people. Ukrainian oligarchs who wanted to take power. In Ukraine, people with money hold the power.'

I don't disagree, but it is interesting to note that there was no mention from them about the massive state run corruption that Ukraine has suffered for decades under its old pro-Russian leaders. That, I feel, is what has held back Ukraine, not pro-democracy protesters in 2004 or 2014.

'If Ukraine had signed this deal, it would be very bad for eastern Ukraine. All the industry for Ukraine comes from the east, the coal, the steel, everything. We fund Kiev with our taxes, they have nothing without us, but we get nothing back.'

I accept that the heart of these old industries lies in the east, but they do not seem to understand that the future of a modern economy is not dirty old state run industries, but modern clean technology. Of course, they are scared about European imports taking away their potential sales of their coal. Again that is what a modern economy is, the free market. I am also surprised that they think all the money that goes to central government comes from their heavy industry. I'm sure much does, but there is also a growing modern business and tourist sector emerging in central and Western Ukraine. Undoubtedly that brings much into the central government coffers.

'I want to ask you about the recently self-proclaimed People's Republics of Donetsk and Lugansk, now claiming independence from Ukraine and run by highly dubious figures armed with guns and unaccountable to no international law. Do you genuinely believe that this has any legitimacy at all?'

'We had a vote there, and we said we didn't recognise the new Kiev government after Maidan. So we go our own way.'

'I understand that, but surely any region or city of any country cannot simply decide to declare its own republic and split from central government just because it doesn't like it. If that were replicated all over the world, there would be international anarchy.'

The only reply was that their little republics are legitimate.

'I've travelled all over Ukraine, and for me, it seems that Western Ukraine and Eastern Ukraine are almost two different countries.' They nodded their heads in agreement. 'The West is European and the East is more Russian. With all the ongoing problems, may Ukraine one day split in two?'

'Maybe. Maybe.' It was said with a heavy heart, not with pleasure.

The father told me that he was so passionate about eastern Ukraine and its connections to Russia, its history, language and culture, that if he was a younger man and not retired, he would be fighting in Lugansk against the Kiev government.

We ended the interview with one last cup of tea, and after I said how much I enjoyed the honey that had been served to accompany the tea, the father produced two large tubs of his homemade honey and presented it to me as a gift. I will say this – despite huge differences on such topics as democracy and the USSR, the hospitality I have received from ordinary Russians in their homes over the years has been second to none.

This family will return home, of that I have no doubt. But to what? Even if their homes are still standing and the water and electricity is back on, what does the future hold for them? I wish them to belong to a more democratic country that looks westward. However, that is not what they want. They want their futures to be tied to their shared past with Russia/ the USSR. I respect their views, but I do not feel positive about their future.

They also invited me to visit Lugansk and stay in their home. One day. I would like to go, but it's under rebel control and extremely unsafe. One day I hope I will visit – but will that area be back in Ukraine, or a separate republic unrecognised by the world? Or even part of mother Russia? No one knows.

Although I have not been to Lugansk or Donbass, I have been in eastern Ukraine. I spent a week in Kharkiv, which is the region just north of the Donbass area. Kharkiv is currently under the control of Kiev and has suffered bombings, yet nothing like the war in Lugansk.

Coming from the Russian city of Belgorod, I crossed the border into Ukraine on foot. A tense border indeed – you could feel the suspicion on both sides. That said, it did produce one of those interesting and human never-a-dull-moments that I seem to experience whilst on the road. Despite the fact my 'do it for a living' tap dancing days are well and truly over, I still occasionally put my shoes on. During the previous week in Moscow, after Nagorno-Karabakh and before heading to Crimea, I had spent some days dance training and did a small performance at one of my old haunts. Therefore, my tap shoes were still in my bag.

I was leaving Russia and my paperwork was in order, so I exited the country without a second look. I walked through the no man's land, surrounded by fences, CCTV and razor wire. Russian and Ukrainian soldiers stood less than 100 metres apart, monitoring the comings and goings. At the Ukrainian side, I was met by Ukrainian soldiers and shown to a nearby hut for document inspection. Inside, the border guards were very suspicious about a foreigner travelling alone and crossing from Russia on foot. I was taken aside, my passport studied in detail and I was asked where I was going and what was I doing. My luggage of course was opened and gone through in detail. No problems... until they found my heavy black well-worn tap shoes.

An armed Ukrainian took said shoes in his hands and looked with fascination at the two metal taps on each shoe. He banged one against a table then asked me with intrigue, 'What is it?' I tried to explain, but wasn't getting very far – so there was only one thing for it, I kicked off my boots, put on my tap shoes and did a ten second combination right there and then.

The border guard looked at me with his mouth hanging open, then clapped his hands, smiled and said 'Cool! Very good! Very good!' He handed me back my passport and told me I could proceed without any more delay. As I walked into Ukraine proper, I smiled to myself, thinking that had to be one of the weirdest places I had ever tap danced in. Then I remembered, in the mid-'90s in a restaurant in Moscow, I tapped danced with a jazz band. It was a private function for what can only be described as the mafia. At one point, much to the mafia diners delight and applause, I danced across the length of the food- and cognac-laden wooden table at which they were sat. As I finished and jumped off, four different guys stuffed notes into my hand. I shoved them in my pocket and it wasn't until I was sat on the metro heading home at 1.00am that I looked at them. They were 100-dollar bills. I had just made $400 – an absolute fortune for me at the time. Moscow in the '90s was a wild place indeed.

The gigantic statue of Lenin in the centre of Kharkiv has been pulled down leaving only one of his boots atop the plinth. Nearby I saw a very provocative poster showing caricatures of Hitler caressing Russian President Vladimir Putin. Ukrainian flags fly everywhere, yet most people speak Russian, not Ukrainian. I did ask around about the possibility of me making the trip south to the Donbass area. I was warned off, too dangerous. Roadblocks with the Ukrainian army on one side and separatist rebels on the other. A very slim chance of getting in, and even if I did manage that, precious little chance of getting safely out again. I did not even attempt it.

Second interview in Moscow prior to Crimea

He was a friend of a friend of a friend. I know his real name, but as agreed with him beforehand, I would not use it. Nor was I to take any photos of him. I will call him Pavel.

Since Pavel does not speak English, an interpreter was also present. We met in the interpreter's apartment. Pavel is my age, but made me look like a boy. He was big and strong, the classic Russian alpha male. Nevertheless, he was also polite and shook my hand when we met. We sat in the living room and once the tea was poured, I began.

'I believe that you left the frontline of the Army in 2001. What is your role now?'

'I train people.'

'Where do you work?'

'I work in a military organisation in Moscow.' I knew by his eyes that he was not willing to divulge any more on this subject, so I did not push it.

'Mr Putin says that there are no Russian soldiers in Ukraine. Most of the world doesn't believe this. So I ask you, are there Russian soldiers in Ukraine?'

'Officially no. Mr Putin does not make anyone go, they are all volunteers, patriotic Russians. There are also support staff like doctors and cooks.'

When I hear the word 'volunteers' I can picture myself and a few mates, a bunch of amateurs with sticks and stones and maybe the odd hand gun. But in Eastern Ukraine, these so-called volunteers are well-organised, trained and armed to the teeth. I am highly sceptical that they are just volunteers.

'Is the Russian government supplying the volunteers with weapons?'

'Yes. There are also specialists there.'

'Like yourself?'

'Yes. I have been in Lugansk and Donetsk, training the volunteers.'

'So there *are* Russian soldiers in Ukraine.' It was a statement, not a question.

'No, not officially.'

It was time to move on.

'Let's talk about the revolution in Kiev's Maidan. I was in Maidan Square in March 2014. I put it to you that what happened in Kiev's Maidan Square was the indiscriminate shooting and killing of civilians by Berkut Special Forces.'

'No. In the streets, there were fascists in the crowd stirring up trouble. Fascists from the US and Europe with weapons and money. They want to take Ukraine and then do the same to Russia.'

'Look, I'm not saying that all those in Maidan were good people, but I saw with my very own eyes thousands of ordinary men and women, demonstrating against a very corrupt government, one they wanted rid of for good. Dozens of them were shot dead in Maidan.'

Pavel's only reply to that was, 'Members of the Berkut died also. I have friends in the Berkut.' That chilled me.

'Can you tell me anything about the tragic shooting down of the Malaysian Jet over East Ukraine?'

'We didn't touch it.'

He constantly talks about fascists. Pavel though, like many Russians, does not seem to understand what the word *really* means. Russian state media are throwing the word fascism around like confetti. It is a label given to near anyone who is against them. Fascism though, is *not* ordinary people demonstrating and trying to throw off a corrupt regime. Quite the opposite.

Pavel also talked a lot about the US, the EU and Israel. He's a fan of none of them. The West, he told me, 'has lost its morals'.

I told him that I am worried and saddened by the path Russia is taking, moving further away from democracy with an authoritative state that controls the press and has an increasing hold on society. Pavel replied,

'This direction is the correct direction. If we have democracy, people will think as individuals and the nation will fail. We must be as one.'

'Can you tell me where your work has taken you over the years?'

'Many places. I can't say all.'

He did however, later admit that he had fought in the very place I had just been detained in, Nagorno-Karabakh.

'In your work, have you personally killed anyone?'

'I killed my first man when I was 19.' He said it so matter of fact, like telling me he'd had eggs for breakfast. Pavel talked openly and in depth with me for an hour and 47 minutes. As physically aggressive as he has undoubtedly been in his 'work', he was calm and courteous with me. I thanked Pavel for his time, we shook hands and he looked me right in the eye, smiled a genuine smile, and wished me luck and safety on my travels.

The photos you see here I took whilst in Maidan Kiev in 2014. The deaths in Maidan were of either innocent pro-democracy protesters or fascists. You decide.

Yalta

I left my old apartment in Simferopol and headed to Yalta by taxi. It was less than 60 miles but it took us nearly two hours. The roads were not good. Yalta is seen as a jewel in the Soviet crown. The very mention of the word 'Yalta' to many Russians makes them go hazy-eyed. It was a place where a lucky few got to escape the grim realities of cities like Moscow. People came down to enjoy the sun, sand, sea and mountains. For many citizens of the former USSR, Yalta is nostalgia.

Parts of Yalta are nice, it has stunning scenery but overall it reminded me of the iconic run-down Scottish Highland resort of Aviemore in the 1980s. Grim. The town's one and only McDonald's is abandoned, closed down when the corporation pulled out following the annexation.

To be fair, there are pleasant parts in the centre and buildings have been renovated along the prom, but it's nothing short of a disgrace that it all feels like 1993 and not 2015. What the blazes have they been doing here for the past 22 years? I expected it to look like this after the USSR fell, but it's been part of Ukraine since then and precious little has been spent on it, nowhere near enough to drag it out of its Soviet past. Yalta is stuck in limbo, teetering on the edge of past decades. What a wasted opportunity. Yalta is not the jewel many think it is, but it so easily could have been.

Due to its place on our planet, it does boast quite a unique, humid, sub-tropical climate and a fascinating environment. It was well below zero when I left Moscow, yet Yalta was almost 20 degrees warmer. I stood in the central square beside the statue of Lenin and took in the magnificent view. Palm trees surrounded him and directly behind were beautiful snow-capped mountains. After a 15-minute walk in the other direction, I sat down on the empty beach, took my shoes and socks off and paddled in the warm Black Sea.

On the Sunday morning, I strolled along the prom and took a photo of local fishermen. It felt like I was in a different era, a gentler time. But of course I wasn't, I was in a land that has been annexed and is now part of Russia. At the roadsides on the outskirts of Yalta, I saw numerous political billboards. Many showed Putin's face and some showed the Russian Communist Zyuganov. These billboards declared 'congratulations' to Crimea for rejoining Russia. I also saw billboards with swastikas pasted on a map of Ukraine. It was propaganda overdrive.

Many shops in Yalta were closed and others lacked products. I spoke with one café owner, a Ukrainian, who told me what she thought of Crimea being part of Russia and now forced to endure Western sanctions. She used to stock Italian biscuits, French cheese, Parma ham and many other delicacies. They are all gone now. The coffee I was served was Italian, but past its best and running low. I was one of only a dozen Westerners she had met in six months and she was dreading the summer season.

The hotel I stayed in would normally have been way above my pay grade as a traveller. It was four-star Western standard with a balcony and en-suite bathroom. A room here in the summer, before the annexation, would cost up to USD100 per night, I was informed. I paid £14. But that wasn't for one night. I paid £14 for four nights. It was an extremely welcoming slice of affordable luxury after a very trying couple of months on the road. But sadly another example of how Crimea has suffered since the annexation.

The tourist industry here is nearly devastated. I cannot imagine anyone from Kiev coming now, it would not be safe for them. In addition, apart from the odd traveller like myself, I can't imagine many from the West making it here either. Before the annexation, all you had to do was take a flight from Europe to Kiev, visa free, and catch a connecting flight to Simferopol. Now you have to apply in advance for a Russian visa, which is timely and expensive and includes getting yourself first to London to be fingerprinted. Once you have your visa, you then to fly to Moscow and catch a connecting flight to Simferopol. Moreover, Western governments say it is not safe to travel here and there are no embassies in Crimea.

I feel the pro-Russian locals have cut off their nose to spite their own face. The majority rely on the tourist money and that has now gone. Anyone here who genuinely voted to join mother Russia seems to have done so out of blind obedience. I saw no other Western tourists while I was in Yalta, only a few Russians. Most people have been scared off and I doubt they will be coming back in their droves again any time soon.

From what I have been told, the Russian government is planning a huge charm offensive to encourage Russians to visit Crimea for their holidays instead of heading to the West. The object being to get money flowing back into Crimea's dilapidated tourist industry.

Time will tell.

Summing up

The Ukrainians feel they have lost part of their land. The Russians feel they have gained back what was theirs in the first place. 'Khrushchev should have never given Crimea away in the first place. He had no right to do so', was what one of my Russian friends told me.

If you say to the average Russian that the referendum in 2014 was a sham, according to locals, and considered highly dubious by the international community, they brush it all off as 'Western propaganda'. They do so because any criticism of Russia is firstly brushed away by the Kremlin as Western propaganda. They also claim that the West is trying to destabilise Russia.

If parents repeatedly tell a child that the Bogeyman lives under his bed, he or she will believe it. They will believe it even if someone else takes their hand, looks under the bed and shows them that he is not there after all. They will believe it because the seed of fear has already been planted. That is how propaganda works and no one does it better than the Kremlin.

I have my own opinion on whether Crimea belongs to Russia or Ukraine, but that is irrelevant here. All of our opinions in the West are irrelevant when it comes to Crimea. Only one thing matters here; will Crimea return to Ukraine? No. Absolutely not. It will simply not happen. There is nothing Ukraine can do, for they are no military match for Russia. As for the West, the Kremlin stopped caring what we think a long time ago.

What truly concerns me is the language used by the Kremlin's state-controlled media. It often claims that those in Kiev, and anyone who disagrees with what Russia is doing, is anti-Russian, a fascist and, at worst, a Nazi.

This language is also used by many Russians to describe outsiders. This is deeply worrying indeed, for it stokes hatred and suspicion. There's nothing wrong with having a small dose of patriotism I guess, but rampant nationalism, as I've come to learn from my research on this book, is an increasingly dangerous thing.

Following Maidan, the Kremlin is not going to give up Crimea. Ukraine and the world simply have to accept it and deal with it. I think the government in Kiev, who are not stupid, have in private accepted the inevitable.

But why is the world not banging on about the Budapest Memorandum of 1994? Signed by Russia, the US and the UK, it was clearly agreed that these powers would 'respect Ukraine's internal borders'. I have rarely heard it even mentioned by the world's movers and shakers. I mentioned it to some Russians – most had never heard of it – while others dismissed it and simply replied 'Crimea is Russian!'

Let us go right back to the Yalta Conference of 1945 when Roosevelt, Stalin and Churchill met to dish up the spoils of victory over Nazi Germany. Personally, I am not so proud of what took place at Yalta. Hindsight is a wonderful thing, but how could they not have known Stalin's intentions? The Soviets actually promised fair and free elections in Eastern Europe and specifically gave guarantees about Poland. Did Churchill really believe this at the time? He was a great man, but I struggle with all this.

The Soviets did make numerous concessions at Yalta, but they were not kept. Post Yalta, the Russian Foreign Minister mentioned to Stalin that he was concerned about the wording of the Yalta agreement. Stalin replied, 'Never mind, we'll do it our own way later.'

As such, no free elections were held and the peoples of Eastern Europe, having being freed from Nazi control, would now suffer Soviet dictatorship for more than 45 years.

Churchill of course 'finally realised' what the Soviets were up to. In that famous speech in Fulton Missouri in 1946, he warned, 'From Stettin in the Baltics, to Trieste in the Adriatic, an iron curtain has descended across the continent'.

However, it was too late. Russia had its plan in place and the once great capitals of Prague, Budapest and Warsaw were cut off from the rest of Europe. What later followed was the disgrace that is the Berlin Wall and the cutting of our continent in two.

The ball for all of this, in my opinion, started rolling at Livadia Palace in Yalta. I think the West let down the people of Eastern Europe immensely, particularly Poland, by allowing huge chunks of territory to fall under communist control. Not one of 'our finest hours'.

Ukraine is in this mess for the long haul. The paths ahead, whatever direction they take, are rocky to say the least. I am reminded of a conversation I had on a night train from Lvov to Kiev in 2005. I shared a cabin with a charming woman named Larissa. Around age 50, she was a schoolteacher, English-speaker and highly intelligent. I asked her, what will change in Ukraine, when will it move into proper democracy and leave its Soviet past behind? Even then, years before the horrors of 2014, she said. 'If you mean the next 20 years, nothing will change. But in 100 years, maybe change. Maybe'.

I wonder what she makes of the situation in her country today.

Who has failed Ukraine? Firstly, Ukraine's corrupt politicians have failed Ukraine on a spectacular scale over the past 20 years. Secondly, the West has failed Ukraine in not helping it more with its transition from communism into democracy. Lastly, Russia has failed Ukraine for dragging it backwards, influencing elections and trying to keep Ukraine as its buffer between Russia and the West.

To sum up the seriousness of the problems between Ukraine and Russia, I would like to mention the following project. A project that has surprisingly been given precious little news space so far. Right now, Ukraine is currently building a wall along its entire border with Russia. Whether it is justified or not, I have no idea. But many in Ukraine are worried. Worried about a full-scale Russian invasion of their country. Construction on the wall started in 2015. It will take four years to complete and is going to be colossal in size and stature. Plans include electrified fences, razor wire, steel turrets, ditches and antipersonnel mines. At roughly 1,200 miles long, this new divide will be one of the biggest on planet Earth.

My heart is heavy for Ukraine, for all of its people and its future. Ukraine is broken.

Update March 2017

Crimea remains 'part of Russia'.

Fighting and violence continue in and around the breakaway republics in Eastern Ukraine.

In December 2016, Ukraine completed a series of missile tests over the Black Sea. Russia called the tests a provocation.

In March 2017, Russia carried out land, air and sea drills involving 2,500 paratroopers.

The British Foreign & Commonwealth Office (FCO) advise **'against all travel'** to Crimea.

4

Kosovo

A circle I could not square

Status	The 'Republic of Kosovo' is a partially recognised parliamentary republic. It is not in the EU but uses the Euro as its official currency
Capital	Pristina
Population	2014 estimated at 1.8 million (around 92% thought to be ethnically Albanian)
Languages	Albanian, Serbian, Bosnian, Turkish
Religion	Islam and Serbian Orthodox

Introduction

AFTER THE BLOODY breakup of Yugoslavia, Kosovo experienced a brutal war with Serbia in 1998–89. With much fanfare, support from many and to the distaste of others, it finally declared independence in 2008.

But is Kosovo *really* an independent country or is it part of Serbia? Officially, it is an independent country, but in reality, on the ground, it's not an easy one to call. Until the early 1990s Kosovo was a province of Serbia and thus part of the wider country of Yugoslavia. When that crumbled, brutal wars ensued. The world was shocked as the horrendous killing of civilians took place on European soil, on a scale not seen since the Second World War. Many call what happened in the Balkans 'genocide' – in particular, what took place in Srebrenica when more than 8,000 Muslim men and boys were massacred by Bosnian Serb forces.

But this chapter is not about the Balkan wars. Much has been and will be written on that by others. This is about one of today's 'Mankind's Great Divides'.

For this chapter, I am concentrating on the Kosovan city of Mitrovica, a symbol of not just Kosovo but of *all* of the old ethnic divisions in Yugoslavia. As of summer 2014, Mitrovica is once again divided by the blockage of the bridge on the River Ibar. The Albanian south of Mitrovica is Muslim, pro-EU, pro-US, pro-NATO and pro-UK. The north of the city is Serbian, pro-Russian, Orthodox and anti-NATO.

The explanation in the above paragraph alone explains why I say that Mitrovica is a circle I just could not square. At this divide, there is no razor wire and no concrete, there are no walls and no watchtowers. The dividing line is a bridge that was once open, but as of 2014, is once again blocked.

Mitrovica is two cities within one, or possibly even two countries within one city.

The What, Where and Why

Yugoslavia came into existence in 1918 after WWI under the name 'Kingdom of Serbs, Croats and Slovenes'. It was renamed the Kingdom of Yugoslavia in October 1929. In 1945 the monarchy was abolished and in 1946 the country was renamed the Federal People's Republic of Yugoslavia by the new communist government. Finally, in 1963 it was renamed the Socialist Federal Republic of Yugoslavia and was ruled by the dictator Tito until his death in 1980. During the Tito years, Kosovo was part of the Socialist Republic of Serbia.

The 1980s saw the rise of the Serbian communist and Nationalist, Slobodan Milosevic. He became President of Serbia in 1989 and stripped Kosovo of its autonomy, putting it back under the direct control of Belgrade.

Ethnic tensions and nationalism bubbled to the surface all across the region and in 1991, Macedonia, Croatia, Slovenia and Bosnia broke away from Yugoslavia. In 1992, only Serbia and Montenegro remained. They formed a new country, naming it the Federal Republic of Yugoslavia.

For most of the '90s, in what became known as the Balkan Wars, the area was subjected to appalling and brutal ethnic fighting. Croats fought Bosnian Muslims, Serbians fought Albanian Kosovans and God only knows what else. These were undoubtedly Europe's deadliest conflicts since WWII. Ethnic cleansing, crimes against humanity and mass rape were the norm. The International Centre for Transitional Justice claims that the Yugoslav wars caused the deaths of around 140,000 people.

By the mid-'90s, The Kosovan Liberation Army fought against Serb control and targeted Serb institutions. This led to a major crackdown by Belgrade and ethnic cleansing of Kosovar Albanians by Serbian authorities. Hundreds of thousands fled to places such as Macedonia and Albania, but many thousands died in Kosovo as a direct result of President Milosevic's actions. This, as we all know, led to a long-awaited response from NATO, as air strikes finally took place on Serb military and government targets. Highly controversial at the time, the air strikes, led by the UK and the US, did the intended job. The Serb military machine was broken and Kosovo became a UN protectorate.

What is fascinating to note here is the influence back then (or lack thereof) from two of the world's biggest players, Russia and China. It is vital to remember that in the 1990s neither of these two countries were the world powers that they are today. The Chinese had yet to step on to the world stage, so to speak. As for Russia, it was a broken society still licking its wounds after the breakup of the USSR. Although Russia huffed and puffed and backed Serbia, under Yeltsin it was in no position to act as it may have wished and reluctantly let NATO take the lead.

As for China, their position can be shown from their passive reaction to the incident when five NATO bombs mistakenly hit the Chinese embassy in Belgrade, killing three. The intended target was a nearby Yugoslav military building. The Chinese were naturally furious and complained to the highest level. They also used the Belgrade incident to their own advantage, ramping up anti-US sentiment at home. Organised and sanctioned demonstrations took place outside the American, British and other Western embassies over a number of days. The Chinese authorities also omitted to tell the Chinese people that President Clinton had apologised unreservedly for the bombings. By the end of 1999, the US had made humanitarian payments to the Chinese families of those who died or were injured to the sum of almost USD5 million. They also paid the Chinese government a reported USD28 million in compensation for the damage to the embassy. Thankfully, the fallout from this tragic mistake blew over rather quickly.

However, let us consider this, if we dare. How do you think today's China, an economic and ever increasing military superpower, would react if the UK or the US mistakenly bombed one of its foreign embassies? It does not bear thinking about.

And what about today's Russia? Taking into account their 'support' for war in East Ukraine and the annexation of Crimea, as well as anti-NATO and Western rhetoric, just how would Putin's strongman Russia react today if Western powers were to bomb Belgrade? It is a terrifying thought. Thankfully, the world was a very different place in the late '90s.

Kosovo's declaration of independence from Serbia was finally enacted on 17 February 2008. NATO peacekeepers, who have been in Kosovo since 1999, are still there on the ground, especially in Mitrovica.

After years of official standoffs, Serbia and Kosovo reached a landmark agreement to normalise relations in 2013. They have also agreed not to block each other's attempts to join the EU. That said, as with the divided communities in Northern Ireland, and in Belfast in particular, the situation on the ground in Mitrovica is far from normal.

Recognition

Getting a country recognised by the world is no easy task. There is a huge difference between Kosovo and say, Nagorno-Karabakh. Nagorno-Karabakh is not recognised by any UN member, but Kosovo is by many. As of 2015, the following countries officially recognise Kosovo as an independent state: 23 EU member states, USA, Canada, Australia, 24 NATO member states, 34 Organisation of Islamic Corporation member states and 108 United Nations member states.

The big players, and those directly involved in the region, that *don't* recognise Kosovo are Serbia and Russia; others include China, India, Iran and Israel.

I initially presumed that all EU countries recognised Kosovo. I was wrong. Spain, Slovakia, Cyprus, Greece and Romania do not. One can only speculate, but it would seem that the reasons for not doing so are not necessarily anti-Kosovo. It is more likely due to their own internal situations.

If Cyprus was to recognise Kosovo, others could say, 'You must now recognise the Turkish Republic of Northern Cyprus', which they will never do. The same goes for Greece. I would imagine that for Romania, if it were to recognise Kosovo, there would be pressure on Bucharest to recognise the Moldovan breakaway region of Transnistria. Israel possibly does not recognise Kosovo for the fear it would be pressured into accepting that Palestine is recognised as a state.

It is complicated geopolitics, yet it seems that there is hypocrisy at work here. Russia, one of Serbia's main allies, was strongly against Kosovo recognition. Yet in 2014, Russia used the Kosovo declaration of independence as a premise for Crimea being recognised as part of Russia. In the same breath, the Russians say the West is hypocritical for recognising Kosovo whilst not recognising Abkhazia.

Whether you personally recognise Kosovo as independent or not, in 2010 the International Court of Justice ruled that Kosovo's declaration of independence from Serbia was not illegal under international law.

Arrival and getting into my stride

Although the focus for this chapter is Mitrovica, my arrival and couple of days in Pristina should be documented. I was flying into the Kosovan capital Pristina via Copenhagen.

With 90 minutes until my flight, I headed to my gate. The only people present were three officials and a young woman. By that I mean three Danish border guard officials and a young woman being physically deported out of Denmark. She was not handcuffed, but it was obvious that she could not move without permission. I chatted to one of the male officers who told me that the woman was Albanian and that she was being deported to Kosovo.

Was she an illegal? Had she broken any other law? I asked one official. He said nothing, but gave me a look that said, *do you really think I'm going to tell you that?*

I sat and observed the woman. She looked desperately sad and resigned to her fate. As other passengers arrived, they were kept well away. I noted that many of the passengers were themselves Albanian. I wondered what they were thinking about one of their own being deported.

I was second last to board, just the deportee behind me. The female officer walked her up the steps to the cabin as the two males stayed on the tarmac. There was no way this girl was getting off the plane. Inside, she was handed over to the crew and paperwork was signed before she was placed in seat 1A. We took off. No escape for her. What happened to her at the other end? I have no idea.

Pristina

Kosovo, Kosovo, Kosovo. If you say 'Kosovo' to most in the West, they react with horror or uncertainty. However, the reality today is that the capital Pristina is stuffed full of UN peacekeeping troops. It is therefore probably one of the safest places on the planet. In addition, it is very welcoming to Americans and Brits who led the NATO bombing of Belgrade. As one Albanian told me, 'If it wasn't for NATO, we wouldn't be here. We would have been completely wiped out by Milosevic.'

On arrival at Pristina airport, I managed to get the border guards not to stamp my passport with a Kosovan entry stamp. There is a very good reason for this.

'Going to Serbia next?' the friendly official asked me.

'Yes, but I am also going to Russia…'

He flicked through my passport and saw the many Russian visas before replying, 'Understand, understand'. He then handed back my passport and I entered Kosovo without an entry stamp.

I knew I would be heading to Serbia next and there can often be problems if they see a Kosovo stamp in your passport. Russia has also made it clear that if you have a Kosovan stamp in your passport, you will be denied entry.

Pristina's town centre is a maze of crooked, winding little streets.

Even though I have been here before, I admit to getting lost a few times when out wandering. Accommodation is actually very expensive in Pristina as it mainly caters for businessmen, EU and NATO officials, so it was rather hard on my traveller's wallet.

Pristina was only a stopover, a means of entry. Nevertheless, I took the opportunity to spend two days in the city to soak up the friendly atmosphere. Since Western intervention in Iraq, Afghanistan and Libya, there are not many countries that openly declare their love and support for the UK and the US. However, they do in Pristina. The lobby of my little hotel, owned and run by Kosovan Albanians, had a British flag flying not just outside the hotel, but in the reception area as well. They have never forgotten the UK's help and support, the numerous troops, the stance against Serbian paramilitaries, and the NATO bombings of Milosevic's government buildings.

Pristina suffered heavy bombardment in the Kosovo war of independence in 1999. Yugoslav forces bombed many residential areas, and Serbian paramilitaries then looted and destroyed homes of ethnic Albanians.

'If it wasn't for NATO, we wouldn't even be here. The Serbs would have killed us all. They tried to wipe us all out.' I was told this numerous times while in Pristina.

A visit to Pristina is not complete without visiting Bill Clinton Avenue. Not a spectacular street by any means, it's dedicated to the man who finally, after much indecision from the West, ordered the bombing of Serbia which halted the ethnic cleansing of Kosovan Albanians. A gleaming ten-foot statue of the former President stands tall and proud, just off the busy street, typically ugly concrete apartment blocks just behind him. I'm not sure what the statue is made of, but when hit by the sun, it glitters like gold. From a Kosovan point of view, Clinton undoubtedly deserves recognition. However, I find it odd to see this kind of statue standing in a former communist country. Maybe a plaque or a photo would have been more appropriate?

In Pristina in 2014, I also saw an old pro-Tony Blair poster. It featured a picture of Blair with the words 'thank you' in Albanian and English. For many, Blair will always be remembered as the British Prime Minister who went into Iraq with George W Bush. But in Kosovo, Blair is a hero for the same reasons as Clinton. That said, for me anyway, it was still rather strange to stand in a predominantly Muslim country and see a pro-Tony Blair poster. I doubt we would see any of these posters in countries such as Iraq or Afghanistan.

The Newborn Monument is a 79-foot long, nine-tonne structure that spells out the word 'Newborn' in English. Built in 2008 to mark Kosovo's declaration of independence, it is decorated with the flags of all the nations around the world that recognise Kosovo as an independent state. A very clever and powerful symbol. However, I cannot see the Russian flag being added any time soon.

Kosovo is in a constant state of rebuilding and much Western cash is pouring into the country. However, it will take many more years to fix roads and rebuild general infrastructure. Not far from the chic restaurants of the city centre are the dilapidated side streets which house the city's not so well off.

It was time to head to Mitrovica, my main reason for coming to Kosovo. I took a taxi from my hotel to the out-of-town, rundown and ugly concrete bus station where I would catch a local bus north. On learning that I was going to Mitrovica, my Albanian taxi driver was more than willing to tell me his thoughts on this unique town.

'The Serbs shouldn't even be there, they are Slavic. They originally come from Russia and should be there.' Strong words indeed.

The roads north were shocking and not much better than when I had visited a few years back. After a very uncomfortable bus ride, I arrived at the bus station in South Mitrovica, the Albanian side. The Albanians don't go to the north of the city and the Serbs don't venture south.

The mind boggles regarding the divide in Mitrovica, and it only fermented my own personal belief that it's not just walls and barbed wire that divide people, it's the walls they create inside the human mind that cause by far the most damage. As I mentioned earlier, there are no walls here; there is no razor wire either, just a blocked bridge and blocked minds.

Mitrovica

Divided by the River Ibar, Mitrovica has been the flashpoint for much violence since the end of the Balkan wars. Although multi ethnic, Albanians make up the lion's share of the population at roughly 70 per cent, with Serbians the second biggest grouping. The overall population is roughly 85,000.

South of the river is the Albanian sector. The north of the town, also known as North Kosovska Mitrovica, is where the Serbs are heavily concentrated.

Almost all Serbs claim that Kosovo is merely a province and thus still part of Serbia. The Kosovan Albanians claim that Kosovo is an official independent country. That said, there is autonomy here, for north of the bridge, the Serbs have their own police and courts. On one side of the bridge are the Kosovan police, on the other side the Serbian police. In the middle, NATO peacekeepers stand guard.

I quickly came to realise that it's all very complicated. The breakup of Yugoslavia, the Balkan wars, the Kosovo war and Kosovo's declaration of independence from Serbia are all very much alive today.

The Albanian side of the bridge

On the Albanian side of Mitrovica, the population is Muslim. Backed by NATO, they are friendly towards the USA and the UK. Considering the world we live in with IS, Iraq and Syria, it took some contemplation to consider this situation. Sat out one evening at a near deserted café, I took in my surroundings. Here I was in a liberal Muslim country, drinking a beer, no women wore burkas that I saw, NATO flags flew, and cool jazz played in English on the café radio. The standards were Western, everything from the service to the quality of the coffee and of the seat I was sat on. When I heard the call to prayer from a nearby Mosque, it summed up the uniqueness of this town.

Is this a blueprint for the future? Who knows? I tried to think of another place where I had experienced this fascinating mix. I could not come up with one.

A quick mention about alcohol in South Mitrovica. Most cafes, restaurants and shops do not sell it, but it's not banned, nor is it illegal. I saw very few locals drinking alcohol, but when I asked for a beer, I was served one with a smile and no ill feeling.

Although peaceful at night, during the day the town centre of South Mitrovica is noisy and hectic. Ethnic Albanian folk and pop music blare out from almost everywhere as people go about the hustle and bustle of their daily routines. People were friendly – very friendly in fact – and they constantly waved and acknowledged that I was a guest in their town.

The Bridge

I spent a lot of time down by the blocked bridge where most officials were happy enough to talk, just as long as I did not use their names. One night, I asked a friendly Albanian police officer the all-important question. 'Who is ultimately in charge here? You guys? The Serb police on the other side of the bridge? Or the NATO peacekeepers in the middle?'

'Good question,' she replied. Yet after much contemplation, she was not able to give a definitive answer.

I attempted to cross the bridge from the Albanian side. When I reached about half way, I could not quite believe what I was looking at. The Albanian half of the bridge is a normal tarmac road, but half way across, the road turns into grass. Turf has been laid on the road along with dozens of potted plants. I had never seen anything like it. For sure, it does not have the immense feeling of division like the separation wall in Bethlehem, but is a very important divide nonetheless. On the Serb side, which was also once the main road, the road is now busted. In 2014, Serbs smashed up the concrete in order to stop traffic (including the authorities) coming over from the Albanian side.

As I walked around taking photos, a member of the KFOR (NATO peace-keeping force), a Swiss soldier on a six-month stint approached me. There was no problem with me taking photos, he was just intrigued because he rarely saw foreigners there. When I explained I was working on a book about division, he was more than willing to chat.

The blocking of the bridge happened just weeks before I was there. Riots and violent clashes took place at this bridge. Tear gas was used and vehicles were set on fire.

'It was very violent, I was on duty that night,' the Swiss soldier told me.

'Who started it? What started it?' I asked.

He shrugged. 'Here? God only knows. It doesn't take much. That's why we always have to be ready. And we are.'

'Can you tell me about that night?'

'The bridge had been blocked by rubble laid down by Serbs for many months. It was always removed by local authorities, but they kept putting more back. This triggered hundreds of people to take to the streets on the Albanian side. They don't want the bridge to be blocked of course. But the Serbians do, they don't want to mix, it's like they are sticking up two fingers at Kosovo and marking their own territory. Both sides taunted each other over the bridge. We were worried the Albanians would try to cross, because it would have gotten very ugly. Riot police were called in as cars were set alight. They came under a hail of petrol bombs and stones and responded with tear gas. Then we were called in to support the riot police. Many were injured, but thankfully there were no deaths that night. Then it all died down pretty quickly. It happens like that here, tensions build up, reach boiling point, explode, fizzle out and then everything returns to normal, whatever 'normal' means.'

I looked at the bridge, blocked by grass and potted plants. In the days following this riot, Serb workmen laid the rolls of turf and brought in potted plants. It's now known as the 'Peace Park'.

'Why can't you guys just remove the whole lot?' I asked totally bemused. 'This town is brimming with NATO and police.'

He held up a hand, the one that had been placed around the barrel of the gun slung around his shoulder.

'No, I can't tell them to stop doing this or to unblock the bridge. I have no say in the daily life here and believe me I don't want it. I'm just here to keep the peace between the two sides.'

From what I was told, it's very safe around the bridge during the day, but not so at night. Depending on the day-to-day political situation, things can change at a moment's notice and standoffs often turn violent. I walked over and started to chat with a Serb police officer.

'Do local people cross over to the other side much?' I asked.

'Many people will never cross to the other side. But those who do, usually for business, do so during the day. At night when it's dark, they stay in their own part of town.'

One evening, workers on the Serb side were laying new turf. A NATO peacekeeper stood by and watched, as did police on the Kosovo side. As we stood watching the laying of new turf, my Serb police officer commented, 'The President of Serbia ordered the bridge to be laid with this stuff.'

'Will this bridge ever be cleared?' I asked him.

'No idea,' he said, before adding quietly, 'who would want to clear it anyway? Not me. North Mitrovica is Serbia, not Kosovo. One day, all of this town and all of Kosovo will once again be part of Serbia.'

I cannot recall ever having experienced such openness amongst officials in and around a divide. Everyone was so willing to speak with me and share their views. Try to get a Transnistrian border guard to chat about the issues of the day. That is like pulling teeth.

Late one calm, warm and balmy evening, I said to the Swiss soldier as we stood on the Serb side by the bridge, 'It's very peaceful here tonight'.

'Don't kid yourself. It can kick off at a moment's notice,' he replied, never taking his hands off his gun nor his eyes off a group of five men who were walking our way.

The Serb side of the bridge

Had I just walked into Russia? It somehow felt like it. Anti-NATO and anti-EU slogans are dubbed on walls, while Serb and Russian flags flutter everywhere. Just metres away, I spied a large billboard, which displayed huge photos of not only Putin and Belarus dictator Lukashenka, but also the smiling face of the very man who was tried for war crimes against the Albanians, Slobodan Milosevic. It is set facing south. Very provocative if you are an Albanian, I would imagine.

I was soon chatting with a local ethnic Serb outside an old café. He told me the complete opposite from the taxi driver in Pristina, who had said the Serbs should not be here but should live in Russia. My man told me, 'The Kosovars are Albanians, they shouldn't be here. They should go and live in Albania.'

Both right? Both wrong? Possibly, they are both right and wrong.

In stark difference to the Albanian side, in the north it was Russian and Serb pop music that blared from apartments and passing cars. As for the cars, they really intrigued me. Whilst some had number plates, the vast majority I saw had no plate whatsoever. An Albanian policeman told me one night when talking about this and other laws not upheld in the Serbian part of Mitrovica, 'It's true, many of the Serb cars don't have number plates, you know, it's a criminal area over there, run by gangsters. There is a huge problem with illegal trade in cars, firearms, cigarette smuggling and many other things. Gangsters, that's what many Serbs are.'

None of the ethnic Serbs in North Mitrovica recognises that they live in an independent Kosovo. They have total allegiance to Belgrade, which I learned provides money for schools, health and courts in North Mitrovica. Despite this support, the town looked and felt far poorer than the other side. A tiny café, located just over the bridge called Café Moct (Moct, meaning bridge) looked exactly like the numerous run-down cafes you find in off-the-beaten-track towns in Russia today.

I headed off and wandered the side streets. Walls painted with pro-

Russian and pro-Serbian murals. The Soviet-style tenement blocks looked run down, and while there were plenty of dilapidated cars, there are also a large number of Mercs and BMWs, again mostly without number plates. I walked the poor neighbourhoods and took photos of tattered Serbian flags fluttering in the streets. It felt like decades ago.

What I saw next stopped me in my tracks. A street with Albanian flags fluttering, strung across the road like British-style bunting. In another area, I saw a giant bollard in the middle of the road with Albanian and American flags attached to it. Hang on! I'm standing in Serb-dominated North Mitrovica and there are Albanian flags? I photographed away, not quite believing it. Suddenly a police patrol came by. The officer checked my documents, told me to be very careful and to leave before nightfall.

I later found out the following, which makes this already complicated place even more confusing. Whilst the north of the city may be Serbian dominated, there is a small enclave of Albanians who still live there. Try to get your head round this: Kosovans say they have their own independent country, while Serbians say Kosovo is part of Serbia. In the town of Mitrovica, Albanians live in the south and Serbians live in the north under a kind of autonomy, yet are still officially part of Kosovo. Then, in that Serb-controlled part of Mitrovica (which officially belongs to Kosovo but is populated by Serbs), there lives a small community of Albanian Kosovans. What a head spin.

The Orthodox Church

Roughly, a half hour walk away from the centre on the Serbian side, I ventured up a small hill and ended up by the Church of Saint Demetrius. Recently renovated, inside it is immaculate with icons and religious artwork. Although I am not religious, I choose to spend much time inside churches, mosques and synagogues all over the world. A Muslim friend of mine once said to me, 'George, I've never met a non-believer who is so interested in religion'. The truth is, I find much solace in these buildings, and here in Mitrovica I appreciated this church, admiring the art, candles and smell of incense. I have to admit though, I prefer the inside of a mosque, where of course there are never paintings or candles. Just stillness.

I stood outside, just to the right of the church and took in the stunning views over Mitrovica. I looked up at the church beside me, then down over

Mitrovica and spotted a mosque on the Albanian side. Two religions, two sets of people, so geographically close, yet poles apart.

While I never felt threatened on the Serb side, I did not feel at peace either. I know it's not Russia, but with the Serbs having tight Slavic connections, it felt 'Soviet' to me in some ways. I wandered over to the north every day and once my research was complete, I would cross back to the Albanian side and feel much more at peace. I don't know why, but that's how I felt. There was no 'them and us' feeling; it was very much live and let live.

As in every divide I researched for this book, if you take away the flags and religious symbols, all that remains is one thing. People. Just ordinary people.

I would like to add here, that during my week in Mitrovica, I took the opportunity to ask various people from both sides of the divide what they thought of the old Yugoslavia and its dictator Tito. What really intrigued me was that I would say 90 per cent, be they Albanians or Serbs, said they thought the old Yugoslavia under Tito belonged to better times.

That really took me aback, but on reflection, it makes sense. Tito's time may not have been democratic, but communities were held together and people lived in peace mostly. Look what happened after the breakup: wars, ethnic cleansing, death and division.

Better the devil you know?

Esat

I first met Esat outside the central Mosque in Mitrovica. Blasting out from speakers high up on the minaret, I was drawn in by the mesmerising and haunting sounds of the Islamic call to prayer, the Adhan. Esat approached me in English and asked if I would like to come in. From that moment, a friendship was struck. I met with Esat on numerous occasions over the following week and we talked in depth about his faith and life in divided Mitrovica.

Esat is a devout Muslim who adheres strictly to his religion. Like most in Kosovo, that means a modern, inclusive and friendly Islam. I attended the Mosque on many occasions, sometimes with Esat, sometimes by myself. Beautiful and peaceful inside, it was obvious I was not a Muslim, yet no one batted an eyelid and I was made extremely welcome.

Esat prays five times a day, and as it was the holy month of Ramadan, he was fasting from dawn till dusk. Not eating all day is one thing, but he did not even take a glass of water when the temperature was over 30 degrees during the day. I truly admired his resolve. I certainly could not have done it. I also felt guilty during Ramadan when I took breakfast and coffee at one of the few Western style cafés. However, there was no animosity shown towards a non-Muslim eating or drinking. During the day, the cafés were near-empty, yet came alive after dusk. I hadn't eaten a cooked meal in days. I ordered a three egg omelette with cheese and side salad, washed down with two fresh coffees. The bill? Approximately £1.50. The prices just go to show how poor Mitrovica is. If they charged anymore, that no one would come and eat, the waitress told me.

Did it bother him that I did not believe? 'No, not one bit,' Esat told me. When I said I believed in evolution, Esat looked at me wryly and humoured, 'Ah evolution...'. Like a parent replying when a child says he just saw pixies in the garden.

I then calmly asked Esat, 'what do you think when a Muslim kills a non-believer in the name of Allah?'

'It is wrong,' he said categorically. 'There is nothing in the Quran that says to kill anyone.'

Esat is a passionate man and it pains him that people kill in the name of his religion. He went on to tell me that he would love to meet with a radical preacher, to challenge him to show where in the Quran it says to kill people. 'They are not reading or quoting from the Quran in any way correctly'.

They of course claim that they are indeed quoting correctly from the Quran. Interpretation of the written word is often a very dangerous thing.

Friday prayers

Not everyone of course is as open as Esat. It was Friday prayers, midday, and the Mosque was full, so the remaining worshippers took their places outside. I asked Esat if I could take photos. 'Sure,' he said. 'It's no problem.' Then off he went to pray.

From inside, the Imam began the call to prayer and the faithful outside lined up their prayer mats on the ground. The call to prayer is mesmerising and I swear that the noise from the nearby cars and trucks melted away. It was like meditation. I stood a respectful distance from the worshippers, across a small path and behind a railing. Everyone was aware I was taking photos, it seemed to bother no one, apart from one man that is.

As the crowd was getting down on their knees, I saw him staring directly at me, roughly 40 feet away. He was very unhappy with my presence and my camera. He angrily jabbed his finger at me and made it clear I should leave. I did not take any more photos, but I did not leave. I had done nothing wrong, but I did feel very uncomfortable. I sat down on the small rusty railing and waited for my friend to finish his prayers.

A smiling Esat finally came over. 'Hi George, did you get some good photos for your book?'

'Eh yeah, kind of,' I said nervously. He made me explain. I did. He was shocked and asked me to point out the man in question. I brushed it off and said I did not want to cause a scene, said it was not important. Esat persisted, telling me it *was* important. He was hurt and offended that I had been treated this way.

'No one has a right to tell you that you cannot take photos here. Show him to me.'

I looked at the now parting congregation and spotted him, still staring right back at me. Esat spotted him. 'Him?' he asked me.

'Yeah, him.' I replied, feeling very uncomfortable.

'Ok,' he said and walked calmly but with purpose towards the man.

It might not have been appropriate considering where I was standing but a voice in my head said, 'Oh Christ.' I walked over just as the conversation was ending. Esat had told him that I was working on a book which included Kosovo and Islam and that I was respectful to both. He told him that I was a guest in their town and that he had no right to tell me not to photograph. The man bowed his head, apologised and left.

Esat is one of the most genuine, non-judgemental and tolerant human beings I have ever met. I am proud to call him my friend.

After this incident, we took shelter from the midday sun. I drank mint tea, yet Esat drank nothing, not even water. I admired his discipline. So what did he think of other locals, the Muslims who were not observing Ramadan and were seen drinking coffee and eating cake? Again showing his tolerance he said, 'It is their decision. It's not my business.'

Esat already knew where I stood on religion. He knew I did not believe in Allah, yet it did not faze him. He even suggested I was a more honest person than those who claim they are Muslim, yet sit sipping tea and eating cake during Ramadan. 'People cannot pick and choose,' he said. 'You have more integrity than some of them.'

Not sure how he would take my next question, I said, 'I want to talk about the lack of tolerance in religion. I want to ask what you think about various magazines that have printed cartoons of the Prophet, the reactions to them and the calling for the deaths of those who printed them.'

He took a deep breath. 'Firstly, I feel it was wrong for those journalists to offend the Prophet like they did. But the violence and calling for their deaths, I totally disagree with. You know, George, when radicals kill non-believers, it breaks my heart every time. The Quran forbids the killing of anyone. Muslims who kill in the name of Allah will experience judgement day when they die and will pay for their killing.'

I am always deeply saddened when religious fanatics burn flags and chant obscene remarks about the other side because they believe that they have been wronged. Believe in what you like, it's not my business; it's no one's business. But in turn, what others believe is not your business either. Believe what you want, but never force it down the throats of others and certainly do not ever inflict pain on someone because they choose to believe differently to you or indeed in no religion at all.

I told Esat of my dinner party idea where a mix of individuals of different religions and faiths are sat around the table. The only rule is they must respect each other and not tell each other how to live their lives. Let the food (and wine for some) flow and conversation commence. Esat liked my idea. I told him he was invited to my dinner party.

Over the course of a week, I had the confidence to engage Esat in topics such as atheism, women's rights, homosexuality and alcohol. He answered all my questions without prejudice. If more people of all religions were like Esat, our world would be a safer and more just place to live.

On the day before I left, he asked me if I would read the Quran, if he could get an official copy in English. I told him I would and am therefore currently reading the Quran whilst on my travels. I have to say, it is heavy stuff indeed and only makes me more confused about religion and what it stands for.

I had planned to end this chapter here, but first I want to share with you what happened to me due to not having a Serbian entry stamp in my passport. This escapade again goes to show just how complicated this part of the world is.

Entry and exit

At midday, a taxi took me the short distance through south Mitrovica to the blocked off bridge. I walked across, past numerous police, but did not see the friendly female Albanian officer. The NATO soldier was there and remembered me. He came over, shook my hand and wished me luck. I told him to keep watching his back.

On the Serb controlled side of Mitrovica, I waited for my bus. I was going up north, still legally in Kosovo, but to the Serb dominated town of Leposavic. Ultimately, I was heading for the Serbian capital Belgrade.

It was a boneshaker of a decades-old bus and I was one of only four on it. Leposavic is only around 40 kilometres north of Mitrovica but once there, it felt many years back in time. The bus station was a dilapidated eyesore, but still operating nonetheless. I got off and walked to the centre. There seemed to be only two motels from what I could see and after wandering back and forth lugging my big case, I settled on one. Run by a friendly enough, yet burly Serbian who looked like an ex-militia man, I paid for my room and settled in. I was the only person staying that night. No food was available, so I headed back out and down the main drag where I took a seat at a small café.

I drank two cold Russian beers, which I paid for with a two Euro coin and the palaver that then happened reminded me of years ago in Russia. The beers were around 75 cents each but the owner could not give me change for a two Euro coin. I just told her to keep the change. She wasn't trying to have me on – there is a serious lack of small change here. I was back in time, back to Eastern Europe 20 years ago. In many Russian shops in the '90s, when they had no coins for change, they gave you penny chew sweets instead. Can you imagine the calamity in Tesco if they handed you your change in Jelly Babies?

The next morning, on another crumbling bus, I soon arrived at the Kosovo/Serbia border. Serbia does not recognise this border because they see 'independent' Kosovo as illegal and still belonging to Belgrade. The Kosovans were not stopping anyone leaving, but on the Serb side, the border guards took my passport and I was told to get off the bus. Within minutes, I was being denied entry to Serbia because I had first flown into Kosovo.

'You can't be serious,' I said, feeling like John McEnroe, although I did say it much friendlier than the great man ever did.

'No entry.' He said deadpan.

'But I'm going to Belgrade, your capital. I've got a flight out of there in a couple of days.'

'Not possible. You try to enter Serbia from Kosovo. We don't recognise Kosovo. We can't let you in from Kosovo.'

'So what the hell am I supposed to do?' I spluttered.

'You must enter Serbia from another country. You go back, all the way to Mitrovica, take a bus east, cross out of Kosovo and get an exit stamp. Then drive to Montenegro and get an entry stamp, then drive through Montenegro and get a Montenegro exit stamp, then finally drive up to our border and no problem, we let you into Serbia.'

He had to be joking, so I played along. I laughed, slapped his upper arm in a friendly manner and said with a smile, 'Yeah right chief.'

Highly amused, he looked at me with a Roger Moore-like raised eyebrow, but said nothing, before handing me my passport and walking off. There is never, in any contested border area, any point in arguing with a border guard. You will not change their mind and if you push it, you can end up being detained. I had no choice. I needed to be in Belgrade as I was booked on a flight to my next divide, but I now had to seriously back track.

Damn, I was stood five feet from the Serbian border, and then I only had a six-hour bus journey to the capital Belgrade. What now? I chatted with three Kosovan border guards who had witnessed me being denied Serbian entry just feet away. They felt for me, but told me there was nothing they could do. Would I really have to make that mammoth journey the Serbian had suggested? 'If you want to get to Belgrade, then yes you'll have to,' was their reply.

I hung around at the border, jumped on the next bus back to Leposavic, changed buses there and eventually found myself back at the divided bridge in Mitrovica. From the Albanian side, I boarded a local bus heading to the town of Pejë close to the Montenegrin border. The bus was small, decades old and struggled going uphill. The roads themselves were rural and basic. It took an agonising two and a half hours. That's 17 miles per hour in the blistering heat. Not fun.

Outside Pejë, I thumbed a lift from an Albanian who was going to Montenegro and who said he would drive me through the mountains. As we drove, the scenery changed from dry and dusty to lush green mountain pastures and I almost forgot about my problems of the day.

Soon we came to a border post high up in the mountains. Cows wandered at will on the road and I got my first visa stamp of the day, a Kosovo exit stamp. After 15 minutes of driving, we approached the Montenegro border and they stamped me in without issue. So far so good. On we drove, down the other side of the mountain, into a tiny hamlet. I thanked the driver Adrianne profusely and offered him cash, but he refused. Adrianne's behaviour was another example of the kindness I have experienced all over the world on my travels. It never does cease to amaze me. I can be travelling in some of the most complicated places on earth and the genuine kindness shown by locals can be remarkable.

It was now late afternoon. I had stood in the hamlet for an hour trying to hitch a lift, and eventually a car stopped. It was an old battered Lada containing four Serbian labourers, who, after a hard day's graft, smelled even worse than I did. They were heading home to Serbia and said they were happy to drive me. We approached the Montenegro border 45 minutes later, where I received my exit stamp. Then, minutes later, I received the all-important Serbian entry stamp that I had been denied in northern Kosovo that morning. I had done it. I was now in Serbia. It was eight hours after I should have arrived and had comprised a detour of 150 kilometres and a heap of stamps in my passport. All just to travel five feet.

Job done? Well, not quite. Although I was in Serbia, I was now a long way off the beaten track and far from Belgrade. The guys dropped me off at a roadside lodge in the mountains, where I was informed that the next bus to Belgrade would not be for another 17 hours. I therefore spent the night in the lodge, which looked and felt like the Bates Motel. The next day, in a series of taxis and buses via Novi Pazar, I finally arrived in Belgrade at seven in the evening.

In total, it had taken me an extra 25 and a half hours to get to Belgrade.

I have since learned that if I had initially flown into Belgrade, received a Serbian entry stamp there, then visited Kosovo and then tried to cross the land border back into Serbia, I would have had no problem at Leposavic. But because the Serbian authorities do not recognise Kosovo as a legal point of entry, my arrival via Pristina airport had made my crossing into Serbia much more complicated.

The Moral of my tale is, if you plan to visit Kosovo and Serbia, *go to Serbia first*. If not, you may well find yourself taking the journey I had to endure.

Summing up

After the tragedies of the Balkan wars and the uncertainties surrounding its declaration of independence, Kosovo is relatively stable now and money is pouring in. That said, it is still hugely underdeveloped and will need billions more in aid to help it rebuild.

Kosovo as an independent state is here to stay. Even the Serbian authorities seem to have accepted that, albeit reluctantly. There will continue to be contentious issues, especially in Mitrovica, and I have no doubt that street clashes and border violence will continue.

As for Mitrovica? I feel it will remain a divided city. Even if they take away the bizarre potted plants and grass from the bridge, and traffic flows again, it will remain divided. Serbs in the north of the city will feel like they are in Serbia, whilst the Albanians in the South will say they live in Kosovo. That is not going to change in a hurry, and probably not in my lifetime.

While the circumstances of division are different, I am inclined to compare Mitrovica to Belfast in the sense that it is no longer officially at war, yet it's not at peace either. That phrase will be explained in detail in the Belfast chapter.

The ongoing backing of NATO has to be Kosovo's ultimate guarantee of its safety and continuity. That said, with all that's going on in Eastern Ukraine, Russia's re-emergence as a military power, and the West seemingly going in the other direction, let's consider the following: What if NATO leaves Kosovo and Russia steps in under the pretence that it's protecting ethnic Serbs in Northern Mitrovica?

A silly thought? Possibly, but then again, would you bet your life savings against it? I wouldn't.

In today's political climate, the only thing we can guarantee about Europe, statehood and recognition is that there are no guarantees.

Update March 2017

The bridge in Mitrovica is still divided by grass and plant pots. However, as I write, work is currently under way to clear it after an EU-facilitated agreement between Belgrade and Pristina was reached. It is hoped that the bridge will finally be opened in May.

Meanwhile, police and peacekeepers remain vigilant.

Even though it looks as if this physical divide may soon be removed, the mental division between Serbs and Kosovans will be far more difficult to remove.

The British Foreign & Commonwealth Office (FCO) advise **'against all but essential travel'** to Leposavic and northern Mitrovica.

5

Cyprus

Invasion or intervention?

Officially

Status	Republic of Cyprus
Capital	Nicosia
Currency	Euro
Population	Approximately 1.1 million
Language	Greek

North of the divide (Unofficially)

Status	Turkish Republic of Northern Cyprus
Capital	Nicosia
Currency	Turkish Lira
Population	Approximately 300,000
Language	Turkish

Introduction

WHEN THE BERLIN WALL fell, that was supposed to be it. Europe was no longer divided and we would all live in peaceful coexistence. That was back in 1989 and we are now well into the second decade of the 21st century, yet sadly, Europe still has a divided city – Nicosia in Cyprus. The capital city of Cyprus is officially the last divided national capital in the world.

Cyprus is a sun, sea and sand holiday destination for many thousands of tourists. Each year, they flock to the beaches in the south, splash around in the sea and drink the cheap booze blissfully unaware that a short drive north, lies a very different world indeed.

The Greek Cypriots control the southern half of Nicosia, and in the north, behind razor wire and walls (with a UN buffer zone in between) stands the TRNC. The Turkish Republic of Northern Cyprus is not recognised by *any* country in the world, apart from Turkey.

The What, Where and Why

After more than 300 years under Ottoman rule, the British annexed Cyprus in 1914, but it wasn't until 1925 that Cyprus became a full crown colony.

In 1955, trouble flared as Greek Cypriots undertook a war against British rule. The aim of EOAK (National Organisation of Cypriot Combatants) was the unification with the motherland, Greece. To counteract this, the British supported and armed a rival paramilitary force made up of Turkish Cypriots.

Archbishop Makarios, head of the campaign for unification with Greece, was deported to the Seychelles, only to return three years later to be elected as President.

Cyprus (not yet divided) gained its independence from the British in 1960 after Greek and Turkish communities agreed on a constitution. What is fascinating here is a 'clause' called the Treaty of Guarantee, which gave Britain, Greece and Turkey the right to intervene. Britain also retained sovereignty of two military bases on Cyprus and holds them to this day.

Harmony did not last long in the new found independent Cyprus. By 1963, violence erupted between the two communities when Greek Cypriots proposed changes to the constitution. Turkish Cypriots withdrew from the power-sharing government and UN peacekeeping forces were stationed on the island from 1964.

In 1974, all hell broke loose when Greek Nationalists, with support from the Greek military junta, staged a coup. Their aim? To incorporate all of Cyprus into Greece. Turkish troops responded by pouring into the north. The coup collapsed, and after much bloodshed, Turkish forces occupied the top third of the island, while the Greeks held onto the remaining two thirds. Greeks fled the north for the south and Turkish Cypriots fled the south for the north. The UN Security Council unanimously called for Turkey to remove its troops from Cyprus. Turkey refused to do so.

The walls quickly went up and Cyprus was brutally divided. It remains so today, more than 40 years later.

The last divided capital city in the world

As I mentioned above, the Treaty of Guarantee gave Britain, Greece and Turkey the 'right to intervene'. That is one hell of a clause and one which perhaps needs to be reconsidered. How different Cyprus may be today if that very important clause were never put in the treaty in the first place. The right to intervene is what seems to form the legal basis of Turkey's actions in 1974, as far as many Turks are concerned.

Perhaps you have noticed that I am trying very hard not to refer to the conflict as either an invasion or an intervention. You will understand why as you keep reading.

When I talk of Nicosia being divided, I'm not talking about a barrier or a fence or two. This is a seriously hard-core divide that runs the entire breadth of the Island. However, my focus was on the capital Nicosia. Cut in two, it certainly has similarities to the Berlin Wall.

Imagine the town or city you live in. Picture the main street that runs through it. I will pick Aberdeen's Union Street. Aberdeen goes to war with itself and the town is subsequently divided right down the middle. Both sides of Union Street become separate countries, walls topped with razor wire and lookout towers blocking off access from one side to the other. Union Street itself, or the actual road, becomes a no man's land, a forbidden zone, patrolled by UN peacekeepers to prevent further violence. That is Nicosia.

On the Greek side of Nicosia, I stayed a couple of kilometres walk from the divide, in a residential area with a charming, rather old, colonial British feel. In contrast, the main street in the centre is (in my opinion) tacky and touristy. Many waddle aimlessly, buying their fake Rolex watches whilst eating fast food, seemingly uninterested in what is behind the walls that divide this city.

Like the Berlin Wall, the divide in Nicosia cuts through the heart of the city. It considers nothing. It is ruthless and simply divides. Walls, steel gates, oil drums and razor wire block off alleyways between apartment blocks. On the Greek side, just a couple of minutes' walk from the heart of the tourist area, I walked down a small road with houses either side. At the end of the road, just before the buffer zone, a Greek Cypriot barricade.

Tentatively I began to take photos. Suddenly a young soldier came out of his bunker and made it clear, *no photos*. He spoke some English and was happy enough to chat for a few minutes. But no photos. I returned to this spot every day for a week. Every day I saw him, we acknowledged each other and finally he allowed me a photo, even though the sign makes it clear that photos are not allowed.

To get to the TRNC, (Turkish Republic of Northern Cyprus) I went to the border checkpoint at Ledra Palace Gate. Here I exited not only the Republic of Cyprus but the European Union itself, then walked a few hundred metres through the UN-controlled Buffer Zone. Ten minutes later, I approached the TRNC border, got my visa, answered a few questions then stepped into one half of a city located in a 'country' that has been unrecognised for 40 years. And I thought Mitrovica was complicated.

A couple of minutes away from the border checkpoints, there is a lot of ruin and poverty. Against advice, I spent hours every day walking as close to the walls and razor wire as I could get away with. Sometimes I was sent packing. I saw no tourists and was surrounded by decaying buildings. It looked like the 1974 war had happened just days previous.

Each side controls their own gates, fences and walls. What stands between them and separates the two is the demilitarised buffer zone, the *forbidden zone*. Inside the forbidden zone where people once lived worked and played, all is abandoned. It has not been touched since 1974 and it lies there like a morbid museum that no one can see or visit. It is frozen in time.

What did it look like *inside the forbidden zone*, I wondered? As I said, picture the main street of the city where you live, divided, then add a buffer zone into the middle, which has lain untouched for 40 years. I got my photo inside the forbidden zone, just don't ask how I got it. It was very hard to comprehend that is the centre of a European capital city in the second decade of the 21st century.

Back in my hotel on the Greek side, I sat out on my balcony, which gave me a perfect view over the rooftops all the way over to the Turkish side. I sipped a cold beer as I jotted down my thoughts and first impressions of the divide. As night fell, the mountains on the Turkish side faded into darkness and suddenly I saw lights. It took me some minutes to work it out. Emblazoned onto the mountainside, a massive display of lights, in the shape of a gigantic Turkish Cypriot flag. Alongside the flag were words that were also lit up. I am told it translates as: 'How happy is the one who says I am Turkish'.

It is a spectacular sight and on seeing it for the first time, it astounded me. Shining every night directly over to the Greek side, I have no doubt that it does the intended job – to provoke the Greek Cypriots – with a message that implies: *We, the Turkish community, are here – and here to stay!*

A stunning piece of propaganda that would make North Korea proud.

Famagusta

Famagusta is a unique place. A town on the coast of east Cyprus, it was once a destination for holidaymakers and a playground for the rich and famous. International stars such as Richard Burton and Elizabeth Taylor once graced its beaches. It was once *the place* to be in all of Cyprus.

However, those days are long gone. During the fighting in 1974, the inhabitants of Famagusta fled, leaving behind their homes, possessions and their entire lives. Following the partition of Cyprus, Famagusta came under the control of the Turkish forces and remains as such to this very day. Totally fenced off, it is another forbidden zone, under military control and is off limits to all members of the public, even those who used to live there.

Today, Famagusta is a ghost town, lying in limbo, eerily empty and devoid of human life. What a tragic situation.

I had researched Famagusta and wondered if I could manage to get in. I asked folks from both sides of the divide in Nicosia, yet the answer was the same from all: 'You have no chance of getting in, George'. I was warned that if I even attempted to get in, or simply got too close to the razor wire that surrounds it, I could be arrested. Or worse.

I did go to Famagusta, now lying on the TRNC side. I crossed the border from the Greek side and caught a bus on the outskirts of Nicosia. However, once I arrived in a newly built area of Famagusta, it was obvious I was getting nowhere near the fenced off old town. I did not even try.

I cannot even begin to imagine what those who were born and bred there feel, having been barred from entering for the past 40 years. Picture the city you live in… can you imagine being banned from ever entering again? It would have been horrendous at the time if it had been blown up or demolished, but decades later, Famagusta still stands and that makes things more painful I think. If it had been erased, then there would be nothing to go back to. But people's houses still stand there, filled with possessions, beds, furniture, clothes, kid's toys and photos on walls. Unimaginable really.

Famagusta seems like a set in a Hollywood movie where a natural disaster or plague has wiped out the human population and the town is left to slowly die. Bit by bit, it crumbles away as Mother Nature reclaims her land.

Interview with a Greek Cypriot veteran

Through a friend in London, I had secured an interview with Greek Cypriot war veteran, Bakis Mavrou.

As arranged, his nephew Christos picked me up in central Nicosia and we drove south, our conversation soon turning to Cyprus. I asked him what he thought of the huge TRNC flag that shines to the Greek side every night.

'You can't miss it. Every day I drive on this road, I must look it. It's antagonistic to us.'

'Do you want the dividing walls in Nicosia to come down?'

'Of course I want them to come down. I want the armies to go, I want to live in peace with everybody. I don't care if they are Turkish or Greek. I just want to live in one island in peace.'

When Christos introduced me to Bakis, I took an instant liking to him. Bakis was only 20 in 1974, when I interviewed him he was 60. He is a quiet, intelligent and friendly man. Christos left us to our meeting and arranged to meet us later. Bakis was initially concerned about his lack of English, but he need not have been, for he was more than able to communicate with me.

We settled down with coffee in a local café, stuck away in the corner. After some small talk and feeling rather in awe of the man, I asked Bakis to tell me what life was like before 1974.

'Before the war, we all lived together. Before I went to the army I worked in a hotel with Turkish people and there was no problem. I had Turkish friends, most people got on well together.'

Bakis told me that before the intervention/invasion, in the years 1963 to 1974, Nationalists on both sides naturally had their own agendas. Many Greek Cypriots wanted to take Cyprus totally under Greek control, while many Turkish Cypriots wanted Cyprus to join Turkey. Many more though, just ordinary people, wanted to get on with their lives and didn't want extremism. As a result, Nationalists on both sides killed their own people who disagreed with them. Bakis told me, 'Greeks killed the Greeks and Turkish killed the Turkish who disagreed.'

'Did you expect the Turkish army to invade Cyprus?'

'No, it was a big surprise. They came on 15 July 1974.'

'Tell me about this.'

He took a deep breath, exhaled and concentrated as he let his mind wander back.

'I heard on the radio that Turkey had invaded. Soon the planes came, they started from Kyrenia on the north coast and dropped many bombs. They had ships and tanks also which came across from mainland Turkey. Although, as I say, it was a surprise and shock for us, it was obvious they were ready to make this invasion. It was probably planned years in advance.'

'What did the rest of the world say or do?'

Bakis shook his head. 'Nothing. No one came to help. The Turkish army were strong with much equipment, we had only hunting rifles. I fought in Famagusta, but we had no chance, it was something like David and Goliath, but this time David didn't win. When they invaded Famagusta, the women and elderly had to leave, Greeks and Turks. Now, of course, Famagusta is a ghost town. It is lying there in ruins, totally locked up. Many young men, soldiers and civilians, including myself, were held in Famagusta and after some days we cried out for water to drink. They took us in groups to a water storage, something like a swimming pool, and lined us up against a wall. Then ten soldiers came with guns and they were ready to kill us. Thankfully they didn't shoot. But they did beat us with the ends of their guns.'

This was the first time since I had arrived that Cyprus and 1974 really hit me.

'Did you think you were going to die?'

Bakis gave me a look that said he was picturing that scene from 1974. 'Yes. Yes, I thought I was going to die.'

He paused, sipped his coffee and I did likewise, letting the words he had just spoken hang in the air. Bakis then continued.

'We were then moved around and eventually taken by trucks to Nicosia. Initially we slept in a big garage, thousands of us. Then the next day we were blindfolded, put onto buses and our hands tied behind our backs. We were then loaded onto ships at Kyrenia and taken to jails over in mainland Turkey. They took our watches, money, rings, everything. Also on these ships were fridges, cars and many goods they had stolen from the Cypriots.'

'You must have been terrified.'

'I thought I was never going back to Cyprus.'

'What were the conditions like in Turkey?'

'Thousands of men in the jail. In my room, 100 men with three toilets. Also in with us were people under the age of 18.'

'Child prisoners?'

'Yes, boys.'

'How long did you spend in jail?'

'About two and a half months. Then one day a Turkish soldier said they were going to do a prisoner exchange. Over time we were released in groups, taken by train, bus and ships back to Cyprus. I was one of the last to be released.'

'Did they return your personal possessions? The watches and money they had taken?'

Bakis smiled sadly and shook his head.

'Once you were released and returned to Cyprus, it must have been to a very different Cyprus?'

'Oh yes, it was divided by then. Our country cut in two. And it still is.'

When Bakis spoke, he never raised his voice, nor was there a trace of hatred or animosity towards his captors, or to *any* Turkish Cypriots. 'I don't hate any Turkish Cypriots,' he told me. I could have talked with this kind man all day. He really is a gentleman.

Interview complete, Bakis kindly invited me for lunch at a nearby café. It was here I met the cousin of a man who was beaten to death by a mob and the Turkish police. This infamous incident took place at the border in 1996.

I bid farewell to Bakis, and Christos very kindly drove me back to Nicosia. Later, sitting out on my balcony, again I watched the sunset and the huge TRNC flag come to life on the mountainside. I now had a burning desire to get a view of 1974 from the Turkish side...

Interview with a Turkish Cypriot veteran

I had so far failed in my attempts to get an interview with someone from the Turkish side of the divide. I'd tried to chat with Turkish soldiers in the days previous, but for one reason or another, it just was not happening. The situation was also made more difficult as fewer people speak English in the TRNC.

I left my hotel and headed onto the baking-hot streets of Nicosia once again. I was in serious need of a caffeine hit, but ignored the trashy-Western-all-taste-the-same-high-street coffee chains. After crossing the border at Ledra Palace Gate, I ducked into a tiny café and ordered a superbly made traditional Turkish coffee. Why would anyone drink the muck those chains flog for a small fortune, when you can indulge yourself with the real deal? Beats me.

I feel it is worth noting here, that whilst a foreigner can travel back and forth across this divide quite easily, if you initially fly or take a boat into the TRNC from mainland Turkey, the government of Cyprus regards this as an illegal entry. It also reserves the right to fine you if you then choose to cross into 'Greek Cyprus.' Be aware.

I was determined to find someone who would talk with me and give me a Turkish perspective on Cyprus, the divide and 1974. I walked around for three hours, tried to chat with locals, but again, no luck. I realised I may have to accept that an interview was not going to happen. I checked my watch. It was 2.00pm and I could take the heat no more. I decided to cross the border and head back to my hotel on the Greek side.

I checked my maps. I had two maps, both of Nicosia, but both different. The map I picked up from the tourist office on the Greek side, showed Nicosia up to the dividing line. Past that, it showed next to nothing, claiming the land was illegally occupied. The second map, which I got

At the Western Wall in Jerusalem.
Israel / Palestine

The dividing wall in Bethlehem.
Israel / Palestine

Israeli soldiers on patrol in the Jewish sector of Hebron.
Israel / Palestine

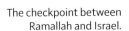

The checkpoint between Ramallah and Israel.
Israel / Palestine

Divided Hebron.
Israel / Palestine

A body search outside Damascus Gate, Friday Prayers.
Israel / Palestine

Bullet holes in the window of a house in Bethlehem with a division wall directly in front.
Israel / Palestine

Tensions build.
Israel / Palestine

Slogan on the
West Bank barrier.
Israel / Palestine

Friday Prayers
and no entry.
Israel / Palestine

Israeli soldier in divided Hebron.
Israel / Palestine

Jew, Muslim, Israeli soldier.
Israel / Palestine

Burned-out stairs in
the old parliament.
The Caucasus / Abkhazia

A girl cycling
in front of the
old parliament
in Sukhumi.
*The Caucasus /
Abkhazia*

Signpost at Abkhaz border.
The Caucasus / Abkhazia

Inside a bombed-out
building in Shusha.
Nagorno–Karabakh

Shusha.
Nagorno–Karabakh

Agdam -
inside the Mosque.
Nagorno–Karabakh

Barricades at central Kiev.
Maidan

The aftermath…
Maidan

The exact spot where a protestor died.
Maidan

Killed. Only 18 years old…
Maidan

Provocative poster in eastern Ukraine.
Crimea

Lukashenko, Putin, Milosevic (Serb side of the bridge).
Kosovo

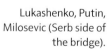

The blocked bridge
in Mitrovica.
Kosovo

Peacekeepers on the bridge.
Kosovo

Serbs show their
solidarity with Russia.
Kosovo

КОСОВСКА МИТРОВИЦА

Косово это Сербия - Крим је Русија

A hacked-up main road on
the Serb side of the bridge.
Kosovo

A Greek Cypriot post in divided Nicosia.
Cyprus

ΤΙΠΟΤΑ ΔΕΝ ΚΕΡΔΙΖΕΤΑΙ ΧΩΡΙΣ ΘΥΣΙΕΣ ΚΑΙ ΕΛΕΥΘΕΡΙΑ ΔΙΧΩΣ ΑΙΜΑ
NOTHING IS GAINED WITHOUT SACRIFICES AND FREEDOM WITHOUT BLOOD

At the Greek side of the divide.
Cyprus

FORBIDDEN ZONE
ZONE INTERDITE

Every street is blocked off in central Nicosia.
Cyprus

Inside the abandoned forbidden zone in Nicosia.
Cyprus

Taner, Mustafa, me.
Cyprus

Left   Lenin outside House of the Soviets.
Below left A dangerous combination.
Below   Proud of their Soviet past.
Transnistria

Russian
'peacekeepers' at
Tighina Bridge.
Transnistria

A sleeping migrant close to the
border.
Ceuta

Moroccan army
huts on the other
side of divide.
Ceuta

A section of the complex fences.
Melilla

Standing in Europe…
looking over at Africa.
Melilla

Spanish tanks on patrol
in Melilla.
Melilla

A UFF mural.
Belfast / Northern Ireland

A reminder of how to
behave.
Belfast / Northern Ireland

A mural in the Ardoyne.
Belfast / Northern Ireland

Deep in the Ardoyne.
Belfast / Northern Ireland

A gas mask mural in Derry.
Belfast / Northern Ireland

'Eddie' mural in Loyalist side of Derry.
Belfast / Northern Ireland

Once open roads, now blocked by walls.

Belfast / Northern Ireland

A peace wall between the Falls and Shankill areas.

Belfast / Northern Ireland

Pro-Palestinian slogan in Belfast.

Belfast / Northern Ireland

The sign leaves you in no doubt where you are…

Belfast / Northern Ireland

Ultra-Loyalist Cluan Place.

Belfast / Northern Ireland

Belarus guards' hut behind a closed border crossing.

Schengen – North

Left   Road blocks close to the border area.

Above   Belarussian house behind the razor wire.

Schengen – North

A shrine to Boris Nemtsov.
Schengen – Middle

The official Ukraine border with Schengen.
Schengen – Middle

The new Hungarian border fence.
Schengen – Middle

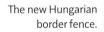

Gates that were used to hold back migrants coming into Hungary.
Schengen – Middle

Soviet reminders near Ukraine border.
Schengen – Middle

Syrian refugees.
Schengen – South

Syrian refugee.
Schengen – South

Closed Turkish–Syrian border.
Schengen – South

from the Turkish authorities, also showed the city, but from their side up to the divide. To work out my way back, I had to use two maps side by side. Two very different maps of exactly the same city.

I was way off the beaten track and far from the border. I stopped for an iced coke, and with a pen borrowed from the bemused café owner, I drew myself a route back to the border. For the next half an hour, I walked down the small side streets of North Nicosia, in baking heat, trying to avoid the sun. Then, a sign hanging outside a building caught my eye. The sign was in Turkish but had an English translation reading 'Cyprus Turkish Pensioners Association.' I slowed down as I read it and did not make it more than five steps before I stopped, feet rooted to the ground.

Pensioners? Hang on a minute, hang on. These guys must be in their 60s or 70s. In 1974 they must have been in their 20s. Therefore, they must have been soldiers in the war…

Within seconds, I was standing inside the air-conditioned lobby of the Cyprus Turkish Pensioners Association.

'Hello? Hello?' I called out, trying not to shout. Well if you don't ask, you don't get.

I explained who I was and what I was writing about. Would someone be so kind as to speak with me? Delighted I was interested in them, an interview (including an interpreter) was arranged for the following day with Mustafa, the man in charge. He wanted to tell me about his brother.

As agreed, I returned at 1.00pm the following afternoon. Mustafa was running late, so I sat with the interpreter and heard again about 1974, but now from a Turkish point of view. His name is Taner and he is a highly intelligent man, with superb English. Taner is 70 years old, yet looks and acts much younger. Very knowledgeable, he naturally had a completely different take on Cyprus from what I had heard on the Greek side. However, like Bakis, the Greek Cypriot I spoke with, Taner had no hatred towards the other side. He made his personal feelings plainly clear. 'I don't hate Greek Cypriots, George. I don't hate. I have Greek friends.'

I believed him.

'The Greek people are good people individually. I can go out and eat, drink, talk and have friendship with them. But when they get together, maybe it is the brainwashing of the church, but when they get together and the political issue comes up, they lose all control.'

Interviewing this man was also the first time that I had heard the term *intervention* used by the Turkish Cypriots to describe what happened in 1974.

'You use the word intervention; they use the word invasion.'

'I use the word intervention because it was done in accordance with the Treaty of Guarantee, which was also agreed by the Athens Court of Appeal. 1974 was *not* an invasion, it was an intervention. Of course there were killings on both sides, but mostly by the Greeks who had the upper hand, they controlled 97 per cent of the island. All the trouble was started by the Greek side. Makarios wanted to change the agreed constitution which meant that Turkish Cypriots would be subjected to minority rights. This is well-documented.'

'Forty years later, this island is still divided. Isn't it time that it was reunited again?'

'Do you know, George, it's not us. Over 20 times, the Greek Cypriots have refused to reunite the island on a federal basis. You can find all this documented in the memoirs of the ex-Foreign Secretary of Greek Cyprus. And you know, each time they have refused, they have lost ground on this issue. At the intervention in 1974, Turkey proposed that there could be a lot of small Turkish areas all over the island to avoid division of the island. They refused. So after 15 days, Turkey got one third of the island and Cyprus became divided. That's why I say they lose control.'

'How many Turkish Cypriots were there in Cyprus in the '60s?'

'About 120,000. And today, 300,000.'

This I know is something that concerns the Greek Cypriots immensely for they see it as Turkey attempting to rebalance the population of the island in their favour. A central concern amongst Greeks is that Ankara is installing a population, which has no connection to Cyprus.

'Do you think the Turkish army should or will leave Cyprus?'

'No.'

'Do you think the dividing walls should come down?'

'Yes.'

'Do you think the island should simply be called Cyprus?'

'Yes.'

It seems we were making progress. 'How can the island be united if the Turkish army remains here?'

'If they remain in a *base*. Not on the streets, but in a *sovereign base*, like the British bases. The Turkish army would be there as guarantors of our safety. Please remember, since 1974, since the Turkish army has been here, there has been no bloodshed, no killing.'

I could not see any Greek I had spoken with accepting Turkish soldiers remaining on the island. Again, Taner reiterated, 'I want the walls to come down and our island to be as one. But the Turkish army *must* remain, albeit in their barracks, but there to protect us.'

'How do you feel when, apart from Turkey of course, none of the world's Islamic countries recognise the TRNC as legitimate?' He took a few seconds before he answered.

'I think many want to, but there is political pressure put on them not to do so. So we have close relations, they recognise us pragmatically but they don't or can't recognise us politically.'

They may well class themselves as Muslims in the TRNC, but the mind-set over religion here is different from Turkey and a long way from, say, Iran.

'We are very laid back, no fundamentalism. We are civilised, our approach is very different. Religion is not an issue here.'

I now wanted to discuss Famagusta. I told him about the Greeks I had met who lived there and who lost all their houses and possessions.

'Famagusta is my area. I know it well. I have all the evidence of what the real history is. I have all the title deeds that show the land belonged to Turkish Cypriots. But they were taken in the early 1900s by Greeks. The Greeks were also encouraged to re-register land and properties when the British ruled. So, the Greek man you spoke with says he lost his home? Yes he did, but they built their property on land that was taken by their ancestors from us. Listen, my family had four houses in what is now Greek Cyprus. Only one is now intact, the others demolished. We lost everything.'

'So you accept that people on both sides lost property?'

'Yes, of course I agree. We need to sort out who owns what, but we should go by original title deeds, not by who bought what house in the colonial times.'

'So Greeks who owned houses here in the north where we are sitting. Do you think they should get compensation?'

'Yes, they will have the title deeds, it's their property. But the Greeks don't recognise our title deeds to houses in Famagusta, our houses that they took and registered as theirs during the British colonial years. It has to work both ways, George. You know, I give lectures on this subject and have done so even in London.'

As well as the ongoing issue of roughly 1,500 people still missing from the 1974 war and families understandably wanting justice for this, a major point of contention is property. It all kicked off when Turkey invaded/intervened, and Turkish Cypriots who lived in the south fled north and left their homes, whilst Greek Cypriots who lived in the north fled south, leaving theirs. Today, untold thousands of people have homes in displaced parts of the island, which they haven't seen in decades. These homes are now either abandoned, rotting, or they now house people from the other side. Turkish Cypriots live in Greek Cypriot houses in the north and vice-versa. How they will ever manage to sort out compensation for this, I simply cannot imagine.

I asked Taner about the huge TRNC flag, the one that lights up at night and shines over to the Greek side.

'Look, I can understand pride, but this flag, is this not just stoking trouble? Is it not just propaganda?'

He smiled. 'Of course. The flag was initially about pride. But now, I tell you why I want it to stay, *to let the Greeks know we are here and we are the equal partners of Greek Cypriots*. Until they accept that, the flag should stay.'

Suddenly in walks Mustafa, late and very apologetic. 'Ah here is the old veteran!' Taner calls out. Mustafa humbly smiles, we shake hands, he apologies profusely, but I tell him not to worry, it's not a problem.

In fact, I am glad Mustafa was late. If he had been on time, I would not have had the opportunity to speak one-on-one with Taner. As they say, things happen for a reason.

Just as Mustafa was getting himself ready for our meeting, I told Taner about my meeting with Bakis. I told him Bakis' story of being held prisoner in Turkey and fearing he would die. Taner took no pride in this tale. He felt for the Greek Cypriot, I could see it in his eyes. He told me he would like to meet Bakis and drink Ouzo with him.

The fascinating thing is that both these men are from opposing sides in Famagusta, yet they have no hatred. Out of all the people I met in all of the divides, what Taner told me about wanting to meet Bakis was one of the most open-minded things I heard during my research for this entire book. A far cry from the blind hatred spewed forth by many.

'If I come back here in say ten years and we meet again, will we be meeting in a country still divided or as one?'

This question made Taner pause the longest. He gave it much thought before replying, 'George, it depends on the Greek Cypriots. It depends if they elect a leadership who doesn't want to rule alone just because they are the majority. I don't think or expect them to give in to the Turks, but they should want to rule jointly with us and see us as equals. It rests with them.'

It was time to interview Mustafa.

I informed Mustafa, due to his lateness, that I already had an in-depth view of the divide from a Turkish perspective. What I now wanted to know was his personal story.

There was so much warmth in that room and again Mustafa apologised for his lateness. Then, having a dig at his friend, Taner remarked, 'You know George, yesterday when you two arranged this interview, he called me seven times. Seven times to remind me to come on time, can you believe it!' We shared a belly laugh at this, but it would be the last laugh of the day. Once delectable Turkish coffee and glasses of chilled water were served, Mustafa told me his 1974 story. A story that engulfs his entire life.

'It all happened in the village of Alaminyo, a mixed village of Turks and Greeks. The village is separated by a stream, around 150 Turkish Cypriots on one side, 600 Greeks on the other. We had only around 30 Turkish volunteers with arms when, one day, 1000 well-armed men walked into the village and attacked the Turkish quarter. Everyone was terrified and many fled. Others were rounded up. My brother, Osman Reis, 27 at the time, was beaten black and blue, and they broke his chin. They then took him into custody. He was newlywed and his young wife, who was pregnant at the time, hid in a nearby hay barn, along with other women and children. They taped shut the mouths of the children, so they wouldn't attract attention from the Greek militia.

'The next day, 13 men who had been captured, including my brother Osman, were taken to a building, lined up and shot in cold blood. The final death toll was 15. The 14th victim was an 82-year-old Turkish Cypriot who tried to hide in his garden. But they found him, killed him, then burned him. The last was a local Imam who was 65 years old. His son was one of the 13 men shot. The Imam came back to find out what had happened to his boy, but they shot the Imam, then beheaded him.'

I was stunned at what I had just heard. The room got quieter and quieter and the air seemed thicker. Taner then went onto explain that even today there are around 1,500 people still unaccounted for from the 1974 war, and that bodies are being discovered all the time. A joint committee was established to help find the missing from both sides. Mustafa was the leading man on the committee to help find the missing from his area.

I cannot imagine the pain this causes for families. What I had just been told, indeed was a reality check against the troubles in my life.

'Am I right in assuming that *you* found your brother's remains? Were you able to give him a proper burial?'

'After they killed him, my brother was buried secretly along with others, under an asphalt road. We didn't know where. But yes, we found my brother, but not until 2006. After much searching over the years, we discovered a grave where we believed he had been killed. Many bodies of young Turkish Cypriots were dug up. After DNA was taken from the bodies and from me, there was a match and my brother was identified. My brother Osman Reiss was finally identified after 32 years.'

I let what had just been said sink in, before asking Taner, 'How did he feel once he finally found his brother?'

'The discovery was both a great grief, and at the same time a great relief,' Mustafa replied, his voice getting quieter all the time. 'My brother Osman Reiss was finally laid to rest in Nicosia and the funeral was attended by the Prime Minister and the President of Cyprus.'

Suddenly, it all got too much for him and he broke down, the pain of his brother still raw inside him. It was heart wrenching to watch as Mustafa heaved and cried. I lowered my head, feeling guilty for intruding on his grief. Mustafa cried for a couple of minutes before composing himself. He then actually apologised to me for crying.

I have the interview with Mustafa on my Dictaphone and I must have listened to it a dozen times whilst writing this. Each time I hear it I can see his face, kind and warm, and when it comes to the place in the interview when he breaks down and cries, something inside me crumbles. Now I have finally written about it, I do not think I ever want to hear the interview again.

Mustafa looked better for letting his emotions spill out. He then kindly invited me to stay and share lunch with him. Soon, his office was full of superb local takeaway food and the three of us sat down, munching on various local styles of kebab and salad, washed down with ice-cold coke. I tried to contribute to the bill, but they would not hear of it.

All this, just because I'd had the nerve to walk into a pensioners club down a side street one hot afternoon.

Mustafa Tolga is a quiet man, who, despite what he has experienced, is full of dignity and warmth. During that interview and on the other two occasions I met him, he never once expressed a single ounce of hatred towards anyone from the other side.

As I walked back through the baking heat of the TRNC towards the border, recalling what Mustafa had just told me, I had that sense of contemplation about life that one can get whilst sitting in silence in a church or mosque or synagogue. Alternatively, for me, atop a mountain.

Listening to Mustafa talk about his brother was one of the most humbling experiences of my life.

Forty years to the day

This was the big day. Exactly 40 years to the day that Turkey invaded, or intervened, in Cyprus. On the Greek side it was 40 years of pain, 'Our island was cut in two by the occupying Turks'. On the Turkish side, a sense of giving thanks for the intervention of the Turkish army that had, 'saved us from Greek oppression'.

During the early evening, I crossed over to the Turkish sector once again, via Ledra Palace Gate. What a transformation! The streets were bathed in the flags of the TRNC and Turkey. There was also a larger military presence than I had seen previously. Definitely a day for propaganda on both sides. I spent a couple of hours wandering the streets and trying to engage people.

One Turkish Cypriot in his 70s was more than happy to tell me his thoughts on the world. I wanted to hear his views on this divide, but after a few minutes he was banging on about his hatred of Israel. 'What on earth did that have to do with Cyprus?' I thought, but I let him rant. He was also very anti-West. I asked him what he thought of the thousands of Hamas rockets fired indiscriminately into Israel. Taken aback by such a question, he brushed it off and said he wanted Russia to back Gaza against the West. Thank God this man was not in a position of power. I thanked him for his time, shook his hand and walked off.

The streets of the TRNC were covered in flags and all things red. The people were ready to celebrate their 40th anniversary and their republic. The Turkish army were very visible that day in the TRNC. Trucks were full of soldiers, but the atmosphere was calm. Most shops and businesses were closed for the day.

Eventually, I headed back to the border. Just as I was getting my TRNC exit stamp, two UN peacekeepers approached the border from the buffer zone. They saluted the Turkish official and one said in English, 'Just coming over to say hello. Everything all right tonight?'

The UN does not take sides here. It simply has the onerous task of keeping the two 'countries' apart, especially at sensitive anniversaries. I got my exit stamp and headed back through no man's land, but something felt different, a sense of tension hung in the air. There was also much activity going on inside the buffer zone I was walking through. Teams of UN peacekeeping soldiers in full riot gear were getting ready. But ready for what?

It soon became apparent. After crossing into the Greek side, I was standing amongst hundreds of young protesters dressed in black with white armbands. Unlike the feeling in the Turkish sector, these people were not in a party mood and certainly not ready to celebrate 40 years of the TRNC.

A man who looked like an organiser walked up to me. He was nervous and wary about who I was, where I was from and what I was doing there. I told him I was not working for any organisation related to Turkey, and that I would like to speak with him to hear his views on Cyprus for my book. He soon opened up and told me where he stood, with burning passion. He was helping to organise the demo for ELAM, The National Popular Front (who are closely aligned to the infamous ultra-right wing Greek party, Golden Dawn).

'We demand full Turkish withdrawal from Cyprus!' he said staring into my eyes, as if I myself were Turkish.

We were standing metres from the border at Ledra Palace gate. 'You are free to travel through that border to the Turkish part of this city, have you ever been there?' I asked.

'No, and I would never go, not until it's all Greek again.'

'Do you want this divide to come down?'

'Of course. All of Cyprus is Greece.'

'So, if or when the walls came down, would you mix with the Turkish Cypriots?'

That threw him and he did not answer. When I asked another protester the same question later, he said that he hated the Turkish so much he did not even want the walls to come down. He wanted *no* mixing with the Turkish Cypriot community whatsoever.

The organiser and other individuals present warned me on half a dozen occasions, that although I was allowed to photograph them and their flags, I must *not* photograph their faces. These people were deadly serious, and while they were never physically aggressive towards me, I had no desire to get on the wrong side of them.

They erected loudspeakers and got their flags ready, while the Greek Cypriot police were busy arranging crash barriers directly in front of their own border. Meanwhile, my camera and I were drawing attention. The police chief asked what I was doing and who I was. I explained about my book, showed him my press card and said I wanted some photos.

'Hmm, Ok, but come behind here, stand behind us.'

It was all set. Hundreds of very fired up ELAM supporters with flags fluttering, standing 50 feet away from the border. Just behind makeshift barriers were four lines of police and me. Everyone, on both sides, was getting ready for whatever was going to happen next. I looked at the police officer to my left – he looked determined but also nervous. Suddenly a tap on my shoulder and a very perplexed voice indeed from behind me said in heavily accented English, 'Can I ask what you are doing standing here?'

He was Ukrainian, smartly dressed in cream trousers and a crisp clean shirt. He introduced himself as the UN official in charge of operations that night. I told him I had permission from the police and then asked what he thought of the situation unfolding before us.

He looked at the crowd of ELAM supporters, standing on the other sides of the police lines. 'The intention of these people is to intimidate. They want to cross over to the Turkish side and cause problems. But right here,' he pointed to where we are standing, 'it's up to the Greek Cypriot police to stop them. But if they get past them and enter the UN buffer zone, then it's up to me to stop them making it to the TRNC border.'

Suddenly, after a shout from the ELAM organiser, the mob came to life, chanting, carrying huge flags and lit torches.

'Be careful,' the Ukrainian UN official said, before walking behind a wall that hid dozens of UN soldiers now in full riot gear.

As the protesters walked slowly towards us, I glanced over my shoulder at the UN riot police 20 feet behind me. Behind them, was a couple hundred metres of buffer zone, then the TRNC border and the Turkish army behind that. This could get really ugly, I thought.

I could feel the police line stiffen as the mob came to a stop directly in front of us. Flags aloft, they chanted in unison with all their might and pointed over my head in the direction of the Turkish side, where their chants could undoubtedly be heard. They claim they are being patriotic, but their body language was very aggressive. Thankfully, they did not attempt to go further. Instead, they performed a kind of marching ritual on their own side.

Close to the border, numerous speeches by various individuals followed over the next hour or so. The organiser appeared beside me. 'You pleased with everything so far?' I asked him. 'Great,' he said with a sparkle in his eye before barking out a chant that was repeated by the crowd in parrot fashion. The speeches were in Greek, which I did not understand, but every minute or so, cheers and chants came from the crowd in support of what was being said.

Maybe they *were* simply being patriotic, but I have to say that there was *not* a good vibe at the border that night. I had seen enough. I thanked the organiser for his time and left. But it wasn't just me that was on the move. The protesters began to march along a main road. I saw them, an hour later, marching in the dark, chanting and holding aloft burning torches...

Summing up

Cyprus 1974 – was it an invasion or an intervention? For an outsider, it is far too delicate a subject to say one way or another. The legacy is that over 40 years later, Cyprus remains divided and the TRNC remains unrecognised by everyone in the world, apart from Turkey.

I find myself often coming back to individual people when summing up. Taking down walls and razor wire can only happen through governments and UN involvement. Politicians must talk to their so-called enemies. Even the British government and the IRA managed it eventually. But individual people also need to mix and to talk, no more so than in divided Cyprus.

I was humbled to have been in the presence of Greek Bakis and Turkish Mustafa. Two men who both experienced the horrors of 1974. However, not once did I experience any hatred from them. What a contrasting situation to the members of ELAM who I saw demonstrate at the border. Many of these people were in their 20s or younger. They were not even born when the 1974 war happened. For sure, they are entitled to their opinions, but there was way too much hatred towards the Turkish side. For argument's sake, I will give them the benefit of the doubt and say their hatred is justified. Even so, even if it *is* justified, peace will *never ever* come to this tiny island until people stop hating another entire group of people simply because of their ethnicity. I do understand that someone may dislike or even hate a certain member of a certain community for something that individual did. But to hate an entire nation of people, many of whom you have never met and never intend to meet, seems tragic to me.

I get the feeling from researching this book, that while most people say they want reconciliation and peace, many seem to secretly enjoy the current state of the divide. It makes them feel they belong to their group, ethnicity or religion. *I am right and because you are on the other side, you are wrong*! Very tribal.

So, what *should* happen in Cyprus? Many Greek Cypriots want the whole island back. I cannot see that happening. The Turkish Cypriots are there to stay. The more enlightened members on each side want the walls to come down, but the Turkish Cypriot community insist that the Turkish army remain to protect them. However, no Greek Cypriot I met will accept Turkish soldiers remaining in a united Cyprus.

But *could it work*? Consider this scenario: they take down the walls and reunite the island as one; they establish a parliament that represents everyone; they allow a contingent of Turkish troops to remain, confined to barracks, much like the British. The troops could be under a strict UN mandate to remain in their compounds and have no day-to-day role in policing. They would be there as a *last resort* should war break out and the Turkish community were attacked. It would take a forward-thinking Greek Cypriot leader to accept such a proposal, but it *could* be achieved. I think it is workable, but will require compromise from all. If people want a common goal badly enough, they will compromise, but they must genuinely want to better their lives and reunite their country.

If the walls come down, maybe people will start to live side by side again, not as Greek Cypriots or Turkish Cypriots but simply as *Cypriots*. Neighbours and friends, as it once was.

Is this an impossible task? No, it is not. Yet, when dealing with so much personal pain and anger, overcoming division can be very difficult indeed.

This divide has gone on for far too long. This is Europe, we have democracy and rule of law so we should be able to solve this problem for the benefit of both the Turkish and Greek Cypriots who share the island. It is shocking that in this supposedly enlightened time, a capital city of a European country is divided with walls and razor wire. Nicosia is a blight on all of Europe and something that should shame us all.

The current stalemate is not working. Despite numerous UN Security Council Resolutions and the Annan Plan, nothing has produced success. Vested interests remain. For the sake of future generations of all Cypriots, those in power on both sides must be prepared to compromise. Ordinary citizens on both sides must also be willing to compromise, and that may well be even more difficult to achieve than the politicians agreeing.

Update March 2017

New UN-mediated talks have been taking place in Switzerland between the President of Cyprus and the Turkish Cypriot leader. Once again, they are trying to reunite their divided island. This time, the hopes are high, but there are of course huge obstacles to overcome. However, at least they are talking.

As of writing, Nicosia remains the last divided capital city in the world. It is now 43 years and counting…

The British Foreign & Commonwealth Office (FCO) has no specific travel warning on Cyprus. It does state though that the **'Turkish Republic of Northern Cyprus is not recognised by the British government.'**

6

Transnistria

Back in the USSR?

Status	Presidential republic. Officially governed as the PMR – Pridnestrovian Moldavian Republic. Unrecognised by any UN member
Capital	Tiraspol (unrecognised)
Currency	Transnistrian Rouble
Population	Estimated at roughly 500,000 (Approximately one third Russian, one third Moldovan and one third Ukrainian)
Language	Moldovan, Russian, Ukrainian

Introduction

TRANSNISTRIA, or Pridnestrovie as it is known in Russia, is located in the historical region of Bessarabia, on the very outskirts of Europe, and was once a part of the tiny country called Moldova.

After the breakup of the USSR, Moldova claimed independence after decades of Soviet rule, but the region of Transnistria stayed loyal to the Motherland and all things red. After a short but brutal war in the early '90s, Russian troops stayed on to protect their little enclave, a small foothold on European soil.

Transnistria boasts its own border, has its own flag, police and money. Yet in the second decade of the 21st century, it remains a non-entity, an unrecognised limbo state. Never heard of it? Not surprising really. No one, not a single member of the UN recognises Transnistria as a legitimate country.

This country does not officially exist. However, believe me, exist it does.

Not being recognised may be of benefit here, for there is little if any adherence to international law, and Transnistria is fast becoming a haven for money laundering, weapons smuggling and people trafficking.

I had already been Transnistria on two prior occasions, so knew it was a bizarre time warp. Whilst other former Soviet republics have moved on in their own ways, in Transnistria, they just cannot seem to let go of the past.

Today, Pridnestrovie is the closest you are ever going to get to experiencing many aspects of the old USSR. For this chapter, I will refer to it as Transnistria.

The What, Where and Why

In 1924, the Moldovan Autonomous Soviet Socialist Republic (MASSR) was established east of the Dniester River, next to Ukraine. In 1940, Russia annexed Bessarabia and together with MASSR formed the Moldavian Soviet Socialist Republic. And there it stayed, locked behind the iron curtain, cut off from the rest of the world.

Control from Moscow remained absolute until the mid-1980s when Gorbachev's attempts to modernise the USSR influenced the rise of nationalism in Moldova.

As the USSR crumbled, Moldova moved swiftly to declare independence, but the pro-Russian east of Moldova, the Transnistria region, rejected this. With the backing of the huge Russian 14th Army, Transnistria won its battle. Moldova backed off and thus today in the second decade of the 21st century, Transnistria remains an unrecognised entity. A black hole. A little Soviet time warp.

Arrival at Chişinău

Moldova is the poorest country on the European continent. A mix of old Soviet-style policies and corruption has made it so. Chişinău, the capital of Moldova has a small airport outside the city and just off the actual road to Transnistria itself. I arrived late in the afternoon and was met by a driver connected to my hotel in Transnistria. He drove an old Mercedes and I noticed the number plate, not Moldovan, but Transnistrian with the hammer and sickle on it.

Onto the main road, we headed east, where, bar a small number of new Mercs and old Ladas, the roads were nearly empty. With every mile we drove, it felt as if the calendar was flicking backwards in years. I relaxed in my seat and enjoyed the serenity of it all. My Russian is not exactly brilliant but, as always, I managed to communicate with my driver and he seemed impressed I had been in Transnistria before. The first time in 2004, and then again in 2010.

Driving up to the unrecognised Transnistrian border, I stiffened with anticipation, yet managed to sneak some photos whilst my driver told me, 'Camera no, no good.'

We approached a heavily fortified area, blocking the main highway. The official yet unofficial border. Imagine driving on a motorway in the UK, and suddenly looming ahead in the middle of the road, you see tanks, soldiers, barbed wire and artillery strewn everywhere. On the other side of that is another country, unrecognised of course.

There is no British embassy in Transnistria, so if you get into trouble, there is very little that can be done to help you. You are on your own.

Electronic flashing ones have now replaced the old painted Soviet signs that once hung over the border. Transnistria is here to stay. I could not have said that five years ago. Considering what's happening in East Ukraine, I now have no doubts whatsoever.

Out of the car and into the brand new immigration building. On my first visit in 2004, this building was a wooden hut. As my driver helped me with my visa application, it dawned on me that I had never previously been allowed to spend a night in Transnistria. Once, I had been given a six-hour visa and was informed to not outstay my welcome. This time I was planning a four-day visit and already had a hotel booked. One thing you never say at this border is that you are coming here to write about them.

The Transnistrian border-guard flicked through my passport and gave me a dirty look when he came across a Ukrainian stamp. Questions, questions, questions. 'Why do you come to Transnistria?' 'Tourist,' I said. He gave me a look that said, *why the hell would a Western tourist come here*? Nevertheless, as it was not his personal concern, he shrugged and stamped. I had my visa.

We rejoined the car queue and once at the front, our car was duly searched. Another armed official checked my documents again before we finally trundled into the uniqueness that is Transnistria. Had I just stepped through a portal?

Within 100 metres, we stopped at a roadside petrol station. Whilst my driver filled the car up, I got out, walked over to a nearby field and took in the view. In the distance, I could see the top of the old communist tower blocks in Tiraspol. The sky was cloudy grey and heavy. It felt like the USSR.

On entering Tiraspol, we drove up the main street, Lenin still standing proud outside the Presidential Palace. The wide streets in the capital remained nearly empty of traffic and pedestrians. It was eerily quiet.

My hotel? State owned and very Russian. Fearing the worst after experiencing rude, Soviet-style manners in many hotels in places like this, I was pleasantly surprised and had no complaints. It was now 9.00pm and after checking in and leaving my bags, I ventured out to the Russian style shops. Inside, large middle-aged women dressed in old-fashioned overalls served me. It reminded me of photos I have seen depicting life in 1950s provincial Britain.

I changed £20 at a nearby exchange into worthless Transnistrian roubles. Completely unchangeable back into any international currency, the paper notes are filthy, and many are near disintegrating. As for the coins, still the pointless Kopek, plastic with the hammer and sickle on them. I bought two cold Russian Baltica beers and sat outside on the concrete steps. As I drank my beer and took in the smell of cheap Russian diesel, I reminded myself that there are no foreign embassies here, you really are on your own. I could hear my friend Gwen's voice in my ear, 'Why can't you ever go somewhere nice?'

Back in my hotel room, I finished my second beer, climbed into bed and drifted off to sleep in a country that does not officially exist.

Out and about in Transnistria

There were no foreigners that I could see. Everything may be priced in Transnistrian roubles, but the locals often think in hard currency and the US dollar is still king. This is very 1990s thinking. It was like this all over the ex-USSR states, as their fledgling currencies were not worth the paper they were printed on. In 2015, the Transnistrian rouble is still not worth the paper it is printed on.

Outside the Presidential palace, which looks like an ugly British 1960s polytechnic, I stood photographing Lenin and history repeated itself. Exactly like last time I was here, an armed guard came out the palace doors, down the steps and right up to me. He demanded I hand over my camera.

I checked his uniform, he was not Militia so I said, 'No, I have done nothing wrong.'

He spoke in Russian but I got the gist of it. I was talking photos of the Palace, he said. Not allowed. I told him I was taking photos of Lenin only.

He indicated he wanted me to delete my photo of the Palace or he would call the Security Services. I let him watch me delete the photo, but of course, I did not delete the other three I had. I walked on. At the other end of this small city stands the seat of government, but it's not called the Transnistrian Parliament. It's called The House of Soviets, and little old ladies in headscarves tend flower beds that surround it. Honestly, if the long-gone 1970s Soviet leader Leonid Brezhnev had walked round the corner, I would not have batted an eyelid. I *had* stepped through a portal.

Unlike in my previous visits when Transnistria looked like it would crumble, money is now pouring in. Black money, dirty and undeclared money, coming from whom and going to where exactly, is anyone's guess. Brand new Russian banks and the official central bank look worryingly out of place. It adds fuel to the notion that Transnistria is fast becoming a black hole for money laundering and illegal weapons sales. Anything goes here. Transnistria does not seem to have an ounce of legitimacy about it whatsoever.

That said, it is quiet and calm. It is uncommercialised, with no discernible American or European influence. Almost no one here speaks English. Yet when I stop for a coffee, they are friendly to me. Globalisation has not reached here yet. There are no Starbucks, no Burger King. Life is much slower, and a lack of industry and traffic means that the air is clean, even in the city centre.

I sit on a bench in a park just off the main street. Kids play, teenagers sit and chat and couples stroll by, pushing prams. It does not feel like the 21st century and everyone seems blissfully oblivious to the outside world.

I can imagine that if my older Russian friends from Moscow were to come here, they would all feel hugely nostalgic for their Soviet childhoods. For Tiraspol really is like the '70s, '60s, or even '50s.

I hate to admit it, but I perversely like Transnistria. I do not mean its Soviet or Russian leanings, or its bad human rights record or illegal shenanigans. I mean this feeling of life being slower and that it has not yet been sucked into a hectic commercialised world. I am reminded of a line from a song I wrote a few years back: 'Life's never seemed so fast, it was always slower in the past'.

Yet Transnistria is not the impoverished place it was in 2004. In those days, I remember buying a fresh coffee for 9p. Not so today, there is much more cash around. But it seems to be held by a very few and I don't think we'll see a trickle down of cash to the poor folks who cling onto old socialist values. No, the money will stay with a connected few. The corrupt authorities, their backers and whoever else is involved in the illegality of it all are no more old-fashioned Socialists than I am. So why all the USSR kitsch? I think it is all just an act. The majority of the people are old and yearn for the old days, so the authorities keep the image alive, keep close to Russia and keep the West at bay. Even young people, who are not necessarily Socialist, jump on the patriotic bandwagon and fly the hammer and sickle. It's not so much pro-Soviet Socialism, as more anti-West. And the system seems to work.

Transnistria will not become westernised, but will remain this little time warp, where the old Soviet world mixes with increasing amounts of dirty, undeclared sacks of cash. Could Transnistria become a bolthole for big Russian players? Could it become a place to invest in, to build huge houses, to hide money, to live in a clean environment, like a criminal retreat hidden away from the prying eyes of the rest of the world?

What do I mean *could*? It seems to be that now.

Bendery

Close to the de facto capital Tiraspol is the town of Bendery, the scene of much fierce fighting in 1991. Between the two stands the all-important Tighina Bridge that straddles the Dniester River. Control this bridge and you control access to the capital Tiraspol.

A Russian peacekeeping force is very visible at the bridge. Photography is *strictly prohibited* and I had failed on my two visits previous to get a shot. This time though, I got my photo, which looks like it was taken in 1970. Just metres away from where I was stood is an old fort that is still used by troops. Large metal gates keep hidden well away whatever is inside.

As I approached and started to take photos, a verbally aggressive Russian soldier came out and made it clear I had to stop and leave. I did not hang around. The idea of being arrested in Transnistria did not appeal to me. Off I walked, heading to the nearby town of Bendery, and 20 minutes later, I stood in the central market. What took me by surprise was the amount of produce on display, it certainly was not like this is 2004. Lots of fruit and veg, also huge chunks of local cheese which sat out in the open without refrigeration, whilst the temperature must have been around 30 degrees.

The meat section of the market was *not* for the faint hearted. Great big slabs of bloodied meat hung on hooks and piles of offal lay on cardboard boxes, which are used to soak up the blood. Pigs' heads, feet and all manner of bits lay there as women who looked like they were straight out of a 1960s Soviet movie hacked up the meat with bare hands. My stomach lurched. I would not have eaten meat from there if you'd paid me.

I headed back into the fresh air and wandered Bendery's main square. Rickety trolleybuses drove people around and lots of old Ladas sat parked at the roadsides. This could have been any provincial Soviet city 30 years ago. I photographed at will and no one questioned me. Finally, I sat in a Russian-style café and wrote up my notes from the past couple of days.

I have learned that Russia is pumping tens of millions into Transnistria. I did not need to find that out though, as I could see it for myself. It helps to keep Transnistria reliant on Moscow. Much of the cash was meant to aid the local population, but corrupt officials have syphoned it off. Russian prosecutors investigating the embezzlement of financial aid even questioned the son of the Transnistrian President.

Cigarette smuggling on a tsunami level also goes on here. Literally billions of cigarettes are coming in from Russia and elsewhere. These cheap, nasty, illegal and often dangerous cigarettes are now flooding into Moldova and eventually into the EU. I bought a packet of Marlboro red for around 60p. Real Marlboro? I doubt it. You can also buy numerous Russian brands of cigarette of course; one brand is even called 'USSR.'

Far more concerning is the amount of armaments left in Transnistria in 1991 by the departing Red Army. It is claimed that Transnistria is stuffed-full of thousands of tons of grenades, explosives and tank ammunition. No one really knows who controls this and to whom it is being sold. In addition, corruption in Transnistria is on a scale like no other. Untold billions are divided up, unaccounted for, and un-declared.

By far the most depressing aspect of Transnistria, something that is still very much a taboo subject, is human trafficking. The locals either do not know about it, or most likely are not willing to talk about it and just accept that it happens. The authorities or those with connections to the security services must surely be in on it. Yet the outside world, in particular the West, seems to be doing precious little to stop this vile trade. I am talking not only about adult women for prostitution, but also child prostitution. Many from Transnistria and Moldova are shipped off to Russia, Ukraine and the Middle East as sex slaves. There is now legislation against this, which from what I could gather only came into force in 2010. As a result, these activities have decreased dramatically, but forced prostitution and even some say, the trafficking of human organs, continues behind the scenes. Moldova also suffers from the organised crime of forced prostitution.

Transnistria is *not* an old-fashioned Soviet dream as many of its residents seem to think it is. To be honest, I wouldn't mind if it actually was. If someone wants to live in a red utopia, then good luck to them. But behind the façade, away from Lenin and the red flags, Transnistria has all the hallmarks of a criminal 'country' that is using its unrecognised status to get away with organised crime on every level possible. Maybe the UN should call the Transnistrian government's bluff and grant them recognition as a country? Why not? At least then, they would be forced to come in from the cold, and begin adhering to international law.

USSR *breakup and the Transnistrian war*

During the late '80s, the USSR was dying, and under Gorbachev, changes were happening. Nationalism was on the rise in many of the Soviet republics, where people could see the imminent demise of an empire. This was no more so than in the Moldavian Soviet Socialist Republic. Considering the history here, there was a resurgent feeling amongst many to realign themselves with Romania. This naturally worried the pro-Russian communities living in this part of Moldova. Yet no one knew what was going to happen, and various groups started to plan how they wanted it all to move forward. It soon became tribal.

Here is what happened in this part of the disintegrating USSR: In August 1989, the authorities, still under the banner of the Supreme Soviet of the Moldavian SSR, made Moldovan the official language once again, replacing Russian. The Latin alphabet was also to make a comeback, replacing the Russian Cyrillic. Change moved at a fast pace and in 1990 the Soviet flag was replaced by the Moldovan tricolour. By the end of 1990, the words Soviet and Socialist were dropped and the official name of the country now became The Republic of Moldova.

With the bloody end of the brutal Ceausescu regime in neighbouring Romania, it now seemed to many that some sort of union between Moldova and Romania would take place. The large Russian population in the east of Moldova (the Transnistrian region) wanted no part of this.

Protests started as early as 1989 and soon there were separatist movements in Transnistria who wanted autonomy for their little area in the newly emerging world. Those in charge in the Transnistria region declared themselves independent from the newly independent Moldova and expressed a desire to re-join or remain in (it is difficult to say which) the nearly-dead USSR.

In September 1990, they declared their new country. It would officially be called the Pridnestrovian Moldavian Soviet Socialist Republic. Transnistria now became another unrecognised state along with the likes of Abkhazia and Nagorno-Karabakh, all because of infighting during the breakup of the Soviet empire. The first fighting between the Moldovan government and Transnistrian separatists took place in December 1990.

As the world knows, a last gasp attempt by plotters in Moscow to keep the USSR alive resulted in a failed coup in August 1991. Although Gorbachev did not sign the death warrant until the end of the year, it was already game over for the Soviet Union and the new Moldovan Parliament was quick off the mark in adopting a declaration of independence.

The Russian 14th Army, a battalion of the USSR, was based in what was up until 1991, the Moldavian Soviet Socialist Republic. However, by 1992, they were soldiers of a country that had collapsed and were now on the territory of the new Moldova, a country that did not want them there. Previous pleas to Moscow to remove these troops had failed. The reactions of Russia in Transnistria seem to be very similar to the actions taken over Crimea and in particular East Ukraine. The stance being: 'We are keeping our troops here to protect Russian people.' This is a classic Kremlin guise to keep a foothold in areas it deems under its sphere of influence.

The new Transnistrian authorities managed to muster an impressive 9,000-militia men. Many came from Russia and pro-Russian sympathisers just over the border in Ukraine. The official Russian 14th Army who numbered another 14,000 was training this new Transnistrian 'army'. In total 23,000 men were ready to fight to keep this part of Moldova red.

By 1992, Moldova, who had now joined the United Nations, claimed it had troops numbering up to 35,000. This included professional soldiers, conscripts, police, reservists and volunteers, especially those Moldovans living close to Transnistria. Whatever weaponry both sides used, it undoubtedly came from what was left over from the USSR. How ironic that both sides were fighting each other with weapons that used to belong to them all.

By April 1992, with the USSR dead, Russia had more than enough problems of its own. Nevertheless, the 14th Army stayed in Transnistria and senior ministers in the new Russian government openly called for Transnistrians to claim their independence. It seems that even then, the broken state of Russia knew that one day it would possibly rise again and would require loyal pockets of supporters on European soil. There have been numerous calls for Russian troop withdrawal from Transnistria. The first deadline was set for 2002. It did not happen. An extension was given to 2003, then again to 2004.

After vicious fighting in early 1992, a ceasefire was negotiated in early June, yet it did not last. All hell broke loose in Bendery as the Moldovan police arrested the head of the Russian 14th Army, resulting in Transnistrian troops opening fire on the police station. Moldovan troops subsequently poured in to retake Bendery and urban warfare took place in the densely populated town. Many civilians were killed or injured. Arguments abound to this very day as to who shot more civilians and who was to blame for the bloodshed in Bendery. I guess we will never get the real truth. Very much like today's East Ukraine.

The news regarding the fighting in Bendery quickly spread to Tiraspol, the seat of the Transnistrian government, and they asked Moscow for help. The new Russian Vice President Rutskoy told Russian forces in Transnistria to storm Bendery. Within days, a mix of forces loyal to Transnistria and Mother Russia retook Bendery and the all-important bridge.

A ceasefire was finally declared in July 1992. Moldovan troops retreated to the capital Chişinău and soon the divide went up as Transnistria started to build its own 'country' with borders, passports, flags and money.

Exact figures for casualties in the Transnistrian war, as in many conflicts, vary wildly. However, it seems the accepted figure is roughly 1,000 dead with thousands injured, many of whom were civilians. A tragedy in itself. Yet what happened here was short-lived and had much less bloodshed than many other breakup wars, Nagorno-Karabakh and Abkhazia being prime examples. There is no doubt that without the Russian 14th Army and its thousands of troops, 'independence' for Transnistria would not have succeeded. What should have been an easy victory for Moldova did not happen and the tables were turned. Without outside support for Transnistria, Moldovan troops could have easily overrun the rebels and Moldova today would be one country. Instead, part of it, which is Transnistria, remains unrecognised and cut off from the world.

The Russian 14th Army are now finally gone, yet more than 1,000 Russian troops still remain in Transnistria today. Ironically, they are there as *self-imposed peacekeepers*. Russian troops on European soil in 2015 – who would have thought so back in 1991? Not me, nor very few, I would imagine. I just wonder how far they had thought ahead on this one. I guess we will never know.

As it happens, I discovered that the BBC's Steven Sackur, who presents the programme 'Hard Talk' on BBC World was in Transnistria at the same time I was. He was set to interview the President of this so-called country. I smirked to myself as I imagined he would be flown into Moldova, whipped along by official car, enjoy a hassle-free border crossing and be driven to the Presidential Palace where he'd do an hour's interview, then be whisked out again to Chişinău airport and back to London in time for tea.

I really *do* enjoy Steven Sackur's programme. It is very hard-hitting, so *was* I jealous that he was interviewing the President when I would simply have no hope of achieving that? No. When I started out planning *Mankind's Great Divides*, I realised that what would really make this book legitimate and hopefully compelling, would be the interviews. Not interviews with officials or those in power, but interviews with *real people*. Real people whose lives are affected on a daily basis by the divides in which they live.

I was set to interview Tatiana, a citizen of Transnistria, born in Tiraspol in 1970. It took a bit of coaxing but she finally agreed to speak with me openly about Transnistria, Ukraine, Putin and the West. In all my interviews, I try to let the interviewee tell their story from their point of view. I try not to judge them, but in the following interview you will see that I simply could not fail to show my frustration at what Tatiana said. Attitudes like hers are sadly the norm in today's Russia.

Interview with Tatiana

'Do you think of yourself as a Transnistrian, Russian or...'

She proudly replied, 'In Soviet times, we were all Russian.'

'Oh, I would ask you to never say to an Armenian, or Georgian, or Latvian or Estonian that they were all Russian.'

'Ok, ok. But we were 15 republics, all together in the USSR. Like sisters.'

'Sisters that all wanted to break away from you. They all wanted to move towards the West.'

She paused and gave me the classic line I had heard numerous times, 'In the Soviet Union there were many good things. My childhood was good, I don't remember bad times.'

We talked about the war in the early '90s. She had been living in Tiraspol, which had been relatively calm compared to the intense fighting in nearby Bendery.

'This was a terrible time for us. The USSR should not break up and we didn't want to be part of Moldova.'

'But this is Moldova. It never wanted to be in the USSR in the first place and it finally got its independence.'

'Maybe, but we didn't want to be part of it.'

'I'm sorry, but this land you live on is part of Moldova, whether you like it or not. If you wanted so much to join Russia and if the Kremlin cared so much for Transnistrian citizens, why didn't they offer you all asylum? You could have gone and lived there?'

'But this is my land, I am from Transnistria.'

'Exactly and Transnistria is part of the Republic of Moldova, not Russia.'

She smiled at me, a knowing smile before pouring more tea. I then said, 'Transnistria is not recognised by any country in the world. According to numerous international bodies, it's an illegal state. That said, would you like Transnistria to join Russia?'

'I want to join Russia, like Crimea and Kaliningrad.'

'Hang on, we need to remember our history here. Kaliningrad was German. It didn't willingly join Russia.'

'I don't like this history,' was her awkward reply.

We then discussed the ongoing war in Ukraine. I accepted that people are dying on both sides and that all killing was wrong. Did she really believe the Kremlin line that fascists in Kiev started all this?

'Yes, I believe the Russian TV. We all saw it, we all saw the fascists in Kiev, in Maidan.'

I had to interrupt her. 'I was in Maidan during this time, I didn't see any Nazis running around. So if I didn't see them, how did you manage?'

'On TV of course.'

'Ah of course. Russian state news, by any chance?'

'Of course.' She replied.

I tried to explain to her that in Kiev and other cities, hundreds of thousands of ordinary men and women took to the streets to protest against a very corrupt government controlled by Moscow. I asked her if she knew the reasons for the initial demonstrations against the government and their going back on the EU trade deal. She did not. I explained that Ukraine had been about to sign a deal to trade with the EU but after immense pressure from the Big Brother in the Kremlin, they dropped it and pledged to stay close to Russia. That was why the people took to the streets. But Tatiana was having none of it and said to me, 'Putin has done so much for Ukraine, why do they want to move towards Europe?'

Tatiana, of course, like millions of other pro-Russians, has access to the internet, to news that is not controlled by governments. They have access to organisations that have decades of professional journalism and reporting behind them. Do they watch them and make up their own minds? Millions do not. They watch Russian TV and believe what they are told.

Tatiana then said, 'What good things has America ever done for Europe?'

'Helped saved it from the Nazis for one thing.' However, I have to admit that I just didn't have a reply, when she told me out of the blue that America started the First World War. I thought I'd 'heard it all before', but this one stumped me.

'What do you personally think of Mr Putin?'

Her eyes lit up. 'Oh he is very educated man. He is clever, he is very strong character. I really like him. He is good for the Russian people. I can see no one who is better than him.'

For all of Tatiana's love of Russia, she admitted that her son, who now lives in Canada, has a much better life and whilst missing him, she is very glad he does not live in Transnistria anymore. That spoke volumes.

With regard to the recent anti-gay laws in Russia, I ask her what she thinks of homosexuality. Her face turns to a very uncomfortable look. 'I don't like these people.'

When I've heard some fellow Scots say, 'I hate the English,' I try to show how ignorant a sweeping statement that is by replying, 'Really, wow I didn't realise you'd met them all?'. I think of using this on Tatiana to try help break down the prejudice, but I decide on another line. I lean across the table where she is pouring tea and say calmly, 'What if your son telephoned you and told you he was gay?'. Initially she was shocked at my question, but then it turned to uncertainty. She simply said, which I honestly believe, 'I have no answer to that question.'

What did she think of Transnistria being a black hole for arms sales, massive state-run corruption, organised prostitution and child trafficking?

She dismissed it, saying it was anti-Russian propaganda. I asked her to read the reports from Human Rights Watch amongst others.

'Transnistria is part of Moldova. This little state you have created with flags and borders is illegal, surely you accept that?'

'I don't want to be part of Moldova. I want Mr Putin to take us into Russia.'

'You do know that the newspapers you read and news channels you watch are controlled by the Kremlin? Only recently, brave presenters resigned live on air saying that they were no longer prepared to keep reporting what they were told to report by government?'

'Who is to say that the Western governments don't control the TV and the press?'

Knowing I will never break down these mental walls, I simply invite her to look online at any British newspaper or news channel where she will see scathing criticism of the British government. But I'm wasting my time, for the concept of a free press is just so alien to many in these parts.

'I just want to be told the truth,' Tatiana said to me. I replied, 'I don't think so, I think you want to hear what you want to hear.'

Tatiana, along with millions of Russians, has a deep distrust of the West. It was not like this in the '90s when they welcomed the Western lifestyle. It's all gone backwards now, helped by very clever anti-Western propaganda. Many Russians think the West is out to destroy them. They believe and fear this.

I am reminded of something the Nazi strongman Goebbels once said: 'Tell a lie often enough and people will eventually believe it'.

Despite our differences, Tatiana and I did get on well. She is a kind woman and we talked every day while I was in Tiraspol. Of course, her closed-off mind did frustrate me, for it's this that holds back not just her country, but also her own life. To be fair, I understand and accept that Tatiana is a product of the system she has lived under all her life. But what brought down the Berlin Wall? Guns and war? No, it was people, people power; no violence needed. The controlling East German regime, backed by the ruthless Stasi, crumbled overnight when the people finally stood up to their own repressive government.

This also happened in Moscow when the hard-line Soviet coup failed in 1991. I firmly believe that Mr Putin is nowhere near as invincible as news from both sides claim. He is a very clever man indeed, and I think he is also very much aware how Russian attitudes to him could change. I passionately believe that this is why the current Kremlin propaganda that spews out is top class and intense, for they know and fear that if they do not keep the population on side, it could be 1991 all over again.

Bad regimes are ultimately broken from within.

Summing up

We have had the civil war in East Ukraine with its supposedly Russian-backed separatists and the Russian annexation of Crimea. Now the Transnistrian government have asked Moscow to allow them to become part of Russia. Yes, you read that correctly: Transnistria has asked Moscow to bring it into the Russian Federation.

It is interesting to note that while I said at the beginning of this chapter that 'no one recognises Transnistria as a legitimate state', that is not quite true. Some of the other 'states in limbo', do recognise Transnistria as an independent state. They are, Abkhazia, Nagorno-Karabakh and South Ossetia. Unrecognised states recognising other unrecognised states...

Transnistria is geographically nowhere near mainland Russia. It is sandwiched between Moldova and Ukraine. Understandably, Kiev is already concerned at Transnistrian wishes, but with Moscow in control in nearby Crimea, who is going to stop it? Tiny impoverished Moldova will huff and puff at losing part of their country, but they are unable to stop the might of Moscow. The West? We have all seen that Mr Putin isn't scared of the West, and with Moldova not a member of NATO, we, apart from complaining, will do pretty much nothing, I'd guess. Novorossiya, 'New Russia' is coming.

Much pressure has been put on Moldova over the past years to keep it close to Russia and away from the West. The problem for the Kremlin is that Moldova yearns to move on from its Soviet past. It is poor, under-funded and its infrastructure is crumbling. It desperately wants to align itself with the West and to enter the modern world. This terrifies Moscow, for it fears Moldova may join not just the EU, but also NATO. The last thing Moscow wants is to have another NATO country just over the water from Crimea.

The pressure exerted on Moldova is similar to Russian tactics used against Georgia and Ukraine and East Europe. For example, in January 2006, Russian giant Gazprom cut gas supplies when Moldova refused to pay double the previous price. Later that year, Russia banned Moldovan wine on 'health grounds'. Wine is one of Moldova's main exports, and because most of its wine was exported to Russia, the ban hit the already weak economy very hard indeed. I remember living in Moscow during the wine ban time and seeing shelves, which were once full of Moldovan fine wines, totally empty. The wine ban was eventually lifted, but in 2013, Russia banned Moldovan wine once again.

The current status is confusing, as I have seen Moldovan wines in Moscow in 2016, yet my Russian friends say they are not real.

We know the effects that the revolution in Kiev's Maidan had on East Ukraine and Crimea, but it also affected the situation in Moldova and Transnistria. As events were unfurling in Kiev in November 2013, tiny Moldova stood tall, brave, and negotiated a trade agreement with the EU.

Moldova would now finally get the chance to trade with the EU, including finding markets for its wine and other products.

In 2014, as Russia annexed Crimea, the Moldovan President warned Russia against trying to annex Transnistria. Moldova also called on the EU to fast track Moldova's membership.

I feel it is only a matter of time before a vote to join the Russian Federation, with the blessing of the Kremlin, is held in Transnistria. Unlike Crimea, nearly everybody in Transnistria wants to join Russia. The Kremlin and many of my Russian friends will claim it is all above board because the vote was democratic, quoting the UN right to self-determination.

The problem is, Transnistria is part of Moldova, but is stuffed full of pro-Russians. How would the Kremlin feel if a far-flung part of Russia that had a significant Welsh population held a vote and decided it was going to join the UK on the basis of the UN right to self-determination? The result would last five seconds.

Kiev, I am sure is very concerned about Transnistria. If it does join Russia, then Ukraine will be hemmed in on both sides. Transnistria may be tiny and seen as unimportant, but that may be about to change, turning Transnistria into a highly significant strategic piece of land.

Novorossiya, the New Russia, is coming, and in some ways, it is already here. By that I mean the way Russia thinks about itself and its neighbours. Physically, it could also mean the annexing of more lands that it sees as under its sphere of influence. Look at the map of Eastern Europe. Eastern Ukraine could split from the West and join Russia, Crimea to the south is already gone and Belarus is basically Russian territory too. Russia is once again expanding and I do not think anyone can stop it.

Perhaps Transnistria will *not* officially join Russia. Maybe it would suit the Kremlin better to keep this little black hole under the radar, hidden away from prying eyes.

One thing I am certain of is that Transnistria will not be re-joining Moldova. It is an old Cold War conflict zone and like Nagorno-Karabakh, this atmosphere will only intensify in the current political climate.

Update March 2017

As is. Transnistria retains its self-imposed international isolation. There has been no vote, as of yet, to join Russia, but many look on with growing concern.

In November 2016, the Moldovan people elected Igor Dodon as their next President. This is a huge turn around in Moldovan politics, for unlike recent leaders, Dodon is pro-Russian. The plot now thickens over not just the future of Transnistria, but also the path which Moldova may now take.

The British Foreign & Commonwealth Office (FCO) **'advises caution if travelling to Transnistria'**. It also states that if you find yourself in trouble with the Transnistrian authorities, any help the UK government can offer you will be **'very limited'**.

7

Ceuta and Melilla

Europe's Final Frontier?

Territories	Ceuta and Melilla
Status	Spanish territory
Population	77,000 (Ceuta) 70,000 (Melilla)
Major languages	Spanish, Arabic
Major religions	Christianity, Islam

Introduction

SANDWICHED INTO the northern coast of the great continent of Africa are the Spanish enclaves of Ceuta and Melilla: the EU's final frontier when it comes to immigration. Surrounded by metres high razor wire fences, the authorities struggle to hold back the tide of the constant and growing numbers of refugees fleeing sub-Saharan Africa. Desperate for a better life in the West, these people will do anything to get into the Spanish enclaves, whilst the authorities try everything to keep them out.

Ceuta is a tiny Spanish outpost stuck onto the northern tip of Africa. Held for roughly 500 years by Spain (who are in no hurry to hand it back) the enclave is still disputed and Spanish sovereignty is not recognised by Morocco. When I say *hand it back*, that in itself is a controversial statement, for many say that Ceuta and Melilla were never Moroccan in the first place.

Just across the water is mainland Europe, and, of course, Spain, which has another piece of foreign land stuck onto the end of it. For here stands the Rock, British Gibraltar. Originally part of Spain, the British have held the Rock for 300 years. The Spanish do not accept British sovereignty of Gibraltar. Double standards here? Maybe.

So, if you're British and want to get a debate going, whilst not trying to start World War III, the next time your Spanish friend says that Gibraltar is Spanish, just say to them, 'Then Ceuta is Moroccan, isn't it?'

Ceuta and Melilla – Spain's African Gibraltar?

The What, Where and Why

Africa. From the late 1800s to the early 1900s, the big European players invaded, colonised and annexed nearly the entire continent. In 1880, the vast majority of African land still lay unclaimed, but by 1914, only 34 years later, it was estimated that 90 per cent of Africa was under the thumb of its 'white European masters.' The French, British, Belgians, Portuguese and even the Germans were at it. Only Ethiopia and Liberia managed to hold back the tide and retain their independence.

France held huge swathes of the continent, including Morocco, but the Spanish had been there first for a long time prior. As Africa's most northerly tip, Ceuta's strategic position had made it a commercial and military hot-spot for centuries. Originally controlled by the Romans for hundreds of years, Ceuta was then conquered by Muslim armies around AD 710. Squabbles between various factions continued for another 700 years, until, in 1415, the Portuguese captured Ceuta. Interestingly, it was a Spaniard, Philip II of Spain, who ascended to the Portuguese throne and therefore ruled Ceuta. That aside, Ceuta remained part of the Portuguese Empire for the next two centuries. Finally, after bitter wars between Spain and Portugal, Ceuta was ceded to Spain in 1668.

Ceuta has been Spanish ever since. Has it ever been Moroccan?

Ceuta

The Ceuta border fence was constructed by Spain to control smuggling and illegal immigration from Africa into its little corner of the continent. The Moroccans naturally complained about the building of the fences. Well, if someone were building great big fences on land you believed to be yours, you would complain too, wouldn't you?

The border fence consists of three parallel three-metre fences topped with razor wire. Underground cables to a central control booth connect all spotlights, video cameras, and noise and movement sensors. A road runs in-between the fences, which is used by police patrols and the ambulance service, if needed. Keeping the fences secure is primarily the job of the Civil Guard, the Spanish military force charged with police duties. Known commonly as *the Guardia*, dozens of their officers, alongside normal police, patrol the borders. The seas around the Spanish enclaves are also patrolled by Guardia boats. Quite an operation. A border that would be near impossible to breach you may think? Not so.

First constructed in 1993, the original fence was merely barbed wire, and therefore very easy to cross. A new, more elaborate system began construction in 1995. However, the border was still seen as an easy option to enter Europe and word soon spread through the African continent. Camps of refugees set up around the buffer zone on the Moroccan side, as more and more would-be migrants made the journey north. There was no more need to make a perilous journey by boat to Europe's shores. One now only needed to head north to Morocco and get across those fences. Once over them and your toes touched the soil, you are in the EU itself, and all without leaving the African continent. You can see the attraction.

It is estimated that in the first nine months of 2005, 11,000 Africans attempted to get over the fences. In September of that year, when hundreds of desperate souls attempted to make it over, they were caught in the middle between Spanish rubber bullets and Moroccan gunfire. Differing figures put the dead at anywhere between three and 18 people. Up to 50 were injured, some severely. It is claimed that two died on the Spanish side of the fence, apparently shot from the Moroccan side. Like many statistics in this book, especially deaths tolls, it is nearly impossible to find the exact truth, for each side spins its own stats. This infamous 2005 event is the subject of a documentary film called *Victimes de nos richesses*. It is well worth watching.

Ceuta feels like mainland Spain decades before the invasion of globalisation. In the colonial town centre, although there is one McDonald's down by the port, that was it. No coffee shop chains, no Tesco or Pizza Hut. I tried to think back to my summer holidays in Spain as a kid with my parents in the 1970s. I can remember almost nothing British then, everything was Spanish. I looked around at the tapas bars where old men in fedora hats sat out in the shade drinking a morning brandy with their coffee. It really did feel like Spain from days gone by.

As I observed tables filled with Spanish tourists from places like Málaga and Almería, I wondered if the draw was to visit a part of their country that looked like it used to. It made sense to me, after all, huge swathes of Southern Spain are near overrun by millions of Brits and their imported culture. So, if you are Spanish, why not jump on a ferry to the Spanish part of Africa for a nostalgia trip. I was beginning to get a feel for Ceuta.

Ceuta is a one-city state, and in the centre, it is rather beautiful. There's a Spanish colonial feel to the place, almost like an old Spanish outpost in Latin America. Palm trees dot around old colonial buildings, while Spanish and Ceuta flags flutter in the breeze. All very laid back.

I walked for 45 minutes, hugging the coastline to the border area. Beautiful beaches with crystal clear waters. It all looked rather idyllic. Yet, this is a contrasting place, and as I drew closer to the border, the scenery changed dramatically. While the centre of Ceuta is immaculate, with every 100 metres I approached the border, the scenery became dirtier and more run down. Migrant beggars sat by the roadside, a mix of African nationalities I could not make out. The border area was as expected, busy and chaotic. However, it was not like other divides I had visited, and there was much trade going on. Free-market capitalism in full flow.

Women carrying giant loads on their backs, men with rickety bikes piled high with nappies, trainers, crates of Pringles and all manner of goods. The Moroccans with passports are allowed into Spain, there they buy up Western products and head back into Africa to sell them on. Trade flourishes and it seems to benefit both sides, for while Spain is more prosperous than Morocco, Spain's economy is also in bad shape. Therefore, the Spanish have no problem with day-trippers coming over and buying goods, just as long as they go back home at the end of the day.

The beach area just inside the Spanish side is extremely dirty, rubbish is strewn everywhere from Moroccan day traders and there's a foul smell of human excrement. The fences run right down to the water's edge on the Spanish side. There is a complex border checkpoint with various passport security checks and baggage searches. On completion, I then had to walk through metal cages, exit 'Spain', walk through no-man's land and then up to the Moroccan border for more passport checks and stamps. Only then did I finally step into Africa proper, and it really did feel different from 'Spain' just metres behind me. I had not come this far to just go back, so decided on a day trip to the city of Tetouan.

Close to the border crossing sat dozens of old Mercedes taxis all vying for business. Tetouan was 35 kilometres away and I paid €2 to join four locals in a car. I was stuck in the back, the car was near falling to bits. The old timer beside me was wearing an anorak that looked about as old as he was, and even though the temperature was around 35 degrees, his anorak was zipped right up to his neck.

A hot sweaty ride, it took almost an hour, but it was interesting to note the pockets of wealth not so far away from the border. Newly built apartment blocks and plenty of 4x4s driving around. I learned later that this area is a playground for the newly wealthy Moroccans.

My taxi dropped me off close to the centre of Tetouan, a UNESCO World Heritage Town, hundreds of years old. My first impression of Tetouan? Oh yeah, this is Africa – very Arabic and full of charm. The air was thick with the smell of exotic spices and the smoke from hookah pipes wafted around and mingled with the vehicle pollution to make quite a heady mix.

Past the Moroccan Kings Palace, I entered the bazaar and quickly lost myself in another world. I had been in Tangier a few years back but it's pretty much geared up for day tripping Western tourists from Spain and I found it rather disappointing. Not so here, no tourists, very authentic, just locals out doing their shopping. Carpets, spices and clothes vied for position in the tiny narrow streets. Animal welfare? Forget it, chickens, rabbits, all kinds of poor creatures were stuffed into cages that lay on the dirty ground. I came across a chicken shop, filled with cages of birds somehow quietly waiting their fate as the old man behind the counter slit the throat of yet another bird. As he let it bleed out, he turned to me and waved a friendly smile.

The streets seemed to get narrower with every turn and I eventually found the tiny old Jewish quarter, which, even to this day in Islamic Morocco, is still inhabited by a small community of Jews. Considering that the Royal Palace stands just outside the old town, the security was visible and on every little street corner stood at least three or four guys in different uniform, some police, some army, some I don't know, but all were armed. I stopped and chatted with one who was relaxed, open and in fact delighted to chat in English.

'You will have no problem here,' he told me. 'Morocco is a peaceful country, there's no war here.' I asked him about Ceuta. 'Even after 500 years of Spanish control, do you still think of it as part of Morocco?'

'For sure,' he said.

'Will it ever be part of Morocco again?' I asked.

'Probably not,' he said with an accepting smile. I wandered on and spent almost four hours just soaking up the atmosphere of a bygone era. There was of course also immense poverty in the old town, and some people with hideous deformities sat out begging for a pittance.

One smartly dressed man approached me, he spoke decent English and said he would be my guide. I was not interested, I'm more than capable of wandering around myself. Therefore, he just walked with me and we simply talked. Then suddenly we approached a small door and he produced a young boy of about nine from seemingly out of nowhere. The child was both severely physically and mentally handicapped. He told me the boy was his son. The man took the boy by the hand and they walked alongside me. Well, the poor boy walked as best he could, making gurgling noises and giving out short high-pitched yelps every minute or so. Fifteen minutes later, the man said to me 'Could you give me money to pay for nappies for my boy? He goes through so many.'

Feeling very uncomfortable, I gave him a handful of coins and made my exit.

Deciding I did not want to share a crammed taxi back, I hailed a cab, did a deal for €10 and was back at the border in only 30 minutes. After thorough document checks, then searching of my bag to make sure I wasn't carrying any aromatic herb like substances from Tetouan, I was back on so called Spanish soil.

Twenty minutes later, I was sat out with a cold beer in the old colonial central square of Spanish Ceuta. Two very different worlds indeed.

I spent four days in Ceuta, having morning coffee in the splendour of the old centre, then walking to the border and soaking it all in. I crossed daily into Morocco and photographed at ease without being reprimanded. In the evening, I sat back in the centre of Ceuta and drank Spanish beer, a million miles yet only a few kilometres from the border fences and Africa.

The border fences run for almost nine kilometres around Ceuta. One afternoon, I headed off-track from the border crossing, trying to get as close as possible to the fences. It was eerily quiet, not a soul, yet I knew the fences were rigged with cameras, sound and movement sensors.

I climbed a slope some metres away and got a perfect view of the great divide. Standing on Spanish soil, I looked out over the fences into Africa and could clearly see the Moroccan soldiers stationed in tiny huts staring right at me. Suddenly, a Guardia patrol jeep pulled up. The Guardia have a reputation in Spain for being tough, and, in the sensitive area where I was photographing, they could easily have arrested me. However, they were surprisingly polite and, after initially questioning me at the fences, took me to a nearby building where they checked my passport, visas and press card. My details were logged in a book. The room was filled with guns, handcuffs and huge torches, the tools they need to help deter immigrants that attempt to cross the fences every night. After a chat with the officer, I was free to go, but was told to keep well away from the fences, especially come night.

It was time for me to move on to the second enclave of Melilla. If I'd thought Ceuta hard-core, my eyes were about to be opened in Melilla.

Melilla

Depending on the route you take, the Spanish enclave of Melilla is a 400-kilometre drive down the North African coast from Ceuta. As with Ceuta, Morocco does not recognise Spanish sovereignty in Melilla and has strongly objected to the construction of the fences.

Like the situation in Ceuta, the Melilla fences have been beefed up over the years to hold back the onslaught. Before this, the mountainous buffer zone between the Spanish and Moroccan positions that lay next to the fence was a hectic area with many refugees from sub-Saharan Africa camped out in the open. Hundreds, at times even thousands, have camped there, using tactics of running en masse to outnumber and spook the border patrols.

Long before the European banking crash, bailouts, and the Spanish economy crashing, the mass intrusion of refugees into Melilla became a huge concern for Madrid. Even the EU started to take heed. On visiting Melilla it became clear to me that it is not just a Spanish problem, it's a problem for the entire EU. It may seem a million miles from the UK, but the British should take it seriously and offer up money, troops and help via Gibraltar. Why? Because once migrants/refugees get into Melilla and are then moved onto mainland Spain, many have a desire to make it into Britain.

In 2005, the Spanish government of José Luis Rodríguez Zapatero, built a third fence next to the two deteriorating ones, at a cost of €33 million. In some areas, these fences have been doubled to a huge, six metres in height.

In 2015, is it stopping the refugees? Well, it might be deterring some and slowing the flow, but it is not stopping them. It is simply a dam holding back a growing and powerful tide.

With regard to the people who used to live in and around the old camp sites situated around the buffer zone, both Amnesty International and Médecins Sans Frontières have accused the Moroccan government of taking migrants and refugees from various areas and dumping them in an uninhabited section of the desert, often without food or water. The phrase 'not in my back yard' springs to mind.

There have been numerous deaths in and around these fences over the years. People have been shot, not only with rubber bullets but also with live ammunition. The Moroccans blame the Spanish and the Spanish the Moroccans. This is also the situation further south at the Algerian/Moroccan border where each side blames the other for deaths of those attempting to make it to Melilla.

As I have already mentioned, Ceuta did not feel like mainland Spain; it had a colonial atmosphere to it. As for Melilla, it is much more Arabic in style.

I arrived in Melilla after a ten-hour drive in a 30-year-old Mercedes taxi. A spectacular journey along the North African coast. My driver, Khalil, dropped me off around 100 metres from the very congested and polluted border. I was standing in the blistering heat on African soil, yet beyond the intense border control and razor wire was Melilla and Spanish soil. I dragged my case between the lines of cars and joined a queue. The Moroccan border guards were wary of my press card and the numerous stamps in my passport. I was led to a room in a nearby building and kept there for almost an hour as they studied my passport with interest. I was questioned about where I had been, where I was going and why. However, it was my press card that caused the most problems. These guards were suspicious and unfriendly. What did I write about? Had I written anything about Morocco?

'Not yet,' I said.

'Will you write anything about Morocco?'

'Yes.'

'What will you write?'

'Well that depends on how long you hold me for,' I replied, beginning now to lose my patience. I was hot, sweaty and exhausted, and I just wanted to get to my destination. It had been a long day and this was the last thing I needed or expected.

Reluctantly they let me pass, and one of kinder ones walked me towards the Melilla border. I asked him, 'What was that all about?'

'Next time you come here, don't say anything about writing or journalism. Just say you are a tourist. Make it easier for yourself.'

I walked a handful of metres to the Melilla border where my EU passport was given a cursory glance by the Spanish official and, moments later, I was on Spanish soil. In reality, my crossing over had only been a slight hassle, absolutely nothing compared to the ordeal that thousands go through as they attempt to get into Melilla by scaling dangerously high fences. Three sets of fences that are the final frontier of Europe. Their task, to stem the tide of people fleeing sub-Saharan Africa, is a colossal one.

Over my five days in Melilla, I must have walked the length of at least eight kilometres of the fences, back and forth many times. It was not without its problems though. Not far from Ceti Refugee Camp (already bursting at the seams, as this is where those who make it over are housed) I headed off with my camera, hugging the fence up a steep part of the road. I got a perfect view of both sides and what lay in the middle. There I was, standing on the continent of Africa, but on Spanish and EU soil. On the other side of the fences was Africa. As I watched the Moroccan military personnel and hardware close to the fence, it hit me just how big this divide was. Some sections had watchtowers and I was reminded of the Berlin Wall.

It is true that Europe and Africa are two continents separated by sea. But in Melilla, Europe and Africa are only a few feet apart from each other. It was very hard to get my head around it all.

On the very edge of Melilla, away from the beautiful colonial town centre, is the Ceti refugee camp. I was drawn to this camp every morning. One day around 11.00am, I stepped off the local bus as three Spanish army tanks came rumbling right in front of me. Something was going on, something had happened. I asked around and spoke with a French news reporter who told me that 700 migrants had stormed the fences at 5.00am. Only 30 had made it over, the Moroccan border guards had pulled the rest back. Tensions were high.

I walked a few hundred metres away from the camp, as close to the border fences as I could get. You cannot just walk up and touch them, as there is a small road that runs parallel to the fences which is for Guardia only. I did once step into that zone and, within 30 seconds, a Guardia officer appeared on a motorbike from absolutely nowhere, followed by a jeep containing two more officers. I was questioned on the spot. One of them spoke English, and after I showed my press card, it calmed matters. Nonetheless, I was informed that I should not be where I was standing.

'You need permission,' the officer told me. They phoned in my details. Once they were satisfied I was who I said I was, they returned my documents. I apologised and thought that would be it. However, as I turned to go, one of them said:

'Go to this address, you can ask permission from the Guardia's press department. If they approve you, we will then take you on escorted tour of the fences, even inside them and you can ask questions.' I wrote down the information and was soon in a taxi heading back into Melilla town centre.

After spending time in an official building, phone calls were made, the ball was in motion and my details had been sent to Madrid. I was told to go to Guardia HQ at 10.00am the following morning for a meeting.

Next morning, Guardia HQ

I was woken by the unmistakable sound of helicopters at 5.00am. They were flying low and the sound was intense. I was convinced it was something connected with the border fences. By 9.30am, I was standing outside Guardia HQ, only a ten-minute walk from my hotel. There was high security outside the building, but I was expected and, after my documents checked, I was ushered into the main building where I passed a bust of the Spanish dictator Franco, then into the lift and up to the Press Office. The official Press Officer greeted me with a stressed look. He shook my hand and beckoned me to sit before apologising if he looked tired, but he had been there all night.

'With 700 people hitting the fences yesterday, I'm not surprised you're stressed,' I said to him. He looked at me a bit perplexed.

'Yesterday was yesterday. But now we have more problems.'

He slid over the desk to me an official press release from this very morning. It was in Spanish, so he started to translate.

'This morning we had another 600 try to storm the fences.'

I knew it. The helicopters. 'At 5.00am?' I said

'Yes, but how did you know?'

'I heard helicopters.'

'That's correct, Guardia helicopters were called in to assist our men on the ground as it was happening.'

'How many made it over?'

He replied with resolve. 'None. No one made it over today.'

He then sighed, rubbed his tired face and said, 'But tomorrow, we don't know how many. And the next day and the next day and the next day and so on... There are thousands of them just waiting in the Moroccan countryside. More and more are coming all the time. I am trying to get clearance from Madrid for you to be taken to the fences, but today, as you know, is a crazy time for us.'

In the end, I was granted official permission for a personal tour of the fences but was told that it was just not possible, the Guardia could not spare the men. I was disappointed, but, considering the pressure they were under, I understood.

Almost 1,400 people stormed the fences while I was there and it's only going to get more intense as civil war, famine, disease and political oppression continue unabated in Africa.

It became clear to me that the Guardia are fighting a battle that, in the long term, they simply cannot win.

A Chance meeting

I first met David in downtown Melilla. I had got talking to an American woman, an evangelistic Christian, who, along with her husband, was in Melilla to bring the word of God to refugees . Once I had explained what I was doing there, she introduced me to David. 'This guy's got a story to tell,' she said, 'you should go talk to him.'

David was smartly dressed, spoke English and was obviously very intelligent. He explained to me that he was one of the few who had made it over the razor wire fences. We agreed to meet on Tuesday outside Ceti refugee camp.

I went to bed that night, my head swimming with questions.

The Ceti refugee camp

I took the bus the short distance from Melilla town centre to the Ceti refugee camp, a stone's throw from the very border fences these folks had climbed over to get into the Spanish territory. I had already been told that I would not be allowed to enter the camp.

Directly across the road from the camp, families take cover from the fierce African heat under bushes and dirty scrub land. Many make fires and there is much cooking going on. Of course, I looked out of place, with my camera slung over my shoulder and my general look of a Westerner. I kept a respectful distance and told myself not to take photos of these people. The last thing they needed was for me to make them feel like they were living in a zoo.

I stopped by a group of six, two young men and two young women with two small children. One of the young men waved at me, so I slowly walked over. They were Syrian, spoke almost no English and no Spanish, only Arabic. I wished I could have communicated properly with them. They were very friendly towards me and I did manage to establish that they had fled the Assad regime and the brutal war in Syria. I guessed these people had not always been poor. They looked like middle-class Syrians who, up until the war, may well have lived in a wealthy suburb of Damascus. They obviously held valid international passports and I learned that their journey to Melilla was nothing short of remarkable. They had flown out of Syria and landed in Egypt. Then by road, they travelled through Egypt and into Libya, through Libya and into Algeria, crossed into Morocco and finally made it into Melilla and the safety of EU soil. But how on earth had they managed to get in here?

I did not doubt that the men could have scaled the fences, but there was no way the two young women with small children had done so. They must have somehow crossed the same land border that I had done previously. I did some asking around during my time in Melilla and learned that money talks. Had they bribed the Moroccan border guards to let them leave Morocco? It seems possible; all they would then have had to do was to walk right up to the Melilla/Spanish border and claim asylum. Another way in is by sea, through smugglers who know the area and how to avoid the boat patrols. Their entry must have been by one of these methods, for as I said there is no way they could have scaled the treacherous fences.

Each day I came back to the area just outside Ceti. The young Syrian family always waved, smiled and beckoned me over. I did not want to patronise them by offering material things, but asked the adults if I could give sugar-free sweets to the children. It was a small gesture, but much appreciated.

There is a small bridge with an underpass close to the camp. Many families sit there, some cook and eat, some just chat away. There is much squalor and rubbish around them but they just get on with it. The atmosphere is relaxed and does not seem to represent the situation of these people's lives. As I stood at the bridge near another family of Syrians who were quietly cooking their food, their two children kicked a football towards me. With their family looking on, the kids and I had a kick around for some minutes. They then indicated that they wanted their photos taken. I was unsure, so looked over at their father for approval. He beamed a smile and nodded his head, so I took photos of the kids and they took great pleasure in seeing them on my camera's viewfinder. After handing over some more sugar-free sweets, the kids ran off delighted and the father came over, shook my hand and said, 'Thank you,' in French.

I simply must mention the golf course. Recap the last few paragraphs. Try to picture it in your mind's eye, and then add, in front of it, a perfectly manicured lush green golf course. I kid you not. It looks uncomfortably out of place set beside the refugee camp and the fences. I felt depressed as I contemplated the inequalities of life all around me.

My interview with David

We met in a small café, not far from the Ceti refugee camp. I explained to the café owner that I was doing an interview and asked if we could sit in the corner in peace. The kind owner then beckoned us through to a large separate room where we got total peace and quiet.

Where was David from? He would not tell me, even after I asked twice. Accepting that he had his reasons, I respected his decision and did not push it further. However, as you read, you will see that David was very open about how he got to Melilla and the trials and tribulations he suffered along the way. It was at this point that, even though he did tell me his real name, I decided not to use it. David, it has to be said, impressed me from the very start.

'Why did you make this journey?'

'I wanted to experience a better life. I want to experience European life.'

'How long did your journey take?'

'I've been on the road for years.'

'Did you work along the way?'

'I took any job. I dug roads, anything. But sometimes you have to beg when you have no money for food.'

'How did having to beg make you feel?'

'I had to beg for a few weeks when I was in Morocco. I felt so bad because it is the first time in my life I ever had to beg.'

'Where did you sleep when on the road? Did you ever have to sleep outside?'

'Sure, when I made it to Nador, I was sleeping in the forest by the mountains.'

'Nador is close to the border of Melilla, yes?'

'Yes and this was where we stayed, getting ourselves ready to climb the fences.'

'How many people were there in the forests with you?'

'Thousands.'

'You crossed through many countries to get here. Do you have a passport?'

'Yes I have a passport, but we always try to cross countries without it, we put passport away and don't show.'

'But did that not cause problems if you were ever stopped by the authorities?'

'Yes. In Algeria, I was picked off the streets and put into prison because I showed no official documents.'

'Prison in Algeria doesn't sound like fun.'

'It wasn't, it was horrible. I was there for three weeks before I was released by the judge, who said I had 15 days to leave the country.'

'And if you didn't?'

'Six months in prison.'

'You then crossed into Morocco? How was that?'

'Oh it was bad. We came to the border crossing at Maghina, but the Algerians also built fences to try and stop us. There were 25 of us in our group, we slept in the desert, and it was so cold. One night the border guards spied us, put on lights and held up guns. They searched us and took away anything they liked, our shoes, any good clothes, my watch. We spent one week in the desert trying to cross from Algeria into Morocco.'

'You just slept in the desert? How, where?'

'Just on the ground with our coats on. It was so cold.'

'Before you even got to the fences, you obviously had to first face the Moroccan border patrol?'

'Yes. They capture many people and take you away to a cell in Rabat, which is the other side of Morocco and as far away from Nador as possible.'

'How many times did you attempt to come over?'

David smiled a sad smile as he recalled, 'So many times.'

'Five, six, ten, more?'

'More, more, I can't count, many, many times. Each time I fail.'

'Can you explain how you approached the fences?'

'Always early morning when the light is bad – bad for the authorities. First we have to be organised. The blacks all operate together. We run en masse and the Moroccan police are not so fit.'

'Did the police or border guards on the Moroccan side ever shoot at you as you attempted to leave?'

'No, they didn't shoot, but they used batons, stones, bottles, sticks, anything they could lay their hands on, to injure us and try to stop us. They would even drive their cars into us. But never shoot.'

'On the night that you actually made it over, how many of you were running at the fences?'

'We were four, maybe five hundred.'

'I remember this incident; it was big news, all over the Western media. You were one of these guys?'

'Yes, I guess so. In the early morning, we woke at 3.00am and made our move. Next thing we hear is police helicopters, flying in front of us and shining lights onto us, there were lights everywhere. Some people wanted to abort, but I kept running telling myself, *one spirit, one soul, one body, one mind.*'

My heart was beating faster as David explained this to me. I tried to imagine the scene: hundreds of terrified people, running in the dark towards huge razor-wire fences with helicopter lights raining down on them. Are they criminals? Have they just escaped prison? No, they are simply trying to get a better life for themselves.

'Tell me what happened when you reached the first fence?'

'First, before you get to the fence, the Moroccans put razor wire on the ground, so in the dark, you run into it with your feet. This is what gets so many people, their feet get cut badly, and the hands and the body, some fall on their faces.'

David paused as his mind wandered back to the fences and no doubt saw his friends being caught up in razor wire.

'As we climb the first fence, the Moroccan police are throwing stones at us to make us fall down.'

'Once you are over the first fence, do you feel safe?'

'Oh no, you are not safe, you are in no man's land. There is a middle fence that you must get over, then over the third fence and only then are you in Spain. We always hope that there are journalists there, it helps the Spanish Guardia to take us in and not to put us back to the Moroccan side. Often the Red Cross are there and help us.'

'So, you've made it past the stone-throwing Moroccan police and over the inner fence, now you're climbing the third fence and obviously, the Spanish Guardia are standing watching you. What is their attitude?'

'The Guardia do not fight us back – they are ready to accept us if we can make it.'

This fascinated me. 'Let me just get this right, the Guardia *don't* try to stop you and, in fact, help you?'

'Of course they build the fences to stop us, but, if we make it over, they welcome you.'

This is astonishing for me to learn. Think about it, the Moroccans do not want these refugees in their country, so you would think they might actually help them to get over and out of their country, but they don't and they routinely beat them. The Spanish have built the huge fences to keep the immigrants out, otherwise there would be streams of them just walking onto Spanish soil every day. Yet, if these people actually make it over, the Guardia help them. I have read much criticism about the way those who make it over are treated once they land in Melilla, and, while I have no doubt that incidents have happened in the past, there is always another side to the story. I have it on authority from many sources that the Guardia do in fact help those who make it over and often provide medical aid if they are injured. While I was there, one migrant was seriously injured atop the inner fence. He was bleeding to death but a quick-thinking Guardia officer saved his life.

'What was the reaction of the Spanish police when you landed on their side?'

'They didn't speak, because they knew I probably didn't speak Spanish, but I could see on his face, he was happy for me.'

'What happened next?'

'We were taken to Ceti refugee camp, the Red Cross were also there and treated anyone with injuries.'

David then showed me some scars, injuries he had received on his numerous attempts at the fences. Unlike many of his friends, he admitted he had gotten off lightly.

'On my first day in the camp we were given an identification tag.'

'Did you give them your real name?'

'Yes I did but they spelled it wrong.'

We laughed at this. 'Can you show me your tag?' I asked.

David was hesitant, but obliged eventually. He did however keep his thumb firmly over some wording on it. I did not understand at first, but it then dawned on me. It must have shown his nationality, which as I have already mentioned he did not want to reveal to me.

'We all had to go to the hospital in the camp, give blood and they checked us for diseases.'

'Ebola' was the first word that sprang to my mind. It was a terrifying thought and made me realise just how easily this deadly virus can be spread.

'Are some refugees diagnosed with diseases?'

'Oh yes.'

'You've been here for a few months now. What's it like to live in the refugee camp?'

'When I remember back to the conditions on the road, living in the forests or desert, the camp is very safe.'

'There are many Nationalists in the camp, are there ever any troubles, any fighting?'

'No, there is no fighting amongst the different people. People from Sudan, Somalia, Syria, Cameroon, Lebanon, Algeria, Niger, Chad, Senegal, Gambia, Liberia, Sierra Leone, so many countries.' He then added with a sly grin, 'But Syrians, well they're always fighting among themselves.'

I simply had to pick David up on something that had fascinated me all the way through the interview, for he had on numerous occasions referred to himself and others from sub-Saharan Africa as 'black men'.

'You keep using the phrase, "black men." If I said to someone in the UK, "Yesterday I interviewed a black man", they may well be offended.'

'Why?'

'Well, it can be confusing, as some may see it as a racist phrase.'

David was astonished 'Wow,' he said. 'But I am black. You are white and I am black. How can it be racist to say someone is black if they are black?'

You know, I am confused as to what is 'correct' to use these days. Some tell me 'black' is an acceptable word and some tell me the complete opposite. Welcome to our ultra sensitive PC world David.

Yet, I understood the honesty and simplicity of what David had just said. I smiled at him and replied, 'I can't argue with that.' How I would love for David to meet a white person who claims the word 'black' is racist. It would make for a very interesting conversation indeed.

'Are there children in the camp?'

'Yes, lots of Syrians have children and many blacks have children also.'

'Inside the camp, where you sleep, is there segregation?'

'Between nationalities, no. But men and women are in different tents.'

'What if people are married with children?'

'The family refugees are inside the building in the camp. But I sleep outside in a tent, a big tent with bunk beds.'

'How many people to a tent?'

'It depends, sometimes ten, others have 20, maybe more.'

'It must get hot inside there?'

'In the day time very, very hot. That's why I don't stay in the day time.'

'I saw many families outside the camp, by the side of the road, under bushes.'

'Yes, they are cooking their food there.'

'Tell me about the food in the camp.'

'The foods are good. For breakfast, I get fresh bread, juice. There is fresh water at the water stand.' Then with a big smile, he told me, 'and I always drink coffee! In the daytime, they cook rice or some Spanish food, but always with bread, too much bread, I think the Spanish eat bread with everything. We get chicken, fish and many good things.'

'What did you eat when you were on the road and living in forests?'

'Anything I could find.'

'After many attempts you made it over these fences. We may still be on the African continent, but we are in Melilla so legally you are in Europe now. What's next for you?'

'Well, the authorities move people out of the camp and over to mainland Spain. So, I want to go there. Málaga, Valencia, I don't mind. I want a job, I want to work.'

David is intelligent, his English good and he has a burning desire to work. He is not interested in handouts. But, I fear for him as the Spanish unemployment rate amongst the young in southern Spain is more than 40 per cent. Yet, I get the feeling David will find work. After what he has gone through, he will not fail at the last hurdle.

'What would you like to do in Spain?'

'First I want to learn Spanish. I'll do anything, I must work. I am not scared of hard work, but I want a stress-free life. I've had enough trouble.'

'In Melilla, how do people react to you? I mean, in Europe there is a huge immigration problem, be it economic or refugees. So, what is the local Spanish reaction to you being here?'

'People are very friendly; they seem to understand what we have gone through to get here. But one day, when I was down by the seaside washing cars, one Spanish man drove past in a BMW and shouted at me in English: "Fuck you, black man!" David laughed a genuine laugh at this, it did not faze him one bit.

I told David that if I mentioned to friends in the UK I was going to a refugee camp full of African immigrants, they would be worried for me. But I was around the camp every day and it felt very safe. No one was going to touch me there. They would not dream of attacking me for money or my camera, because there's the fear of being sent back to Morocco for breaking the law. It's a risk that most will simply not take, especially after the monumental effort they have made to get to Melilla in the first place.

'Will you be given a Spanish passport?'

'No, before they send us off to the mainland, they give us some official documents like an identity card. They set us up in an apartment and give us some money to start off.'

'The Spanish government are very good to the refugees then?'

'Yes they are.'

I've read criticism from Human Rights Watch and other groups about the treatment of refugees dished out by the Spanish authorities, but I didn't experience that while in Melilla. Quite the opposite, I heard nothing but praise. I also found the Guardia officers I met extremely helpful and concerned about the overall situation. Others may disagree with these comments, but I can only report on what I saw and what I experienced.

'Do you have to apply to leave the camp, to go to mainland Spain and get work?'

'No, the officials in the camp decide who will go. When I came here, the camp gave me clothes and essentials, like a toothbrush. Now it's finished so I use money from car washing to buy my own things. I buy some clothes so I can be clean for going to church. I am a Christian.'

David is very proud of his religion. I imagine that his deep belief in God must have helped him immensely throughout his journey to get to where we are sitting. I asked David if there were ever problems in the refugee camp between the Christians, Arabs, Sunni Muslims or Shia Muslims.

'No, thankfully there are no religious problems in our camp. The Muslims pray in the Mosque, the Catholics go to the church down town, and for us, the Pastor comes to the camp every Sunday.'

During my time in Melilla I learnt that whilst many refugees like David make their own journey north through Africa, criminal gangs are also in on the act. Human rights activists claim that many people are brought to Morocco from countries across the continent by smugglers who charge as much as they can get away with. It seems that wherever there is a human tragedy, there is always another human just waiting to cash in.

I thanked David, looked straight into his eyes, shook hands with this remarkable young man and our interview was over.

Summing up

Spain is not going to hand Ceuta or Melilla back to Morocco, and people are not going to stop attempting to scale the fences. The Guardia, whose job it is to keep them out, seems to be at breaking point. It's a battle the Guardia simply cannot win. They can hold it back, keep plugging the gaps, but they can't stop it or beat it.

Just in the short time I was there, 600 people attempted to scale the fences one morning and 700 the next. Some people conclude that the solution is to build the fences even higher and make them more complex or dangerous in order to deter. But where does it all end?

It will only end when poor, corrupt, war-torn and unstable African dictatorships become peaceful democracies. It will only end when people do not want to flee from their countries. It would be the best option for all concerned, not just for the harassed local population, but also massive relief for an already overstretched mainland Europe. Will this happen? 'Highly unlikely' seems to be a phrase that hardly even begins to explain it. Therefore, the problem will never end.

In the UK, the concern is mostly about legal EU free movement. For sure, in the not too distant past, people did flee persecution from the likes of Ceausescu's Romania, but there are no Communist dictatorships in existence in Europe now. Granted, compared to the UK, Romania and Bulgaria are poor, underdeveloped, and corrupt. It is largely for economic reasons that people want to leave, not because they are being persecuted by their government.

In Ceuta and Melilla, it's a totally different ball game, and it's desperate. It is a human tragedy. Young families flee civil war in Syria, violence in Sudan and repressive governments in numerous other countries. No one from Eastern Europe is fleeing that. My heart goes out to them. These people who are fleeing did not ask to be born into these countries. All they want is a chance to live in peace, without persecution.

However, let us look at the other side of the coin. Europe (and yes I do mean Europe, for it's not just Spain's problem, it is a problem for all of Europe) cannot simply be an open door for everyone. For if it were, there would be a stampede of migration on a biblical scale. It would be utter chaos and would swamp a southern Europe already suffering from its own huge economic problems.

Firstly, Morocco needs to do more. It has huge borders with Algeria to the south and needs to plug the gaps there. But how far back do you go? Maybe Algeria should do more with its borders with Libya, Niger and Mali, then they in turn do likewise with Chad and Sudan and so on and so on. However, poorer countries have less resources and often less desire to sort this out. The official line from Morocco is that they are doing all they can. However, I question why Morocco would want to stop people fleeing, it just does not make sense. Once they cross these fences then they are officially in Europe, it's not Morocco's problem anymore. It can wipe its hands and leave it to Europe. I would imagine the last thing Morocco wants is for refugees from all over Africa to stay in Morocco.

I will go a step further and suggest that despite the huffing and puffing from Morocco over sovereignty, I doubt it even wants Ceuta and Melilla back. Could this be the reason that so many make it to the fences in the first place?

Could the official unofficial line be: just let them all get to Melilla and Ceuta and make them the EU's problem! I have my suspicions.

For argument's sake, let us think the unthinkable. Could Spain simply decide enough is enough and pull out of North Africa? It seems a long shot, but the more I think about it, it is something Madrid may decide if the situation continues to deteriorate. Really, what reason, apart from pride, does Spain have for keeping hold of these enclaves? These little pockets of Africa do not have oil, diamonds, or gold. So what do these enclaves bring to the Spanish economy? I would wager that they cost Madrid an absolute fortune.

If Spain decides to pull out, remove the fences and retreat back across the water to the mainland (resulting in Ceuta and Melilla becoming Moroccan sovereign territory) the refugees would still come, still desperate to leave Africa and make to the promised land of Europe. Therefore, would Spain simply be delaying the inevitable? Possibly, but possibly not. What would now stand in front of the migrants would not be merely a set of fences, but the Gibraltar Straits and a vast stretch of water between Melilla and the Spanish coast. It would be damn expensive but maybe, just maybe, easier for the Spanish navy with help from the British via Gibraltar to halt mass immigration.

Currently all that needs to be done, to get to Europe, is to get over these fences. Getting across miles of dangerous water, past Guardia and UK boats, is a far more difficult task indeed.

Would these measures stop people attempting the journey? There doesn't seem to be a week that goes by without the media reporting the loss of life at sea, usually of migrants attempting to get to Italy by coming over from the African coast.

You may have noticed I have used different words/phrases to describe those attempting to make it to another land: refugees, migrants, economic migrants. It is not laziness on my part, there is a reason for it. These words have very different meanings and the people who make the journey are doing it for different reasons. Therefore, I feel it is not up to me to say under which category they all fall. In addition, just to confuse matters, add in the term, 'asylum seeker'.

Update March 2017

Extra funding and an increase in Guardia officers, not to mention the layer of fine mesh the Spanish authorities have added to the fence (which makes it extremely difficult to get a grip of), seem to be working in Melilla. The numbers managing to scale the fences and make it into Melilla have dropped dramatically.

Not so in Ceuta. In early December 2016, 400 people successfully stormed the fences and made it into the EU. In Jan 2017, 1,100 people stormed the fences, but only two were successful. In Feb 2017, 350 successfully got over the fences.

In the months since I interviewed David, we have kept in touch and the most recent news on him is that David is now out of the refugee camp. After some time in mainland Spain, he moved onto Germany where he was set up in a small apartment and is currently working.

Much to my surprise, I could find **no official travel warnings** regarding Ceuta and Melilla.

8

Belfast

Divided in the name of peace

Status	Capital city of Northern Ireland
Population	Per Belfast City Council: 338,907
Currency	British Pound Sterling
Language	English
Religion	Christianity

Introduction

NORTHERN IRELAND is part of the current day United Kingdom and has a bloody history of civil war, famously known as 'The Troubles.' Its capital, Belfast, in the '70s and '80s was one of the most dangerous cities in the world. Sectarian violence between Loyalist and Republican paramilitaries, including bombings, killings of civilians, soldiers and police, took place on a regular and terrifying basis.

'The Troubles' deserve not just a book to themselves, but an encyclopaedia. However this chapter is about the here and now, and the focus is predominantly on Belfast, Northern Ireland's divided capital. With more than 180 so-called peace walls in Belfast, the Nationalist Catholic and Loyalist Protestant communities are in many ways more divided than ever. The war may be officially over, but the peace has not yet been won.

The What, Where and Why

The island of Ireland was partitioned by an act of the British Parliament in 1921. 'Southern Ireland', which is predominantly Catholic, became the Free Irish State, while the largely Protestant Northern Ireland remained part of the United Kingdom.

This chapter is all about the self-imposed division between the Loyalists and Nationalist communities in the north. Most Roman Catholics in Northern Ireland (Nationalists) want a united Ireland and most Protestants (Loyalists) want to remain part of the UK. During 'The Troubles', each side was backed by its own paramilitary groups who would stop at nothing to achieve their goals. 'The Troubles' lasted from the late 1960s until a peace agreement was signed in 1998. During 30 years, violence erupted all over Northern Ireland, sometimes spilling over into the Republic. It is estimated that around 3,500 people lost their lives, many of whom were innocent civilians.

Some of the big players involved in 'The Troubles' include the Provisional IRA (Irish Republican Army) and INLA (Irish National Liberation Army) who fought an armed struggle against the British; the RUC police force (Royal Ulster Constabulary), now disbanded; the British Army (now off the streets); and the Loyalist paramilitary groups who fought the

Republicans: UDA (Ulster Defence Association), UVF (Ulster Volunteer Force), UFF (Ulster Freedom Fighters), UR (Ulster Resistance) and the RHC (Red Hand Commando).

The Good Friday Agreement

Signed on 10 April 1998, the Good Friday Agreement (GFA) sought to end the three-decade's long sectarian conflict in Northern Ireland. It was highly controversial at the time, and according to many, still is.

Signed by the British and Irish governments and backed by many of the main political parties/groupings in Northern Ireland, the agreement proposed a power-sharing executive in the Northern Ireland Assembly, the decommissioning of paramilitary weapons, more cross border cooperation with the Republic and a change of policing in Northern Ireland. The Agreement also saw the Irish Republic finally drop its long-held claim to the six counties that make up Northern Ireland. However, the most controversial aspect of the agreement has to be the releasing of hundreds of paramilitary prisoners from maximum-security jails. Some of the most violent men in the world, many of whom were on life sentences, were simply allowed to walk free. On leaving jail, many were greeted with adulation from their supporters, while the families of their victims could only look on in despair. This happened on both sides, but you will read more about this and reconciliation in the summing up at chapter's end.

A copy of the GFA was sent out to all voters in Northern Ireland and the Republic. The following May it was put to referendum. Seventy-four per cent of voters in Northern Ireland voted for it and 94 per cent in the Irish Republic. It was obvious that the vast majority of people had had enough of the bloodshed. It was time to move on.

The agreement stated, 'We the participants in the multi-party negotiations believe that the agreement we have negotiated offers a truly historic opportunity for a new beginning'.

However, the agreement did not bring an instant halt to the violence. Only four months after the signing, an IRA splinter group (who were against the treaty) bombed the town of Omagh, killing 29 people.

Over time, the GFA has created a new beginning, but as you will discover when you read this chapter, Northern Ireland is still not at peace.

Belfast

I am sure if you were to ask the average British person about Northern Ireland, most would say that the troubles are over. Officially they'd be right: we have the peace process now; the IRA have disbanded; the RUC gone and replaced by the PSNI (Police Service of Northern Ireland); weapons have been put out of commission; official organised terrorist attacks no more; and the British Army are off the streets.

It must then be all wine and roses in Belfast? Sadly, it is far from that. Suspicion and hatred still prevail amongst the Protestant and Catholic communities in this troubled city and tensions rise to boiling point during the marching season. Revenge beatings and sectarian attacks take place each year and, not so long ago, a 15-year-old boy was shot in both legs in Londonderry (or Derry if you prefer).

I had one week planned in Belfast and accepted from the off that I would only be scratching the surface of Belfast in that time. I decided not to spread myself too thin, and I carefully chose the following areas to visit: The Shankill Road, The Falls Road, Crumlin Road, Cluan Place, Cupar Way, Tiger's Bay, and the Ardoyne and its surrounding area.

I stayed in a B&B in the south of the city, a middle-class area removed from the troubles and segregation. Walking around there, mixing with international students going to the university, one could easily have been forgiven in thinking that there had never been any 'troubles' here. On my first morning, after a stomach-bursting Ulster fry up, I headed out onto the streets and soon entered another world.

Tiger's Bay

Tiger's Bay is an ultra-Loyalist enclave in north Belfast. As I stood on the pavement taking photos, a car pulled up in the small road in front of me, the driver yanked on his handbrake, opened the door and got out. I was startled.

'Morning,' I said with a smile.

'Who are you?' Not threatening, but very inquisitive.

'Beg your pardon?' I said.

'What you doing here?'

'Just taking pictures of these murals.'

'Where are you from?'

'Aberdeen. Why?'

'You must be very careful around here, it's a tight community and we don't like outsiders. Undercover police come here as do Republicans, to stake us out.'

I assured him I was neither the police nor a Republican. We chatted some and I was relieved to see that he believed who I said I was. He then became friendly enough.

'Just round there is a memorial to members of the UDF. Go and see it, but stay at a respectful distance. We have CCTV in houses, you will be watched. But look, if anyone stops you or causes you problems or asks you to get in a car or go into a house, just tell them that you were speaking with Dave and that it's Ok to take photos. They'll know who I am.' Dave had obviously been involved in the Loyalist cause.

Nearby, I saw one particular mural that showed Belfast during the bombings it endured in WWII. It was stunning. These murals are, of course, political and some are very violent, but no one can deny the talent of the artist who painted them. That said, I do not think they help the situation, as they help keep the city locked in the past and segregation firmly in place. I also viewed the nearby memorial that was dedicated to members of Loyalist paramilitaries. I did not stay long. I had the feeling that eyes were watching me.

I met Dave again later that day, back in the centre outside City Hall, where he and around 20 people were holding a protest over the banning of the Union Flag over City Hall.

'What about a compromise?' I suggested to one of the protesters. He looked at me, full of intrigue. 'Go on,' he said.

Choosing my words very carefully, I said, 'I accept that Belfast is part of Northern Ireland and that is part of the UK. But I can also see how the flying of the Union Flag may not represent the large Catholic community in Belfast. How about a new Northern Ireland flag that represents all people and you can fly the British flag back at your house?'

He dismissed my idea as if I were a lunatic. 'We are British and we will never give in to republicanism. Never!' To me he sounded like the now deceased preacher Ian Paisley. The group were friendly enough to me, especially when they realised that I had met Dave earlier and that I was no threat to them. Whilst they did allow me to photograph their flags and slogans, I was not allowed to photograph their faces.

Ardoyne

The Crumlin Road is a major road that runs four miles from Belfast city centre to the west of the city. It stands between the Catholic Ardoyne housing estate and just across the narrow road, Twaddle Avenue (which is the start of a Loyalist area). In Belfast, such places are known as a 'sectarian interface'.

Over in the Ardoyne sit terraced houses, mostly with neat little gardens. It all seemed normal enough, until you saw the murals on the sides on the houses at the end of each block. Many religious murals of the Virgin Mary, but also numerous pro-republican ones. I was standing in Belfast, which is UK territory, yet it certainly did not feel it. A slogan painted on a wall makes it abundantly clear what they thought of the police. *PSNI are not welcome in Ardoyne.* I have to say in their defence, the police have an extremely difficult job here. From talking with both sides, it became obvious to me that the PSNI are on a hiding to nothing. The Nationalists claim the police are pro-British and against them. The Loyalists feel the police favour the Republicans. The police have a difficult task at the best of times, but here in Northern Ireland, they must feel that they are walking on eggshells.

I ventured deeper into the Ardoyne and soon saw anti-British stickers attached to lampposts, 'Brits out of Ireland'. Near a painted green pub, huge pro-IRA slogans adorned the sidewalls of houses. I photographed at will and, although feeling slightly nervous, no one bothered me. I did get a couple of stares but also a few acknowledgments and one 'Good morning'.

I had been swigging water from my plastic bottle all morning and suddenly found myself in serious need of a toilet, deep in the Ardoyne. I was stood directly outside the painted green pub. Should I go in, buy a coke or something and ask to use the toilet? A little voice in my head said, *Na, you can hold it.* Always listen to your inner voice and you won't go far wrong.

I kept walking through the estate, reading the murals and taking photos as time evaporated. Two hours later, I found myself back on the main road. I crossed over and seconds later was stood outside a Loyalist camp. Union Flags, Scottish Flags, English flags, the Red Hand of Ulster flag and numerous other flags with orange and purple fluttered in the breeze. Lastly, and bizarrely, the Israeli flag.

What would my acquaintances in Israel/Palestine make of all this? In numerous areas of the Nationalist community, I saw pro-Palestine slogans. Palestinian flags flying outside houses, slogans painted on walls saying 'Free Palestine', and anti-Israeli rhetoric. On the Loyalists side, where I was presently standing, the complete opposite and very pro-Israel. How many people, I wondered, from either community, had ever been to Palestine? Do they understand the situation and do they really know why they are backing who they claim to support?

Twaddell Loyalist camp

Set just off the interface, not far from the main roundabout at the edge of Twaddell Avenue, lies the Twaddell Loyalist protest camp. It is hard-core Loyalist, and has been there since mid-2013. According to people I spoke with who help man the camp, they have no intention of leaving. They have been camped out here day and night in what looks like an area of scrubland with a couple of small caravans and a fence dripping in flags and slogans in support of their cause. So, what is all the fuss about?

Marching.

In 2013, the Northern Ireland Parades Commission barred the Orange Order from marching past the Catholic Ardoyne. A protest was set up and the volunteers said they would stay until the end of the year. By mid-2015, as I said, they are still there and it is costing a fortune to police.

At a time of austerity across the UK, police have not escaped the cuts either. Therefore, the cost of policing this camp is a huge controversy. The police claim that it costs them £40,000 per night to patrol this standoff. The protesters refute this and say the figure is nearer £27,000. Even if they are right, £27,000 per night is a huge amount of money.

The writer in me would like to be in Belfast during the infamous July marching season, to experience it first-hand. However, the neutral human being in me does not want to see this. I do not want to hear bigoted chants and regressive attitudes. I do not want to see the burning of bonfires with effigies of the Pope.

I recently watched a documentary on YouTube. It was set in Belfast during the marching season and the presenter spoke with numerous youths who wore Glasgow Rangers football tops on one side and Celtic ones on the other. They spewed out hatred and abuse to each other. When asked why they held these views, apart from the obvious answers such as, 'Because they are Tims or Huns', most had no clue as to why they hated each other.

Such knee-jerk tribalism would be easy to dismiss as nonsense if it were not so tragic.

Having got my bearings during the day, I came back to this spot at around 5.00pm in the evening. There would be a demonstration, as there is every evening. A few dozen protesters had gathered around outside the gates to the camp. I feel the need to point out here that everywhere I went in Belfast, I was always asked by locals where I was from. It was never aggressive, but always with a sense of suspicion and slight nervousness.

With my camera slung over my shoulder and inquisitive demeanour, they were very wary of me at first. I chatted with a couple of people for a good 20 minutes until I got their approval. Only then were they willing to share their views and get their point across.

Pointing over at the Catholic Ardoyne housing estate, which is just a few metres across the road, I asked a man, 'Would you ever go over there?'

He looked across the street in disgust. 'No, it's not safe, and you shouldn't either.'

I told him I had done so that very morning and mentioned I nearly went into that green pub to use the toilet.

'You made the right choice by not going in there,' he said.

We discussed the troubles and politics in general. One old man told me that he really liked Margaret Thatcher when she first came into office, but that after she had signed the Anglo-Irish agreement, she could 'Go to hell'. To be fair, I did not hear anti-Catholic views, just a burning passion to protect what they see as their culture. The general view I got regarding the Ardoyne was that, 'They should keep to their side and let us get on with our traditions.'

Soaking up as much information as I could, I was astonished by the scale of the actual marching ban that is causing this nightly standoff. It is minuscule. They have not been banned from marching full stop, only from marching past the end of their road. The banned distance cannot be more than a couple of hundred metres. It seemed madness to be carrying on like this. Nevertheless, for these people, it is a matter of principle.

'You're not being stopped from marching in your own area, just past here, which is directly in front of the Catholic area. Is this all really worth it?' I asked my man.

'This is the Queen's highway,' he spluttered, jabbing a finger at the road in question. 'It is my right to walk down it and I shall!'

They are convinced they are going to overturn the ban and will march again. I asked one resident in the Ardoyne earlier that day what he thought of the camp. He told me that he did not give a damn if the Loyalists marched in their own area, but they had no right to do so in front of the Ardoyne. 'They just want to antagonise us,' he told me.

I asked another Loyalist what would happen if the authorities did not allow them to march down the road in the future. 'There's going to be a war,' he replied.

More residents of the Loyalist area soon arrived at the camp, many doing so every single evening. Around 50 people were now present and almost as many police. I walked over and started chatting with a suited and booted member of the PSNI. 'You expecting any trouble here tonight?'

'I always expect the unexpected here,' he told me wryly. 'Be careful around here, all it takes is for you to walk down the wrong street, get into a conversation with a bunch of people, then say the wrong thing to the wrong person and if they're that way inclined, well, you know. Look, be under no illusion, there's still violence here. You don't want to find yourself in the situation I just explained.' He then snapped shut his visor and walked off to join his comrades.

I walked back over to the camp and watched the proceedings. Around 100 metres away, down the Loyalist road, men and boys were ready to march. Dressed in clothes that represented the Orange Order, men held flags that portrayed the famous battle of the Boyne in 1690. Other men in bowler hats played flutes. On a call from the man in charge, flags on poles were held aloft, the music started and at a very steady slow pace, they marched. Their destination? Right up to the line of police that were stopping them from heading to the Ardoyne. Suddenly I remembered the demo at Ledra Place gate in divided Nicosia. Surely they are not going to try to get though?

Thankfully, they did not, they just marched right up to the line of police and stopped. They stood for a few moments, turned and marched back down the road. It was symbolic, nothing more, no violence that night thankfully. At the roadside, I stood with numerous residents, all dressed in something that had a Union flag on it. It was a friendly enough atmosphere, but I did not take to a couple of woman beside me who started to sing the sectarian song *The Sash*.

There were only 50 or so marchers there that night, but, on other nights, it's different. Sometimes hundreds and on special occasions like political or cultural anniversaries, the numbers go into four figures. I was told that one night in the week prior to me being there, there had been 4,000 marchers present.

'Now that was a great night,' the man beside me commented, his face beaming with pride.

It was now dark, the small demo was dispersing and the police vans were cautiously moving off. Calm was once again returning to this troubled interface.

East Belfast

The wall runs the length of the street and has a real Cold War feel to it. A community cut in two. As I stood in the Nationalist side, just feet from the wall, end terrace houses again displayed pro-Irish slogans and murals. Behind the wall and wire, a Union flag fluttered defiantly just behind the partition on the Loyalist side. I walked down the street, past the wall and around the corner. The murals on the end of small terraced houses made it abundantly clear of where you were now standing. I ventured into a huddle of streets and saw not only kerbstones painted red white and blue, but also parts of lampposts painted blue. Numerous Union flags hung from houses and lampposts.

After walking for around half an hour, I made it to Cluan Place, which is a one street cul-de-sac, a tiny ultra-Loyalist enclave in a predominantly Nationalist area. It is almost barricaded. A ripped Union flag and a sign saying – Loyalist Cluan Place, unbowed, unbroken, greets you.

As I walked down the tiny street, curtains twitched on either side and I felt nervous. Within minutes, a woman came out, stood in her front garden smoking a cigarette and watched me. I was now at the end of the street and taking photographs of a giant mural painted on the end of the last house. A powerful slogan with the peace fence directly to its left, which is at the end of the house owner's back garden. These people claim they have been hounded, shot at and bombed over the years by the IRA and other organisations. 'No Surrender', they say, and claim to be 'Always British'.

The residents over the fence on the Nationalist side claim differently. They claim they have been bombarded with missiles from the residents of Cluan Place. In and around Cluan Place, as in every part of Belfast, you will get a very different answer to every question depending on whom you talk with. I smiled to the woman as I walked past and back the way I'd came.

'Morning,' I said.

She nodded and replied, 'Where are you from?'

'Aberdeen,' I said. I did attempt to engage her in conversation about Cluan Place and the divide behind it, but she would not talk and quickly went back inside, then locked her door. I moved on.

Derry or Londonderry?

The city of Derry is the second largest city in Northern Ireland. Or is it *Londonderry*? It all depends on your point of view. Nationalists always call it Derry and Loyalists often use the name Londonderry. Yet, I found that whilst in the city, most refer to it simply as Derry. 'London' was added to the name after Derry gained a royal charter from King James I in 1613. I am not making a judgement as to which name is the correct one, so I apologise if in this chapter I refer to the city by using either name. Officially, in the UK anyway, the name is Londonderry. The best advice I was given was that when I was in Derry, just call it Derry: 'For your own safety, don't say Londonderry. A protestant won't give a damn if you call it Derry, but if you call it Londonderry to a Catholic, you're asking for trouble.'

I was feeling stifled by Belfast and needed a day away. Granted it was not to a place that is any more peaceful, but at least it was a change of scenery. I took the bus from the central station and was soon out of the city and deep in the countryside. I tried to let my mind wander and forget division for a couple of hours.

Once I got closer to Derry, I spotted a sign out of the dirty bus window, just a typical UK road sign, but the 'London' part of the word Londonderry has been spray painted over. Only the Derry part remained visible.

Bogside

Once in Derry, I made my way to the famous Derry Walls and glanced down at the main reason for coming here, the Bogside, a Nationalist working-class stronghold. The history of the Bogside is particularly bloody and brutal. It was here in 1969 that the so-called *Battle of the Bogside* took place.

The battle of the Bogside was fought between the residents of the area and the RUC (Royal Ulster Constabulary). Tensions finally exploded when Nationalists threw stones and other missiles at a Unionist apprentice-boys march near the walls. The RUC, stuck in the middle, had to battle with both sides to protect themselves and keep each side apart. After rioting went on for days, the RUC who could not contain it any longer, withdrew and the British army entered. The Battle of the Bogside is seen as one of the first defining moments of 'The Troubles'. It was also in the Bogside that British soldiers shot dead 13 civilians in 1972, in what became known as Bloody Sunday.

Wandering the Bogside, I felt like I had left the UK and entered the Republic. The difference in feel and look is overwhelming. You cannot fail to notice Free Derry Corner, with its gigantic murals and slogan of 'You are now entering Free Derry'. It is as if this part of the city had declared itself a self-autonomous area. The slogan was first painted on the side of a freestanding gable wall in 1969.

There were anti-British slogans, pro-IRA slogans, pro-civil rights march murals and religious ones. The most poignant for me was the gas mask mural. I stood and looked at this for a long ten minutes. Painted on the side of a house, it towered over me, a painting of a boy wearing a gas mask and holding what I think is a homemade Molotov cocktail. I walked deep into the anti-British Bogside and photographed at will. No one bothered me, a few locals did stop and say a friendly hello, which was always followed by the now customary: 'Where are you from?'.

I had been warned from various Loyalists in Belfast about Derry. It ranged from, 'Don't go to Derry' to 'They're all mad there' to 'Go, but don't venture into the Bogside'.

The most sensible information I got was from a taxi driver in Belfast. Born and bred in Derry (I have no idea if he was Catholic or Protestant) he told me, 'Don't be stupid and get into a political or religious conversation. There's nothing to be afraid of in Derry, so don't be scared, just be careful. Be careful with what you are wearing, always go neutral. Wearing anything remotely British-looking in the Bogside will be suicidal, likewise wearing a Celtic football top over in the Protestant area would not exactly be beneficial for your health either. Oh, and don't tell them you're writing about them, not worth the hassle.'

To be honest, he did not tell me anything I did not know already, but it was good to hear some unbiased friendly advice. As always, in controversial places such as Northern Ireland, Palestine and Crimea, it is essential to know your political history. Then simply use common sense when out in the streets.

Late in the afternoon, as the sun was fading, an old dear who I got chatting with, a resident of Bogside, said to me in a caring manner, 'You and your camera don't want to be wandering around here at night, son. Not the safest of places for you.'

Peace bridge

Officially opened on 25 June 2011, this ultra-modern peace bridge is the latest effort to bring the two communities closer. It is a nice gesture, and whilst I applaud all efforts to bring communities together, I doubt it will be a huge success. The many people who live in the centre, mix regularly and have no truck with belonging to either side will welcome the new bridge. But why would people living deep in the tribal working-class areas use it? What purpose would anyone from the Bogside have in wanting to cross a bridge that takes him into the heart of Loyalist Londonderry? None whatsoever, I would imagine. I do not mean to knock the bridge, but it seems more symbolic than anything else. The only thing that will truly bring people together here is the breaking down of mental barriers.

Waterside

On the east side of the river Foyle, it is predominantly Unionist Protestant and like in Belfast, the murals change. Kerbstones were once again painted red, white and blue, bunting hung on streets, and I came face to face with one of the most aggressive murals I had seen yet.

The British heavy metal group Iron Maiden have used the image of a character called Eddie for decades. Eddie is a rather menacing human skeleton. A Union Flag, in some shape or another, usually accompanies him. Well, here was Eddie being used as a sectarian football. A huge painting of him is painted on the side of a house, looking as fierce as any Iron Maiden album cover. He holds a sword in one hand and a ripped Union Flag in the other. On the ground he is trampling on, lie the dead bodies of Irishmen and the famous Free Derry sign lies in ruins.

What message does this give to local children? It simply helps to sow the seeds of hatred and division, as it continues into the next generation, and the next and the next. I walked the small streets of the Loyalist area, closely watched by a few youths as I photographed the murals. I did not feel threatened, I felt depressed.

Late afternoon, I decided not to take the direct bus back to Belfast, I choose one that went through the countryside and small towns. I was in no rush and wanted to get a sense of escapism. It did the trick. My mind quickly relaxed as the hatred melted into beautiful greenery and I switched off, forgetting all about politics religion and division.

Belfast and Derry are unique divides as in they are not totally partitioned like, say, the West Bank in Bethlehem. Everyone is free to walk and go where they wish. The real divide here is a mental one. A resident from the Loyalist Twaddle area is not going to walk through the Catholic housing estate and pop into that green pub for a pint. Likewise, a Catholic resident of the Falls Road is not going to walk over to the Shankill and nip into the shop that sells everything Orange. They can all do so if they wish, but most choose not to. I feel it proves my point that the biggest divides are not physical walls, but the ones that we create in the human mind.

Back in Belfast, I headed straight to a pub near my B&B and treated myself to a couple of pints of well-earned Guinness. As I took to my bed that night, I thought about the next day's trip into the Nationalist Falls Road and nearby Loyalist Shankill, and the words to an old song came into my head. A song I have heard Glasgow Rangers fans chat for many years...

'Do you know where hell is? Hell is in the Falls! Heaven is the Shankill and we'll guard those Derry Walls, oh I was born under a Union Jack, a Union Union Jack'.

The Shankill and the Falls Road

The Nationalist Catholic Falls Road and the Loyalist Protestant Shankill are in West Belfast. They may only be metres apart at certain points, yet they are poles apart. I started my day in the Falls. Irish flags were everywhere and I saw a stunning mural of Bobby Sands, famous for the Maze prison hunger strike. He is buried in Milltown Cemetery at the very far end of the Falls Road. However, Milltown cemetery will forever be remembered as the place where the Loyalist paramilitary maniac Michael Stone ran amok with grenades and a pistol during an IRA funeral in 1988. He injured 60 and killed three. It is believed his targets were Gerry Adams and Martin McGuinness.

In July 1970, during an operation called the Falls Curfew, the British army entered the Falls to search for weapons stashes. Attacked by locals with petrol bombs, they responded with CS Gas, which led to gun battles between the British Army and the IRA. The area was sealed off and house-to-house searches began. Pistols, rifles, shotguns, machine guns, grenades, explosives and much ammo was confiscated, most of it belonging to the IRA. On the streets, many soldiers were injured and four civilians died. This incident did much to turn the local Falls residents against the British. A small garden of remembrance commemorates members of the IRA who died whilst fighting the Army.

The peace wall that separates the Falls with the neighbouring Shankill is one of the most prominent in all Belfast. The wall runs the length of Cupar Way and stretches for more than three miles. It is a depressing reminder of the segregation here.

I left the Falls Road and walked down a side street. Billboards lined the way. 'Free Palestine,' read a slogan alongside other pro-republican murals. I came to a set of gates, which were open, but I am told get locked at night. I walked through, it was very quiet and no one was around. I turned to my left and saw the dividing wall. The Falls on one side, Loyalist Shankill the other. The area surrounding the wall is grim and for some reason reminded me of East Germany.

'Welcome to the Shankill', read the mural on a nearby wall. On I walked into a housing estate. British flags, murals of King Billy and Loyalist paramilitaries were all on display. A hand painted warning on a wall makes it very clear how you must behave in Belfast's tight knit communities. See my photo of this chilling warning.

The IRA subjected the people of the Shankill to numerous bombings and shootings during 'The Troubles', and even into the 1990s. Pubs and shops were bombed and scores of civilians died, hence why the Shankill became a hotbed of Loyalist paramilitaries such as the UVF, UDA and Red Hand Commando.

Walking through the Shankill, I felt like I was in the Rangers end of Glasgow. I stopped at junctions to take photos of various murals, then suddenly spied what can only be described as an orange shop. No, I do not mean a mobile phone shop, but an actual shop that sold everything to do with the Orange/Loyalist cause. Inside, a CD played marching tunes, the walls were adorned with UK flags, orange flags, 'No Surrender' scarves and all manner of things orange.

Three men were in the shop. I got a nod of the head from one, a hello from the next and, from the one working, an inquisitive look and the inevitable, 'Where are you from?' After a week of this, I was thinking of getting a t-shirt printed.

We chatted about the area and I asked the most approachable of the three, 'Would you ever go to the Falls Road?'

'Not if I can help it,' he replied.

By late afternoon, I left the two segregated worlds, walked back towards the normality of central Belfast, sat in a café and wrote up my notes. To live under a self-imposed apartheid, in a street shrouded in either British or Irish flags, seems depressing. There is most definitely an 'us and them' mentality. Unless that changes, I feel there will always be division here. Undoubtedly both sides have suffered immensely. With many perpetrators of violence having never been brought to account, or been released as part of the controversial Good Friday Agreement, many people in Belfast feel that they have had no justice at all.

The Peace Walls

The first peace walls were built in 1969 at the start of The Troubles. These walls range in length from a few hundred metres to a staggering three miles in places. They are made of iron, brick or steel and are up to 25 feet high. Built as temporary structures only to last a few months, the walls have actually increased in height and number since the Good Friday Agreement.

The walls cut right through the heart of communities. Many residents' back gardens are caged in with metal fences to stop missiles being thrown over from the other side.

These so called peace walls are, to me, like a pill given for depression. The pill helps you in the short term but does not solve the underlying issues. Peace walls? Short term – yes they maybe are – but long term they are walls of division that cause more suspicion and hatred due to a lack of integration.

There has been a pledge to remove these peace walls, all of them, by 2020, but I really cannot see that happening. They have to change the mind-set of the residents on both sides or all hell will break loose if they do bring down these walls without first doing so.

Can people change their mind-set? Of course, it is possible, but much harder than removing a physical wall.

It was time for me to leave Belfast and to be honest I was not sad to go. It had been great research and I enjoyed the charm and calm of the city centre, but after immersing myself deep in the tribal feelings in Belfast, I felt despondent. Whilst there, I went to my bed each night, feeling rather depressed. Depressed that in the 21st century, a city on UK soil, which, despite coming on leaps and bounds and moving on from organised violence, is still divided. Belfast has won the war with itself, but not yet secured peace and harmony. There is still much to do here.

Summing up

I am extremely grateful for not being born in and around this divide. Belfast in the 1970s must have been hell. Aberdeenshire in the 1970s was peaceful bliss.

The attitudes of some in Belfast were sadly, from what I experienced, on a par with Azerbaijanis and Armenians over Nagorno-Karabakh. Hatred and suspicion. But what makes Belfast very different and almost unique compared to most other divides, is that some people cling onto such things as battles from hundreds of years ago, claiming it as their own culture today in the 21st century. I think it holds not just them, but the city and the entire country back. Many really do seem to be living in the shadows of the past.

Large parts of the city are segregated and it seems a breeding ground for bigotry and suspicion. There is light at the end of the tunnel, though. There are many good people in this city and it has to be said that every-one I met from both communities, once they got over their initial suspicion regarding who I was and what I was doing there with my camera and notebook, were all friendly towards me. Pity they cannot be as friendly with each other.

I have spoken with friends who have visited Belfast and they said, 'Oh it's great. Lovely city'. Ok, look, I do not expect everyone to be interested in wandering places such as Tigers Bay and the Ardoyne, asking questions, chatting with locals and getting under the skin of the city. However, if all that outsiders do is simply stroll around the city centre, visiting the stunning Titanic Quarter and eating in the lovely restaurants, they may kid themselves that it is all peace and love in Belfast. Does that or should that matter to the average tourist? I guess it does not matter, but it should, especially if they are British or Irish. I feel people really need to know about and understand the immense division that still goes on here.

With countless unsolved shootings, bombings, stabbings and killings, there is so much pain here for both communities. People want to know what happened to their loved ones. Many want justice, be it from the UK government or the Sinn Féin leadership. While it was clear that many involved in the violence were paid-up members of either Republican or Loyalist armed groups, many innocent civilians also died, and in terrible circumstances. People want to know why their son or daughter was mown down in the street or blown up by a car bomb. Families are still battling for truths over past killings. Will they ever get it? Will this land ever be at peace?

Am I being naive when I say people must learn to live together? Maybe. But look at the alternative: more division and a continuation of hatred. People from both sides should remind themselves that revenge leads to revenge leads to revenge... Life, for too many decades, has been far too cheap in Northern Ireland.

Away from the partisans, many good people are trying to heal the wounds of the past and move forward. I watched a superb documentary on YouTube, it follows two men, one an ex-Loyalist paramilitary and one ex-IRA. Both have killed and been in jail but have since renounced violence. Hard men, brought up in the absolute height of The Troubles, they reflect on their past hatred, what was done to them and what they did to others. If men like this can forgive and move on, surely today's generation can?

I also watched a very moving documentary mediated by Archbishop Desmond Tutu. Convicted extremists, now released from jail and who have since turned their backs on their sectarian past, were sat at one side of a table. Directly opposite them, only feet away, sat the relatives of victims of The Troubles. I watched this programme on my laptop one evening whilst still in Belfast which made it even more real.

Statements such as, 'I was out to kill as many British soldiers as I could', or 'I wanted to kill Catholics', sent a chill through me. This was brutal honesty. Brutal honesty. One of the killers, full of emotion, even asked the victim's family to forgive him. Then there was Tutu, judging no one, he seemed to have the patience of a saint. This programme is a must see. I guarantee that when you start watching this, hear the stories and look into the eyes of the people on both sides, the outside world will completely vanish and you will be totally submerged. I was stunned, speechless, emotional and ultimately very humbled. I have since watched this programme a further three times during the writing of this chapter. It has helped me to try to understand what people went through. Yet it also makes me sad and angry that out in the streets the sectarian hate still prevails in far too many areas of Belfast. I would like to force all those bigots, often young people who were not even alive during The Troubles, to watch this and get some perspective into their lives.

I believe that this documentary should be on the Northern Ireland school curriculum and it should be compulsory for each child to watch it. No exceptions.

I wish every person in every divide I have researched would watch it. The first people that spring to my mind are the two wonderful men I interviewed in divided Cyprus. Bakis, who was taken prisoner by the Turks, and Mustafa, whose brother was killed by Greeks. So much healing could be achieved. What could meetings like this achieve in Israel/Palestine I wonder?

I had nothing but total admiration for the families of victims in the documentary. They sat directly opposite these men of violence. The phrase, 'It can't have been easy for them', does not even come close to describing how painful it must have been. The entire programme was nothing short of remarkable. Could I have done it? If someone had killed my dad simply because he was a Catholic or Protestant, could I sit there, talk calmly with, and shake the hand of someone who was part of the organisation that killed him? I do not know, I would like to think I could, but hand on heart, I honestly do not know.

I also had respect for a few of the convicted killers, who talked about what they had done and showed genuine regret about the death of the individual concerned. Most were remorseful, but others not so. Both sides were very courageous for being in the same room together, let alone sitting around the same table and communicating. The human decency shown by both sides at this meeting overpowered my senses.

Without any doubt, the most difficult meeting comes in the second programme, where the notorious Loyalist killer Michael Stone, who was sentenced to over 600 years in prison but released early under the Good Friday Agreement, comes face to face with the family of a Catholic man he killed. The way the wife of the murdered man conducted herself at this meeting, her utter courage to be in the same room as Stone, and then forgive him, overwhelmed me.

At the very end of the meeting, through floods of tears, she actually managed to shake Stone's hand. I am in awe of that woman. Please, watch this programme. It will blow you away and rip your heart to pieces, yet at the same time give you some sense of hope. You can find it on YouTube. It's called *Facing the Truth*, and comes in two parts.

As I tried to think of something to write to sum up the suspicion and ignorance of hatred, I suddenly remembered an old Irish joke.

A man is walking through Belfast late one night and suddenly a masked man appears from behind and sticks a pistol in his back

'Right mister, so what are you? Catholic or Protestant?'

The terrified man replies, 'Neither, I'm an atheist.' After a few seconds of contemplation, the masked man says slowly, 'Aye, but are you a Catholic atheist or a Protestant atheist?'

It may be a funny joke, and I remember when I first heard it years ago, I laughed. But I don't laugh now. It's too realistic.

No one should demonise anyone else who happens to believe in some other version of religion or no religion at all. On this point, I will leave the last word to the late great Irish comedian Dave Allen, himself an atheist, who used to say at the end of his programme, 'May your god go with you.'

Update March 2017

On a positive note, the standoff at Twaddell Avenue seems to have finally ended. Only time will tell if the agreement reached over parades holds. The policing of this standoff has cost taxpayers an estimated £20 million.

On 23 June 2016, Northern Ireland voted narrowly to remain in the EU but, of course, the collective UK vote was to leave. Within days, senior figures in Sinn Fein started to talk about having a referendum for a united Ireland. I cannot imagine any Loyalist in Northern Ireland buying that. I think the division here is only going to get more tribal.

People from both the Loyalist and Nationalist communities continue to seek truth and justice over historic killings.

Sporadic sectarian violent attacks continue.

The so-called 'peace walls' remain in place.

Belfast. No longer at war, yet still not at peace.

Of course, there are no Foreign Office travel warnings for Belfast, as Belfast is in the United Kingdom.

9

Schengen

A false sense of security?

The Schengen Area comprises the 26 following member states:
Austria, Belgium, Czech Republic, Denmark, Estonia, Finland,
France, Germany, Greece, Hungary, Iceland, Italy, Latvia, Lithuania,
Luxembourg, Malta, Netherlands, Norway, Poland, Portugal,
Slovakia, Slovenia, Spain, Sweden, Switzerland and Liechtenstein.

Introduction

THE SCHENGEN AGREEMENT. Conceived in 1985 when East and West were still divided by the Berlin Wall, the USSR existed and the Cold War was being played out, it was initially signed by France, West Germany, Belgium, Luxembourg and the Netherlands. It was seen as a great step forward in the evolution of Europe. But no one, not even its pioneers, could have dreamed that three decades later it would incorporate countries that, at the time of its conception, lay deep behind the iron curtain. Then again, maybe that is exactly what they dreamed of...

To the pro-Europeans, the Schengen Agreement had always been seen as a progressive step in the free movement of peoples and goods. To Euro-sceptics, Schengen was seen as (along with the EU itself) a step towards a 'one nation Europe', a one-size-fits-all state. People of this view were for many years laughed at, ridiculed and brushed off. Not anymore.

The issue is not only the millions of people coming from poor ex-communist countries to richer Western Europe (that in itself is an issue for some), but now and more pressing is the issue with countries just beyond Schengen. The country I speak of is Turkey and its neigh-bour, which is the disaster of war torn Syria. What does that have to do with Schengen? Simply this: millions of people have fled Syria and many are making their way through Turkey to the border into the EU. More mouths to feed and people to house. Problematic, but doable. However, what is, or should be, of real concern, is that alongside genuine refugees from Syria, members of so-called Islamic State now also have the potential for easy entry into the European Union. Many point to the numerous violent attacks in not just Turkey, France, and as I write this, Germany, claiming that IS members have already crossed unnoticed into the EU.

As already mentioned in the book's introduction, I decided not to give my own opinion at the end of each chapter by saying which side if any I 'backed'. My opinion on, say, Cyprus or Nagorno-Karabakh or Palestine is not important. But on Schengen I most certainly give my opinion. I am all for the taking down of walls, razor wire and such like to re-unite divided lands. However, it is important that we make the distinction between that and the issue of open borders in the EU. They are two very different things indeed. My views on Schengen have been formed over a period of many years. You might agree with them, or you might not.

Section A
Down South. The Turkish/Bulgarian border

Edirne is a city at a very important crossroad. It is the furthest north-Western city in Turkey and is the gateway to Europe, sharing a border with both Bulgaria and Greece. Only a small city, Edirne was once the capital of the Ottoman Empire. Today, it is of much less importance when compared to Istanbul, but it's got a feel of giving you a genuine experience of real Turkey. In many ways, it's a mini-Istanbul, minus the tourists. The small centre with pedestrian streets, bazaars and grand Mosques is beautiful, full of culture and old world charm. However, walk only 20 minutes away to the outskirts of town and it's altogether different. Poor Turks and Syrian refugees are living in what can only be described as squalor. I wandered the narrow streets of shanty-style accommodation, middle-aged women sat outside and kids played in and around garbage. There were lots of scruffy dogs, many cats and the odd rat. A far cry from the charming centre of this town. Kids ran up to me as I walked. They had dirty, smiling faces and wanted their photos taken. I looked around for an adult and managed to make eye contact with a group of old women who seemed to understand the situation. They nodded their approval. I took photos and showed them to the kids through the viewfinder, much to their delight. Nobody begged, nobody asked me for anything.

The Turkish people are proud people who have no desire to leave their homeland. The problem for the European countries that share a border with Turkey is the refugees from Syria. The Turkish people I met were not only kind to me, but sympathetic to the plight of their Syrian brothers. That said, there is only so much people can or will take. I wonder how long it will take or for how many more Syrian refugees to arrive before the welcoming hand of the Turkish population is removed?

I took a local bus for around 12 miles and got off 100 metres from the gigantic land border. There were numerous lanes for cars, trucks and pedestrians. There was a trickle of cars, three kilometres of trucks, but as for individuals walking over, it was just me at that time.

I had to go through three different types of Turkish passport and visa checks. Thankfully, I had a multiple entry Turkish visa, so I could come and go as I pleased. I walked through the no-man's land and up to the Bulgarian border. After more passport checks, I walked easily into the European Union.

Just inside the border, I soon got chatting with a Bulgarian driver and we agreed a payment of €30 for him to drive me around for the day, initially heading to the nearest town of Svilengrad. The outskirts reminded me of being in rural Romania, lots of run down and abandoned communist-era factories. Not attractive at all. I had thought the three-kilometre queue of lorries into the Turkish side was long, but on the Bulgarian side, heading to Turkey, the queue was a staggering ten to 15 kilometres long. My driver told me it takes the trucks an entire day to cross over. It never stops. Are they all checked? Are all the trucks coming into the EU checked? Is each and every one opened up and searched? I do not know.

How many people come over to the EU inside those trucks I wondered? I asked my man, 'More than we know,' he replied.

In Svilengrad, we found a small café near the centre and ordered coffee. My driver had little English, so once again my broken Russian was put to the test. I always surprise myself though, because when there is no other option, I seem to get by. In his 50s, John told me that while he accepts Bulgaria is poor and corrupt, he does not like the EU. He also told me he does not want to give up the Bulgarian Lev and join the Euro. He has strong political views and after having lived through communism, he hates it with a passion. Like millions in former communist countries, he admires the former British Prime Minister, Margaret Thatcher, who stood up to the Soviets. He also made it clear, he does not like Turkey, or Islam.

As we chatted, I looked around and took in my surroundings. While Svilengrad may be in the EU, it does not feel European. It has a somewhat Russian feel to it. This is where the EU one-size-fits-all project struggles to make sense to me. It may be fine for, say, a Spaniard to go border free to France, or a Czech citizen to enjoy travel anywhere in the EU after the Cold War. But it is countries on the perimeter, the likes of Hungary, Poland and Lithuania amongst others who now have the sole responsibility of manning the outer Schengen border. Sure, they get money and support from the EU, but is it acceptable in the uncertainty of our times that there is only one outer ring border for so many countries? The more I look into it and see the pressure on the ground, I do not think so. I need to point out here, that although Bulgaria is in the EU, it is not yet in Schengen. It is expected to join in the very near future.

Just over the border in Turkey, Edirne is near dry and what little alcohol is sold is hidden away. Here in Svilengrad, in typical Bulgarian style, café culture with alcohol was flowing freely. Fascinating things, borders. One minute you are in one world, then a few steps away, you are in another.

With Turkey, Greece and Bulgaria so close to each other, John was happy to drive me the half-hour to the Bulgarian border with Greece where his mate was a border guard. When we arrived, I got out and while John and his mate had a chat, I took the opportunity to take photos.

One would think that the non-EU country would be poor and the EU country richer. Not so here. On crossing from non-EU Turkey to EU Bulgaria, it was very evident which was the poorer of the two (and it's not Turkey). I was in Bulgaria for the first time in the communist era in the '80s, and if I am honest, parts of it do not look much different today.

As he drove me back to the border with Turkey, I asked John if he and others were worried about IS militants making their way into Turkey from Syria, then ending up at this border and getting into the EU via Bulgaria.

'Yes, of course. It's only a matter of time. Maybe it's even happening now'. He pointed at numerous vehicles that were trundling into Bulgaria from Turkey. 'Who knows what or who is inside these?'

Back in Turkey, the owner and staff in my little hotel in central Edirne were extremely kind to me. As Muslims, they were very interested to learn of my travels to such places as Palestine. They invited me to join them for meals out back in the little courtyard and never once charged me for food. We talked every day and I joined the men at the Mosque on three occasions. Watching them pray, I sat quietly on the thick carpet at the back and enjoyed the serenity.

One of the young men who worked in the hotel tried his best to get me to take Islam into my heart. We chatted about this many times during the week I was there. He was such a nice guy, so full of passion and not a fundamentalist in any way whatsoever, he just oozed genuine love for Allah. He smiled warmly as he saw me sitting in the comfy area of the hotel landing each night with a beer or two. Of course, I had asked the owner in advance if this was Ok and was told that it was not a problem. On my last day, knowing he was not going to succeed, he hugged me, kissed me on the cheek and lastly put his hand on my chest. He looked me in the eye and said that, even though I did not believe, I had a good heart. For me, that sounded far better than being told I was going to hell.

One day whilst in Edirne, just after prayer, I was standing outside the Mosque with the owner of my hotel, the passionate young guy, and another man from the hotel. The Mosque's huge minaret towered above us.

'It's beautiful, yes?' my friend said.

'Oh yes,' I replied.

'You want to go up inside?' His eyes sparkled.

'Are you serious?'

'Yes, wait, I get the Imam, he is a friend of mine.'

Ten minutes later, he returned with the Imam, who greeted me with a nod of the head and a smile.

'Is this allowed?' I gestured towards the minaret.

'Normally not allowed, but I have key!' replied the smiling Imam.

Entering through a small door at street level, I was soon climbing up inside the minaret and up a set of spiral stone stairs, which were built hundreds of years ago. It was extremely narrow with only room for one person at a time. Up and up and up we climbed, it seemed to go on forever. Eventually we came to a tiny door, opened it and stepped out onto a minuscule little round balcony. We were up almost 150 feet. Oh my giddy aunt, it was high. My Turkish friends told me that almost no one gets up here and it was a first even for them.

I would guess that I might have been the first Western non-believer to have had the honour of climbing up inside this hundreds-of-years-old minaret. It was exhilarating. Thank you guys.

Turkish/Greek border

After a wickedly sweet breakfast of baklava, yoghurt and honey in the little courtyard of my hotel, I was soon on an old local bus heading out of Edirne. An hour or so later, after a pot-holed bumpy journey, I was dropped off at the border. I had been the only person on the bus. I love that. Why? I do not really know, but I guess it is that sense of adventure, an off the beaten track feeling. It seems that nothing pleases me more when I am the only one present, or when no one in the town, wherever I was, spoke English. Ultimately, I'm at my happiest when I'm not surrounded by throngs of tourists. Mind you, you don't exactly get many sun worshipping tourists in, say, Transnistria.

I stood in the middle of nowhere on a country road. Yet a mile or so away was Greek territory and the official EU Schengen border. That single border that is supposed to protect the entire EU from uncontrolled immigration and the growing threat of terrorism.

I walked over to the passport control building. It was painless. I got my Turkish exit stamp and walked back onto the single road that led to Greece. There were lots of military around in the fields either side, plus plenty of signs saying 'no photography'. I walked down the empty road, past a sentry guard with a large Turkish sign above the road and continued on until I passed under a similar set-up with Greek signs and flags. Past that, signs in English claimed I was now in a restricted zone. They reminded me of the signs in Turkish-controlled North Cyprus. I walked alone, fences either side of the solitary road.

Eventually I came to the EU border and passport control. The guard was rather bemused as to why I was there. He spoke decent enough English and asked what I was doing and where I was going.

'Just crossing the border to go for a walk, grab a coffee then come back to Turkey later,' I said. He shrugged, handed me back my passport, I thanked him and stepped onto EU soil, into a quiet Greek village.

I swear there was almost no one around in that village. The few shops there were, all closed. It was lunchtime, so this was very traditional I guessed. There were a few decent enough homes around with well-tended gardens, but overall it was poor and there were many abandoned farm buildings. I got the impression that anyone young here would leave at the first opportunity and head to a big city in search of work and money. Not the best economic climate in Greece these days. I wandered past sleepy dogs, three people and pretty much nothing else. Was this really one of the Schengen secure entry points into the EU? I couldn't see a well-equipped IS terrorist having huge problems getting in here. It was hardly Fort Knox.

It was all very calm at this border crossing in this sleepy lost-in-time village, but it is not like that elsewhere along this border. Greece and Turkey share a border around 200 kilometres in length and, like Bulgaria, Greece is also concerned with immigration and people coming from Syria and further afield through Turkey. The flash point area is the Orestiada region, south of here where Greece has been building its own walls. Fences, to be precise – huge razor wire fences along its border with Turkey. They are patrolled by Greek foot patrols who have thermal vision cameras to spot people who approach the fences at night. It seems to be working and the number of migrants attempting to enter Greece from this area has fallen dramatically. Prior to 2012, thousands were arrested for attempting to cross. By 2013, after the fences were erected, only a handful were arrested. The Greeks claim it a huge success and say that one of the EU's worst areas for illegal immigration has been sealed. While the fences have drawn the usual criticism from certain quarters for their severity, the Greek population seem to be mostly happy with them.

It seems that, at least here anyway, the EU and, in particular, Greek efforts to stop illegal immigration are working. That said, it is probably just pushing the problem onto other less policed areas, like the largely un-policed Turkish/Bulgaria border to the north east.

I walked back through the deserted village to the border area, exited Greece, headed through the restricted zone road, waved at the bemused Turkish soldiers who had seen me cross only two hours prior, got a new Turkish entry stamp and arrived back in Turkey. My time in Edirne was ending and it was time to move onto an area that is anything but calm and sleepy.

I was headed to south Turkey and its border with war torn Syria.

Turkish/Syrian border

I made my way from Edirne back to Istanbul by bus and by lunchtime (against advice), I was on a plane for a short flight to the city of Gaziantep. Formerly known as (and still sometimes referred to as) Antep, Gaziantep is a city in south-eastern Turkey. Rich in culture, it is one of the oldest inhabited cities in the world. In another time, it would have been a cultural trip, but the reality today is that Gaziantep is only 60 miles from the Syrian city of Aleppo, where brutal fighting has taken place in recent years. Gaziantep is a city that is now feeling very nervous indeed.

Over the border in Syria, untold thousands of people have died in Aleppo. If fighting between rebels and the Assad regime weren't enough, we've recently seen the bombardment of the city by Russian forces. Regarding Gaziantep, the British government currently advises against 'all but essential travel', and that the area has a 'high threat of terrorism'. Understandable really.

In the old town of Gaziantep, traders sell fresh spices, coffee, tea, tobacco, baklava and proper Turkish delight. My senses were dancing with delight. It felt so calm and peaceful, and one could so easily have forgotten about Syria being so close.

Although my new Turkish friends in Edirne told me not to go to

Gaziantep, it felt like a must for this book. I also felt I was seeing the authentic Turkey and certainly not the tourist version in holiday resorts or even Western-friendly central Istanbul. As I sat out at one of Gaziantep's traditional cafés drinking my delicious Arabic coffee and puffing on a hookah pipe, I noticed a teenage boy racking through bins for whatever scraps he could find.

'Syrian refugee,' my waiter told me.

Later, that night, I could not sleep because of the heat and no air con in my cheap hotel, so at 4.00am I headed out onto the streets, to find some fresh coffee. The streets were nearly empty, except for the odd taxi driver. Then, in the middle of the road, walking towards me came a rag tag mix of youths and boys with barrows and contraptions like luggage trolleys. They were Syrian refugees who go out at night to scavenge around for recyclables like glass, paper and plastic to sell on. They keep the streets clean, earn some cash and help to maintain what little dignity they have left. The oldest in the group must have been roughly 16 and the youngest, no more than eight. I waved at them and they smiled, waved back and continued down the road, picking up their wares. They did not look downtrodden, in fact they looked alert, positive and had that look about them that said, 'At least we're doing something'.

Suddenly a police car stopped at the side of the road and asked to check my documents. In English, the officer said, 'You shouldn't walk around at this time. Turkish people are no problem, most refugees are no problem, but others, well, we don't know who else is here. Best to go to your hotel, ok?'

Islamic State fighters are known to have crossed the border and are already operating in Gaziantep. I was also told that the kidnapping of a westerner and driving them back across the border into Syria was not out of the question.

I headed back, fell asleep for a couple of hours and, after a weak shower but strong coffee, was waiting for my driver at 9.00am. He had been arranged in advance through a contact in Edirne and knew where he was being asked to take me. We were heading south to a huge Syrian refugee camp, but I also wanted to get as close as possible as I could to the actual Syrian border, which I knew was totally sealed off. With official advice to not even come to the city of Gaziantep, was I really in a car hurtling towards the Syrian border? Hands up to being slightly nervous.

I chatted with my driver, a local from Gaziantep, and asked him about the refugee situation and war in Syria.

'Big problem here now, many many Arabs,' he said with a heavy heart.

'Does that bother you? I mean you are all Muslims and they are in need of help.'

'Muslims yes, but Turks and Arabs are very different and we are not so rich country. Turkey has its own problems. We help these people, but we can't do it forever. The rich west must help more. Britain must help more.'

Turkey has a huge border with Syria, over 900 kilometres in length and, if the civil war and flood of refugees was not a headache enough, they are very concerned about IS coming across the border undetected. Currently, Turkey is building a four-metre-high wall in the Gaziantep province to help deter this. To the east, they are also constructing a similar wall in the border town of Nusaybin. However, much of the border, especially in vast rugged countryside, is very porous indeed.

Events in Turkey/Syria are changing with lightning speed. For the record, I was at this border in 2015 and initially wrote this chapter at that time.

Turkey though, has another immense problem to deal with: the foreign citizens, often Western and British, wanting to come to Syria to fight for IS. They can't fly into Syria, and the borders with Israel would not be a good idea, so how do they do it? Simple. They fly from the UK to Istanbul with an easy-to-get online tourist visa, make the same trip down south that I did and get themselves smuggled across the border. We have seen specific examples of this with young fighters, even teenage girls, making the trip. So not only are the Turks trying to stop IS coming in, they are trying to stop radicalised Westerns from leaving Turkey and joining IS. What a situation Turkey finds itself in.

Critics have said that Turkey is not doing enough. Maybe, I do not know, but what I do know is that Turkey cannot fight this alone. The fight is too big and too important. Foreign intelligence has reportedly passed onto Turkey the names of 10,000 suspects who may be linked to extremism. But the fight-back surely has to start back home in places like the UK and the rest of the EU. Not allowing known or suspected people to leave in the first place would help. No wonder, the main roads in and around the Turkish/Syria border are being chillingly referred to as highways to jihad.

Although Turkey graciously opened its border and hearts to the Syrian people at the start of the civil war in Syria, once it became apparent that

IS and other terrorist organisations were taking footholds in the region, it understandably tightened security measures. There has even been talk that if Syria descends into even more chaos, Turkey may have to build a wall the entire length of its 900-kilometre border.

Around 100 metres from the border, my driver pulled over and stopped. I got out of the car and looked across at the border walls and gates, all locked up. Locked up for good it would seem. No one was around and it was eerily quiet. Suddenly I felt chilled that on the other side of that wall was Syria. The area I was standing in has a FCO warning of 'advise against all travel'.

This border is totally sealed shut and I cannot see it opening again for many years, if ever. The security risk is too high. The once busy nearby railway tracks sit empty of life. I took photos as we drove along the perimeter of the border wall, but my driver got increasingly nervous and we left ten minutes later.

If anyone in the West thinks it is 'not our problem,' or that it's so far away that it doesn't really concern us, they need to take their heads out of the sand. Even if they are not concerned with the plight of the Syrians, they should at least think of the consequences of untold numbers of people making it into Turkey and then potentially moving onto the open borders of Schengen. Schengen really does bother me, it always has. I feel Schengen is already seriously flawed, but if Turkey joins the EU and Schengen (as many EU politicians want it to do), it means that Europe's one outer border could be pushed as far back as Syria and Iran. This is serious stuff. Just look at the map, consider the problems we face today and ask yourself if you would be happy with that situation.

We are sleepwalking into chaos, I fear. Surely it is time for a serious grown-up rethink on Schengen and free movement across an entire continent. And surely, it is also time to stop labelling those who are concerned about this as racists.

An hour after leaving the border area but still close to Syria, we finally arrived at a huge refugee camp. It seemed to stretch as far as the eye could see. One gigantic tented area, surrounded by security and wire. Were we going to get in? We tried, but not a chance. Only prior written permission from the Turkish government would allow that. I cannot even begin to imagine the paperwork involved there.

Outside the camp, with the aid of my Turkish driver (who spoke Arabic) I chatted with some Syrian men.

'How long have you been here?' I asked a man in his 60s.

'Four years,' he replied.

'We left everything, our houses, possessions, and friends,' another told me.

'How are conditions in the camp?'

'We are treated very well here and are very grateful to Turkey.'

Turkey, I feel, deserves more praise for its handling of Syrian refugees. No country has done more to help the plight of the Syrian refugees than Turkey.

'We just want the war in Syria to end. We just want to go back to our homeland.'

'Do you really think the war will end?' I asked tentatively.

'When it was just rebels against Assad, there was a possibility of peace. But now, with IS and other militant groups, no I cannot see peace coming to Syria any time soon.' I did not even want to ask if they had lost family for I was told in advance that it is almost a certainty that everyone in this camp would have experienced bloodshed and death, often of children. Instead, I asked one old man if he had friends here, old friends, or maybe new friends made in the camp.

'I have made new friends in the camp, people from Aleppo I had never met before. Also some old friends, but some you know they don't stay in the camp, they prefer to live outside and make their own way.'

My driver told me that this was true and explained that while the camps brought shelter, warmth, food, water and even school for the children, they also came with rules such as curfews. Many, whilst grateful to Turkey, preferred not to go into the camps, but take their chances on the streets, just like the kids in Gaziantep at 4.00am collecting plastic and making money.

Everyone in and around the camp looked well-fed and clean. All were friendly to me yet many had a haunted look in their eyes. I could not even begin to imagine what these people had witnessed and been through in the bloodbath that is Syria.

No one knows the exact figures, for it would be impossible to do so. An educated guess puts the number of Syrian refugees in Turkey at between two and three million, with hundreds of thousands living in refugee camps. They just cannot build camps fast enough and many unfortunate souls are turned away. Living in a refugee camp would not be my first choice of accommodation, but it sure beats sleeping rough in a motorway underpass. The camps, where bedding, food and clean water are dished out for free, is where most seem to want to be.

For those who can't get in, the vast majority simply live where they can. I had already seen them in Istanbul and Edirne, but most seem to stick to down south, around Gaziantep, the poorest region of Turkey. I wonder, if being here, with Syria just over the walls, makes them feel close to their homeland?

However, I fear there is going to be trouble. The Turkish people have been very accommodating thus far, and the Syrians do not want to be here, they want to be back home but can't due to the civil war. Patience within much of Turkish society is wearing thin. Shantytown type scenarios are popping up on the outskirts of many Turkish towns and villages, petty crime is growing and rubbish and sanitation is a huge issue. In the Gaziantep region alone, there is an estimated 400,000 refugees.

Leading Turkish figures are rightly concerned and say the refugee numbers are simply unsustainable. Many refugees have now been in Turkey for more than four years. It seems, through loopholes in Turkish law, that after five years, they can actually get Turkish citizenship. The mind boggles as to the scale of future social problems here.

For the moment, forget about the EU and Schengen and illegal immigrants (all a serious problem of course) and just contemplate the following: Islamic State launching a massive attack on Turkey. Why should that concern the peoples of Western Europe? Because, Turkey is a member of NATO.

We must remember that under Article 5, NATO may have to respond. 'An attack on one is an attack on us all'. But Islamic State is not a country, they are individuals. Who would NATO attack and where? There have been numerous hideous attacks in Turkey already, claimed by IS and other such groups. How far will they go? What will the response be from the West? No one knows.

The situation in Syria is changing day by day. Since I travelled to this border area, Russia has backed Assad with intense bombing of rebel held areas, while the West has been unsure what to do next. As always, it is the innocents that suffer and many more thousands of Syrians have died. Even if Assad does re-take his country, what does the future hold for the refugees who remain inside Turkey? Will they go back/be allowed to go back? Will they want to go back? I have no idea.

Section B
In the middle

To explore this section of the Schengen border, I first headed to Ukraine, where a tiny village is split in two. One side is in Ukraine and the other is in Slovakia, which is an EU member state. I was based in the town of Uzhhorod, Western Ukraine for a week. Out of season and with lots of tourism and money leaving Ukraine since the ongoing fighting in the east, I lived like a king in a four star hotel for a few pounds per night, a big change from my usual accommodation. I have no idea how other 'professional' journalists live whilst on the road or what they eat and where. For me, it's often a banana or two, a tin of tuna, or a local kebab taken back to my room and eaten whilst perched on the edge of a rickety bed. Exploring the world for many years has been utterly fascinating, but glamorous and luxurious it is not.

Kiev is Kiev, but away from the capital, rural Ukraine is very much like it was decades ago. I walked the four kilometres to where Ukraine ends and the Schengen zone begins.

There has been a fundamental change in attitudes of Ukrainian officialdom over the past couple of years. Until very recently, Ukrainian border guards, in my experience, behaved like Soviet throwbacks, grunting and groaning like many of their counterparts in Russia. It's only a few years ago that I was refused entry at a border crossing from Slovakia into Ukraine due to all the dodgy looking visa stamps in my passport. I have also had the classic burly treatment from border guards on trains, but this seems to have changed in Western Ukraine. Since Maidan, Eastern Ukraine and Crimea, there has been a fundamental and highly visible change in the way they treat Western visitors.

Up a long steep road, a couple of kilometres from my hotel, I finally saw the border. A huge classic Soviet statue just off the road stopped me in my tracks. I had not expected this, what a find.

Remember that despite all the current problems with Russia, Ukraine was once part of the USSR. I was standing at what once would have been the old Soviet border. This huge statue, as so often in these parts, is about WWII and the defeat of the Nazis. It stands proud and defiant, looking out westward to Europe. A border gate was slung across the middle of the road, with only the odd car approaching it. I walked towards it. About 20 metres from the border gate, the soldier stiffened, put up his hand and jabbered away in Ukrainian. Realising I didn't understand, he managed in broken English to tell me I couldn't cross here, no one on foot could cross here. As I said, attitudes are changing here and this guy was friendly when he realised I was British. He explained to me if I wanted to cross into the EU I'd have to go south to a pedestrian border crossing as this crossing was vehicles only. I actually knew that anyway, I had just wanted to come up and soak in the atmosphere. As it turned out, my plan for the next day was to visit the border he had just mentioned.

'No problem,' I said. 'I understand. I'm going to Vel'ké Slemence tomorrow anyway. Thanks.'

'Have a good day,' he said, waved and returned to his post.

He was the friendliest Ukrainian border guard I had come across in 20 years.

Vel'ké Slemence

Vel'ké Slemence was sliced in two in 1945, one part going to the Soviet Ukraine and the remaining part to what was then Czechoslovakia. Over 60 years of separation endured, followed by a glimmer of hope and a brief opening of the border for a few years. However, since 2008, it is steadfast once more and is now the official external border of Schengen and modern-day Ukraine, armed with military and fences. More than just a dividing line between Europe and Ukraine, it is a border through the actual lives of families. The reality is that a Ukrainian citizen at one end of the village who wants to visit his family or friend at the other end of the village (which is over the border and thus in Slovakia) needs an EU visa to do so.

I had taken a taxi 45 minutes from Uzhhorod and asked the driver to drop me 50 metres away from the border. The village had one main road through it and directly in front of me was the border. After that, the village and road continued, but not on Ukrainian territory anymore. The road now ran into the European Union country of Slovakia. I approached the border on the Ukrainian side, and, again, I was the only one crossing, the entire place deserted. I handed my passport to the Ukrainian border guard who spent much time looking at my numerous Russian visa stamps, he questioned me politely about where I'd come from and where I was going. Happy enough, he stamped me out of Ukraine and I walked a handful of steps to the EU Schengen border. Standing in between the two borders, I glanced both left and right where I saw land that would have once been back gardens and plots, now dug up with the earth ploughed and either side surrounded by razor wire and cameras. The crossing you see in the picture is just that, an official border crossing, but the new EU fence now runs the entire length of the Slovak/Ukraine border. It is patrolled regularly by troops armed with the best of equipment, their main job being to deter illegal immigrants and of course cross border smuggling.

At the EU border post, similar questions were asked, but they were not so friendly, which really annoyed me, and I was taken aback at the tone of the voice. 'What is your purpose for coming to the EU?'

Was this guy for real? I replied politely, 'Excuse me but I don't need a purpose, I hold an EU passport.'

It was 2015 and long before the Brexit vote, yet this border guard actually said to me, 'Britain is in the EU?'

Trying not to look flabbergasted, I replied sarcastically, 'Yes, unfortunately it is, but we live in hope.'

He didn't get it and handed back my passport with a look that said he thought me slightly mad. I walked out the secure gate and stepped on to European soil. I turned, looked the five metres back at the other side, same village, but in Ukraine and all the problems that go with it. I walked on through the Slovakian side of the village, which due to its long complicated history, had a very Hungarian feel to it.

Only a solitary road with neat little houses and no one around. Nothing to do here, nothing to see, not even a shop. I did a loop and 30 minutes later was back at the border. I never expected to find anything or get any interviews here, I just wanted to experience this little divide for myself. An EU international border slicing a village in half with families on either side; a very strange place indeed.

Back on the Ukrainian side, I was more than happy to flirt with three very attractive Ukrainian female border guards who were now on duty. After granting me a Ukrainian entry stamp, they came out of their hut and we talked East Ukraine, Maidan, Crimea and all sorts. 'Do you want Ukraine to join the EU?' I asked.

'Oh yes,' one replied. 'Ukraine will be in the EU within five years.' I smiled politely.

I asked if she would let me walk behind into the area where the fences were and take some photos. No chance she said, it was more than her job was worth.

It was time for me to head back to Uzhhorod and make my way to south Hungary.

The Hungarian 'Wall'

Although more than 60,000 people entered Hungary illegally in the first six months of 2015, the late summer/autumn brought it all to a head. During July and August, around 90,000 people entered, then in September alone more than 130,000.

Hungary simply could not cope, as migrants moved en masse from Turkey, then made their way through Serbia towards the Hungarian/ Schengen border. At the time, though, apart from the occasional official crossing, this was simply open fields. The EU's outer border, one border for the entire continent – at this place on the map, basically open.

As tens of thousands streamed unchecked into the EU, the Commission dragged its heels and dithered about what to do. Hungary finally took matters into its own hands by erecting a 'protective fence' down south with Serbia. The razor wire fence is 13 foot high and runs for the length of 109 miles.

There were huge riots down here, as angry violent young men tried to get through before the fence was complete. Hungarian security responded with tear gas and water cannon.

Angela Merkel, I fear, gave precious little thought to the havoc it would create in the transit countries like Hungary, as she sent out the message to all would-be migrants: 'Come to Germany! You're all welcome!'

I spent the day driving around the countryside and getting as close to this fence as I could. I parked my car at the end of tiny villages and walked right up to it. The ground was muddy, full of tyre tracks from the ongoing Hungarian border patrols. I touched the actual fence, a fence that has seen illegal entry to the EU fall from 130,000 in Sept 2015 to around 2,000 in March 2016.

Everyone has a right to escape persecution or war and seek asylum. Despite criticism over this fence, the Hungarian authorities have made it clear that they will accept genuine refugees, but it must be done properly, via a border crossing, and with documents, if possible.

Prior to this fence going up, many thousands then made it to Budapest where they camped out beside the international train station. Police were holding them there, preventing them from catching trains to Germany.

According to friends in Budapest, the Hungarian people genuinely felt for the women and young children, but they were highly sceptical and very concerned about the large groups of single men, often aggressive, sporting expensive watches, trainers and iPhones.

'Many were brandishing large bundles of cash, willing to pay up to €400 to be allowed to get on a train to Germany. I don't have this kind of money and I can't afford an iPhone.' Another told me, 'What is happening to people in Syria is a tragedy, but we could see for ourselves that many who got into Hungary didn't seem genuine. It was very scary. Who are we allowing into Europe? Many of the young men refused to be registered, they didn't claim asylum here, nor did they do so in Turkey, Serbia or anywhere else on route. They just wanted to go where they wanted to go. This is not right.'

Turkey may not be exactly democratic, but it is generally a safe country for Syrian refugees. As mentioned previously, I had been right down to the border with Syria and to a refugee camp. I know the refugees are very grateful to Turkey and simply relieved to be safe. No one has done more to help Syrian refugees than Turkey, and according to international law, they should be registering their claim for asylum at first point of entry in a safe country. However, many people, after paying smugglers, are then making a journey onwards, overseas and by land to get to Germany. They are doing so by choice. Granted, it is certainly not a pleasant choice, but they are not fleeing civil war in Turkey. When I had been talking with Syrian refugees in Gaziantep, south Turkey, I asked them what they thought about their compatriots making the dangerous journey across the sea to get to the EU. They told me, 'Sure, they hope to get a better life in the EU, but it's a choice, they don't need to do it. We are safe here in Turkey, Assad and IS are not killing us here. I would not risk my children by doing this journey to Europe.'

They are also not fleeing war in Greece, Serbia, Croatia or anywhere else they land. In addition, the countries they travel through on the way get battered at every turn. Ask Hungarian farmers who have seen crops trashed by thousands of migrants what their opinions are of the refugees' plight.

Ask British lorry drivers about the violence they have faced whilst in Calais. Yes, of course the conditions in these camps are horrendous, but consider the following – if you were fleeing with your young family from a despot regime in Africa, would you not be kissing the very ground as soon as you landed in Spain? You would be safe and taken care of. Would you drag your kids all the way north to a camp on the French/UK border?

The policy of allowing anyone to go anywhere they want has benefited very few. It has not benefited the countries that get trampled in the process, and it's ultimately only encouraging more unfortunate people fleeing war to pay people smugglers and put their own children's lives as risk.

Passions and emotions run deep over this, but we must make the distinction between refugees fleeing war in Syria and making it into Turkey, and those then deciding to continue on a perilous journey across numerous safe European countries. They are two very different situations indeed.

All human suffering due to war is an utter tragedy. I am most definitely for helping people who are caught up in it. We must do everything we can to help as many as we can. Nevertheless, I am highly sceptical of encouraging and allowing what is now hundreds of thousands of people to stream through open European borders with precious little checks on who they are.

Section C
Up North: NATO and 'Russia' with only a fence between them

Belarus, dubbed the 'last dictatorship in Europe', sits sandwiched between Russia in the East, Ukraine to the South and, most importantly, an ever-expanding EU to the north and west. Belarus is most definitely Mr Putin's ultimate buffer zone. Its economy is in a perilous state and has been so for many years. It survives with Russian backing and supplies of cheap gas.

Although Belarus has an EU border with Latvia and Poland, it was its border with Lithuania that fascinated me. To be more precise, a tiny part of that border and place referred to as, 'Stalin's Pipe'. Twenty-odd years ago, Belarus and Lithuania were part of one state, the USSR. There was no real border between these two republics, no divide. But today, 60 kilometres from the Lithuanian capital Vilnius, right down on the Belarus border, lies a remarkable area. For this is where an iron curtain has appeared, *after* the fall of communism.

In 1939, when Lithuania was being taken into the Soviet sphere and Kremlin officials were drawing up a map of various internal borders, Stalin apparently left his pipe on the map. Not a man in the room would dare move it for they were all terrified of him, so they simply drew the borderline around his pipe.

I have no idea if this is true, but it is a wonderful tale and, if it were true, it would not surprise me one bit. The reality is that over the past numerous decades, these borders have constantly changed with the political situation of the day. Without even moving house, older residents like to comment on the fact that they have lived in three different countries. Between the great wars, this area was part of Poland, post WWII it was part of the USSR for many decades, and now it is Lithuania (or Belarus on the other side of the fence).

I took the bus south from Vilnius to the village of Sacl, but I was still 35 kilometres from my destination. After some haggling, I agreed on a price for a taxi to my accommodation. Off we headed into rural countryside and I asked my driver to drive as close to the Belarus border as we could possibly get. Whilst Vilnius is stunning and now European, rural Lithuania is poor, underdeveloped and basic. We drove on decent enough roads, close to forests and suddenly my driver said in Russian, 'My friend, look, Belarus border.'

'Pull over,' I said and got out with my camera. There it was, not a border crossing, there aren't any here, just a border fence. Swathes of forest had been cut away to make it easier for border guards to spot comings and goings. There were also two old signposts feet apart that I learned marked the pre-Schengen border.

Eventually, we arrived at my destination and the only place to stay around there. Norviliskes Castle. A former monastery, around 500 years old, for centuries it was a shelter for Franciscan monks. It then lay empty in the Soviet years and went into near terminal decline. In the years following the collapse of the USSR, it was bought by a businessman and restored.

I had phoned in advance, they were not yet open for business as it was out of season, but they allowed me to spend the night there. There was only one member of staff and I was the only guest. I literally had my own private castle and banquet hall for the night.

After checking in and leaving my gear, I headed off with my camera and was soon standing in the heart of the area known as Stalin's Pipe. Less than 100 feet away and running right around the back of the castle was the Schengen border fence and on the other side, pro-Russian Belarus.

When I say there is nothing else here, I mean *nothing*. Just the castle and the border fence. It felt like the end of the civilised world. I walked down the track from the castle, down a slope and came face-to-face with the fence. Not a soul was around, or none that I could see anyway.

In Russia, the name may have changed from the KGB to the FSB, but they are in many ways the same organisation. In Belarus, they did not even bother to change the name and the KGB still exist in all its glory. 'Be under no illusion,' one contact in Vilnius told me, 'The KGB operates down by this border, the fence may not look like much, but don't even attempt to cross it, for out of the forest they will appear and you won't get ten metres.' I have been in Belarus before, and know about their security services. Therefore, I had no desire to illegally cross into their territory.

Stood at the fence, I took it all in and what struck me was that this is not just a border between Schengen and non-Schengen, this is a border fence between pro-Russian Belarus and NATO. It felt very Cold War. In reality, NATO could put missiles, or shields or anything it wanted right where I was standing, and Russia likewise, just a handful of metres away on the other side. I say 'Russia' could do this, because Belarus and Russia are when you get right down to it, pretty much the same country.

I do not believe the current Russian hype that NATO wishes to attack Russia and take it over, but I can see why many Russians fear that NATO is expanding too far. They also say that NATO broke a promise not to take former Warsaw Pact countries into the Atlantic alliance. Russia was especially angry when the Baltic States joined.

Would Russia ever attempt to take back the Baltics? That seemed a ridiculous prospect just a few years ago, even for hawkish Russian politicians. But now, no one knows. Personally, I don't believe that Russian tanks will simply roll into the Baltics, but, and here is my point, Mr Putin has made it quite clear that he would use the same tactics elsewhere that he used in Crimea, that being to 'go in' to protect Russian citizens. I know how unpredictable Russia can be, and I know the immense support the average Russian would give Putin if he did decide to intervene in the Baltics.

Russia going into the Baltics to 'protect Russians' is a guise, nothing more. Protect them from what? Russian citizens in the Baltics have far more protection, freedom of speech and equal rights in these EU countries then their fellow Russian citizens have back in Russia. Yet it's a highly dangerous situation indeed, for once again we must remember, that if Russian forces did ever walk into the Baltics, under whatever guise, these countries are fully paid up members of NATO, and NATO's Article 5 clearly states, 'An attack on one, is an attack on us all'.

What would NATO's reaction be to Russia walking into the Baltics? I shudder to think.

Down by the Schengen fence, there was not a single human being to be seen or heard. I was now stood right up at the fence and photographed at will. There were obvious tyre tracks in the earth on both sides where border patrols operate and I am sure CCTV was around, but I couldn't see any. That said, I was wary, did not stay long and was soon back at the castle.

The young woman, the only member of staff, whose name is Marina, had already told me that unfortunately the castle kitchen was not open and there was no food. There were also no shops nearby. There was nothing. I had anticipated something like this, so out of my bag I produced the meagre supplies I had bought in Vilnius. Two bananas, a bag of crisps and some almonds. Thankfully, I'd also had the foresight to pack a bottle of wine. In the evening, I sat at the head of a majestic table in the banquet hall, feeling like a Viking or someone important in a Robin Hood film. There was no internet or even phone signal in the area, which did not bother me one bit. As night ascended, I lit dozens of candles that were all round the hall, sat back in my high-backed chair, drank my wine and listened to the sound of rain battering off the castle windows. Would the KGB make an incursion over the fences at night and drag me off deep into Belarus? Strange how the mind works...

The following morning after no breakfast but hot coffee, Marina promised she would take me on a tour of the fences. We drove up to a long straight section of the fence, where just inside Lithuania stood a solitary farmhouse. Metres away, the fence and a Belarus border guard hut. Behind that, a tiny village with houses on neither side of the little road. An old man came out of the farmhouse and walked towards us. Marina knew him and we got talking, her taking on the role of interpreter.

Pointing over the fence at the Belarussian side he said, 'I have friends over there. This used to be one village then, in 2002, the fence went up and border was closed forever. There's a shop over there, I can't go there now.'

'Tell me about your friends.'

'Sometimes we call over the fence to each other. But they can't come here. They must travel hundreds of kilometres to Minsk to get a Schengen visa then cross over at an official border crossing. No one can cross here.'

Knowing that he was old school and had lived through Soviet times, I asked him a question that I was sure I knew the answer to.

'You now live in the European Union, in a democratic country, what do you think of that?'

'I grew up and spent all my life in the USSR, this was part of the USSR,' he said pointing to the very soil on which we were standing. 'I preferred it back then.'

This of course was exactly the answer I had expected. Millions, especially the elderly, are still very nostalgic for the USSR. I thanked him for his time, shook his hand and off we headed.

On we drove, on roads that ran through forests where again huge swathes had been cut away so border guards could see all around. Thirty minutes later we came off the main road, down a dirt track and finally into a small hamlet. The border fence, which now had razor wire on top, cut right through the hamlet and in between houses where people still lived.

I stepped out of Marina's car and began taking photos. Suddenly, out of a mobile hut came a Lithuanian border guard. He was naturally wary of my presence but was polite and in fact spoke excellent English. I told him I just wanted some photos for a book I was writing. He told me I shouldn't really, but he didn't seem too bothered. He did call someone though, his superior I would guess, who soon appeared in a jeep. He was obviously higher up the food chain and came over, gun attached at the hip. We chatted some and then he said in English pointing at the fence, 'Go on, photograph away.' I was pleasantly surprised, I don't think they meet many people this far off-grid and not someone who is interested in what they do.

Old cottages just stood there, some on the EU side, some only metres away in Belarus. In between them, a border fence with razor wire and cameras. It was hard to take in, for this used to be a cosy little hamlet, now its residents – families, friends and neighbours – are divided. They live in separate countries with very different ideologies.

'Don't get too close,' one of the Lithuanian guards called over to me as I ventured feet from the fence.

'Do you ever communicate with the Belarusian border guards?' I called back. He walked over, hand near his gun as he looked through the fence to the Belarusian side.

'Sure, I do. We see them and they see us. I wave and say hello, but usually they don't respond. Not so friendly guys.'

As if thinking aloud, I commented, 'I don't see any Belarusian guards on patrol.'

He smiled, 'Sure you don't, but they'll be watching you.'

'Do people try to get over this fence?'

'Every day, every single day,' he replied. 'Lots of smuggling goods, especially cigarettes, but also people, some Belarussians trying to escape Belarus, but also many other nationalities who come from places such as Pakistan, Afghanistan and many others. They come through Russia and Belarus and try to get into Europe. Every day we have this problem.'

I looked around at the smattering of houses on both sides of the divide. 'This little collection of houses, families and friends, are split in two by this fence. Can you tell me about it?'

'It happened almost overnight. One day no fence, then Lithuania joins Schengen and the fence goes up. Sometimes, people communicate over the fence, you know they shout over, we don't mind, they're not doing any harm, as long as they don't go to close. Sometimes a citizen from our side wants to speak to their brother who lives ten miles away over in another Belarus village. So they get someone from say, that house there,' he said pointing to a cottage over the fence. 'They go to the next village and tell the relative and they come back at a pre-arranged time and over the fence have a chat.' Another guard then joined in the conversation: 'Mostly it's just old people here, so they don't have electronic means to communicate.'

I know how Belarus operates, so even if these people here had internet, it is never a safe bet in Belarus. Online access is heavily controlled and policed. Apps are blocked, social media sites blocked, emails and phone calls listened into, political content blocked and of course, there is little press freedom either. If I was unfortunate enough to live on the other side of this divide, I think I would also communicate by talking over the fence.

I kept photographing and suddenly had a desire to see two people, one from each side of the divide come out of their respective houses and have a conversation over the fence. Now that would have been one hell of a photo. As if reading my thoughts, one of the Lithuanian border guards politely told me that I had gotten my photos and really should leave now. I thanked them for their time, shook hands and we continued our drive back to Vilnius.

In the car, as I scribbled down my notes for the day, it became clear to me that with the West and Russia moving ever further apart from each other, this border is likely to intensify in importance over the coming years.

Granted, the fence here (with regard to the awe factor) is not in the same league as say the walls in Bethlehem. Nor does it have the intensity of the razor wire fences around Melilla in North Africa. Nevertheless, due to my personal interest in the USSR and today's Russia, this border, probably more than most, fascinated me.

This fence is Europe's reminder that with growing Russian expansion and a weakening of the West, the old Cold War could well be about to heat up. Keep your eye on this part of the world.

Summing up

When I mention the word 'Schengen' to friends, whilst they admit to having heard of it, many do not have a full understanding of what it means. When I say it means the free movement of goods and people, no border checks when driving between the likes of France and Spain, they think it is a wonderful idea. It does sound good, doesn't it? However, that's not the full picture by any means. Especially not in the Europe we live in today. Of course, I should acknowledge and confirm here that the UK is not in Schengen.

When during one of my in-depth passionate debates with a friend who says he believes Schengen is a good idea, I tried the following tact to try to put it into personal terms. Interesting to note that while he thinks Schengen is a good idea when it comes to *his* free movement, he also grumbles about the amount of immigration into his European country. Sorry my friend, but if you join the Schengen club, you must accept all the house rules. You cannot pick and choose.

Take Germany and France, both highly successful countries, good business ethics and prosperous. Having a border free system between them for goods and people makes sense I guess. But, that's *not* what's happened with Schengen. I've been intrigued by Schengen for years and if the idea of it had been kept to certain countries with the same work ethics like the example I've just given, then it could have been successful. But no, it was highjacked by European politicians and then the flood-gates were opened to all.

Here is the analogy I gave to my friend regarding Schengen:

'I ask you to picture a giant block of apartments. Naturally, the inhabitants of each apartment are all different. Some apartments contain, for example, a family with four children, some contain a married couple with no children, others have single people in them, whilst in others there are old-age pensioners. In some apartments the inhabitants are working and on minimum wage, others are on state benefits through no fault of their own, some are just downright bone idle and never worked or contributed to the system, and a couple of apartments contain well off people who contribute much. Now, this block of apartments happen to be controlled by a leader, an unelected landlord, let us say, and when the individual tenants signed the lease to their apartment they also signed up to the number one golden rule. Which is... there are *no* locks on the doors of the individual apartments. Everyone is free to come and go into each other's apartment at will. So mate, would you sign up to that?'

I looked at my friend and could almost see the wheels turning in his mind. Had I finally gotten through to him? Damn, why hadn't I come up with this analogy years ago?

We are where we are on Schengen and, right now, much more money needs to be poured into the policing of it. Yet, if the EU ever expands the Schengen border to include such countries as Ukraine or Turkey, I think it would just have signed its own death warrant.

In reality, Schengen is one border for almost the entire European continent. That does not fill me with confidence when it comes to stopping illegal immigration, drugs and money laundering or people smuggling. Once anyone involved in illegal activities crosses the Schengen border, that is it, they are in. They can then travel totally free and unchecked right across country after country.

Schengen was a good idea, or it *could* have been a good idea, but it certainly has not worked out that way. I think it is only a matter of time before countries leave Schengen and reinstate their own borders. Personally, I am prepared to put up with border checks and the showing of my passport on a train from say Berlin to Amsterdam if it means we can properly tackle the above issues. In fact, I do it all the time in numerous other countries, it's not such a hassle really.

This book is about divided lands and the pain and hardship that that brings to many. Is it therefore a contradiction that I think the Schengen Agreement needs dismantling and national borders reinstated? No, because they are two completely different things. Dismantling Schengen would simply put back into place each individual country's long-standing and accepted border. Putting a border check back in between, say, Spain and France would not divide families and cause the problems faced in divided

Cyprus, for example. What it would do is allow each country to check who and what comes and goes. Anyone arriving in southern Spain after fleeing North Africa is now free to walk into France unchecked (or any other country in Schengen). I think in today's current climate, this needs a serious re-think.

With regard to stopping illegal immigration, drugs, money laundering, human trafficking, and the growing threat of terrorism... the sooner the 'one-size-fits-all' Schengen model goes, the better.

Update March 2017

In late November 2016, Turkish President Erdogan accused the EU of breaking promises over an earlier deal in which Turkey was promised visa-free travel for its citizens and accelerated membership talks. Erdogan has also threatened to allow hundreds of thousands more refugees to leave Turkey and travel into the EU.

It seems that not a day goes by without EU borders being at the forefront of news in the UK. Schengen remains, but its future looks bleak. Problems with illegal entry continue, especially in southern Europe, and, inside the EU itself, many thousands legally keep moving from the poorer east to the more prosperous west. Can this continue without change? Is it not time we had a grown-up debate on borders without resulting to cries of 'racism'?

Schengen in my opinion, is not fit for purpose.

10

Today's Russia

Population	Approximately 146.5 million
Currency	Russian ruble (RUB)

I HAVE WRITTEN this chapter over many months, and rewritten it countless times. More effort has gone into this chapter than any other in this book.

You may well be thinking, 'So what makes you qualified, George? How can you give an opinion on another country when you have claimed to be as unbiased as possible in all the divides in this book? In fact, why are you even writing an entire chapter on today's Russia?'

Fair comments, but in my defence I'd say: Russia deserves a chapter all of its own because of its historical connections and current 'influence' in the divides in Transnistria, Abkhazia, Nagorno-Karabakh and Crimea. Secondly, I accept that I am not qualified to talk about Russia like a professor of Political History is. However, I feel it's my time spent there on the ground that legitimises my right to my tuppence worth.

I first travelled to Russia in 1993, and to say it was a culture shock would be an understatement. Over the past 20 odd years, I have lived there, worked there, and have travelled the length and breadth of it. I have mixed and lived with numerous Russian families, often for weeks or months at a time. I know ordinary Russian citizens from all walks of life and social status. I have listened to them and bombarded them with questions about life in Russia. I have always been particularly fascinated to meet with Russians of an older generation, and have enjoyed many nights sitting listening to them tell me about life in the USSR – the good, the bad and the ugly. I have Russia under my skin. I love it yet it annoys me in equal measure. It just fascinates me, I guess I'm addicted to it. There is not a place on earth like it. It is not the West or Asia, it is not even European. It simply is Russia.

My focus for this chapter is the Russia of today and why I feel it is in many ways, almost a mirror image of its own past. I know that many of my Russian friends will not outwardly agree with what I am about to say (even if in private they grudgingly do so). Others will outright refute all of it, especially a certain female friend of mine. For example, in November 2015, we were discussing the Kiev Maidan revolution and she once again refused to believe anything I said about the majority being innocent pro-democracy protesters who did not use any violence whatsoever. I told her I had stood in Maidan with housewives, mothers, students, doctors, nurses, lawyers, people of all walks of life, even priests holding candles. She replied, 'You don't know what you are talking about, George. All you believe is Western propaganda. Don't ever tell me they were innocents. No! No! No! In Kiev, they were fascists.'

As a believer in free speech, of course she is entitled to her opinion. But remember this, I was there, she wasn't. She gets her news from the Kremlin-controlled news channels.

Just for the record, the majority of Russians I have spoken to back Putin's support of Syria's Assad. When I asked them either if they were aware of why and how the Syrian revolution had started and the killings of innocent civilians by the Assad regime, they told me that they did not know about that, or that they didn't believe it, dismissing it, yet again, as more Western propaganda.

Ok, tin hats on my dear Russian friends, for here is my take on Russia. Russia is historically a nation of poets, writers, classical musicians, artists, thinkers, and highly intelligent people. But tragically these creative people had the heart and soul ripped out of them by decades of Communism. As for today, many people from the former USSR are still a product of it and its mind-set.

I have concluded that many Russians do not really understand democracy and all that it entails. Moreover, how could they? They have never lived under a proper democracy, where the law and courts are independent from the government. They have experienced a society where bribery is endemic right through the system, where government controls increasing segments of life and where individuals who dare to speak out are often locked up on trumped up charges.

Churchill, to me, summed up Russia pretty well when he said it was, '... a riddle wrapped in a mystery inside an enigma.'

The Russia of the '90s or even the 2000s is *not* the Russia of today. I'm not talking about structural changes, I'm talking about the mood of the people, the general feel in the air. Suspicion and hatred of the West, and America in particular, is very prevalent in today's Russia.

Whilst there are many differences between the West and Russia, I would say the fundamental difference is this: In the West we value individualism, in Russia it is the complete opposite, it is collectivism that matters. Decades of control under communism did that I guess. Even Vladimir Putin said recently in a TV interview, 'The USA is based on individualism and Russia on collectivism.'

In the '90s, while huge swathes of the population struggled with the alien concept of the free market and capitalism, many, especially the young, wanted everything American and British. Be it a t-shirt, or trainers, or sweatshirts, everyone wanted to have a symbol of the West. It was cool to have a link to the West and the British Union Flag was proudly displayed on everything from numerous items of clothing to school bags. Russia was literally crumbling; no young person would have wanted a t-shirt with a Russian flag on it. They were embarrassed by their own country, which was seen at the time as a joke. Oh, how things have changed.

In the Russia of the early '90s, the immense grip the once all-powerful Soviet elite had vanished overnight. It was as if the population had just woken up from a collective coma that had lasted decades. There was a unique feeling in the air, a mix of excitement, worry, trepidation, uncertainty and bemusement. The gloves were off and it was winner takes all. Not only could people now make money, but they could also do what they wanted, be it legal or not. The system/the authorities, for once, did not control Russia during this time, it was a free for all. The result was that many people felt lost and longed for the controlling influence of big brother.

The wearing of Western symbols in Russia has now almost vanished and is being replaced by the patriotic wearing of everything not just Russian, but, worryingly, Soviet. The hammer and sickle on posters, hats, scarves and clothing is now seen on a regular basis. I have even seen ice cream, all packaged up displaying the hammer and sickle on the wrapper. My Russian friends see no harm in it, 'Just a bit of fun,' they tell me. I struggle to see it that way.

So what happened with Russia, what went wrong? Paradise, of course, did not come with the end of Communism. Many thought they were going to walk into a land of milk and honey, but progress does not work like that. Even in the West, it takes time. It took Britain decades, or even longer, to have a fully functioning democracy. Russia does not have this and I have come to accept that, now, it probably never will.

Many Russians wanted what we had and expected it quick. But that did not happen. Many got poorer, and criminal gangs and mafia ran the roost. Capitalism in Russia in the '90s was like the Wild West; it was not a nice experience. I was there, I saw it first hand. Many became despondent and started to look to the past, not for communism but for reassurance and guidance from those in charge.

Nowadays, when thinking of the West and its values, many Russians seem to think: 'been there, tried it, it didn't work'.

Many Russians needed a saviour in the '90s, and along came Vladimir Putin who started a long process of rebuilding Russian pride. How did he do it? Very cleverly. He started to blame many of Russia's economic problems on those who had benefited from the early days of capitalism. He then slowly but surely brought former state-owned industries back under Kremlin control. Businessmen were accused of tax evasion, and the public lapped it up. He then started spending his new billions on modernising the near obsolete Russian military. The terrible new Russian national anthem was dropped and replaced with the stirring music of the old Soviet anthem, albeit with new words.

The Kremlin then started to blame many of Russia's ills on the West, and, once again, vast swathes of the population lapped it up. 'Everything wrong in Russia is the fault of someone else'. Not all, of course, believe this, but many do. The Kremlin now controls nearly all the media. Anyone who speaks out and, more importantly, is a real threat, is dealt with, often harshly. I remember in the '90s, Russian TV actually showed its own version of the political satire programme *Spitting Image*. Yeltsin was shown as a buffoon and many others in power were targeted. Russians had never seen this before, and they loved being able to poke fun at those who led them. Can you imagine this happening in today's Russia? Not a chance. For all of Yeltsin's failings, one thing is clear, there was freedom of speech during that time, a damn sight more than there is today.

The West does need to come in for criticism when it comes to Russia. More should have been done to help Russia with the painful transition from Communism to the free market and democracy. Back in the '90s, I used to shake my head when I heard British politicians tell us that Russia now had democracy and that everything would be fine. Nothing could have been further from the truth. We could have helped in the early days in a way we simply cannot now – almost no Western help or influence is allowed in Russia today.

The West did not understand Russia in the breakup of the USSR and, even today, it still does not seem to get it. It does not understand what makes the Russian people tick. I think we have lost the battle to take Russia with us into a democratic world. Too little too late, for it doesn't matter what we say or do, our ways are not trusted and we only drive more Russians closer to Vladimir Putin and his vision of a powerful new Russia.

However, let us have a reality check here: do the Russian people really want to return to a communist state ran by the terrifying KGB? While the people in the West were living in relative comfort, enjoying freedom of speech and the ability to kick out their government every few years, the USSR with its vast arsenal of nuclear weapons was struggling to feed its own people. It was a basket-case economy. No freedom of speech for citizens, little freedom of expression for artists, choreographers and composers. No vote, no choice of who governed you. In addition, apart from the privileged few with connections to the Communist Party, there was virtually no foreign travel allowed. People had no access to far superior Western products. Let me clarify that last point, I do not mean superficial luxury items like a BMW, I mean decent clothes, household goods that weren't drab and toilet roll that didn't rip your ass to shreds. Do you remember what you were doing in the late 1980s in the West? Many of my friends in the nuclear superpower USSR were standing in long lines queueing up to buy cheap sausage, bread, milk, butter and all the basics. Often when they got to the front of the queue, the shelves were bare. Socialism is supposed to be about equality and capitalism greed they say. Nonsense. During the Soviet times, people queued and lived a spartan existence, whilst high up members of the Communist Party shopped at stores that had luxury Western products flown in especially for them. Many of those in power did not drink cheap vodka but instead enjoyed Scottish whisky and French Cognac; and instead of vile Soviet-made cigarettes, they smoked Marlboros. Socialism and equality in the USSR? Yeah, right.

To be fair, the USSR did have good state education, albeit one that taught its students a very warped version of history. It paid its pensions on time, everyone had a job and wages and, unlike in the terrible 1990s, they were also paid on time. However, the UK has an excellent state education and pensions a damn sight better than Russia. It also has a health service, which, while not perfect, is the envy of the world. Nothing that Soviet apologists still come out with is worth living under.

Take a society like the old East Germany, which some *still* claim was good. East Berlin was blocked off by a wall and patrolled by guards who had a shoot to kill policy when it came to anyone trying to escape to the freedom of the West. Many viewed East Germany as the biggest political prison camp in the world. I have recently returned from there after having interviewed a very unrepentant ex-Stasi officer. The East German regime, and the way it treated its own people, was an affront to human decency.

Do Russians, Transnistrians and others want to go back to a totally controlled state? No, of course they do not. So, what do they want? Many want Western luxury products; they want the internet and they want access to money; they want the ability to travel to the West, and enjoy the trappings of it, yet they do not want to live by its ethics or way of life. Many Russians who have made it big where money is concerned, take great pride in showing it off. Many of my ordinary Russian friends find that vulgar. Interestingly, I have come across far more money-orientated people in today's Russia than in the West. In Russia, money really is power.

Today, thousands of young men and women in Moscow are happy to sing the Soviet national anthem and fly red flags on May Day. However, I'd bet my life that they would not want to live under a real Stalinist system. They would not last five minutes. Maybe it is time they started to think of the millions of their fellow Russians murdered by Stalin – not just those who spoke out against him, but also the landowners, the intellects and the free-thinkers. Maybe they should learn about the ordinary people who were being locked up in the 1980s as political prisoners. Nobody did this better than the KGB and their comrades in the East German Stasi.

What do many patriotic Russians think about their country? From my experience, something along the lines of: 'We are Russia. We are strong, we have a great history, we don't need the West, we don't want the West. We will do things our way, the Russian way. Take your liberal views and fuck off and leave us alone'. I am sorry if that sounds crude, but that is often the way it is.

Russia, in my opinion, is most definitely evolving backwards. Their tolerance is not good. Alongside the huge rise in patriotism, racism is rampant. Some TV presenters, all indirectly working for the Kremlin, openly spout vile views live on air, especially about the Russian pet hate, homosexuality.

Of course, there are people who are different in Russia – be it gay, or anti-Kremlin, or even pro-West. Nevertheless, they need to remember this golden rule: If you want to have a quiet harassment free life, keep your lifestyle and views to yourself. Your life should be private, not public. Moreover, if you are in any way influential, you should not speak out against the Kremlin or stand in an election. Chances are you will be busted for the classic ruse called 'tax evasion'. Others end up dead like Boris Nemtsov and other numerous journalists over the years. Who is behind these killings? I do not know. But I ask this, is it just coincidence that so many high-profile people who have bravely spoken out and taken a stance against the authorities find themselves dead? Outspoken journalists in Russia, are in my opinion, the bravest of the brave.

Just to clarify, I do not believe that the West is perfect, far from it.

But I do get fed up hearing constant criticism of, say, the UK from Brits themselves who live there and enjoy (compared to many countries around the world) the freedom and safety it provides.

In the West, society has evolved to respect the rights of the individual, to embrace who they are and have equality. It is not perfect, and the West still has much evolving to do, but Russia is moving in the other direction. Today's Russia is in general more homophobic and racist than I could have ever imagined it would turn out to be. Ignorance about other countries and about how others lead their lives is simply staggering.

Vladimir Putin famously said a few years back, 'The breakup of the USSR was the biggest geopolitical disaster of the 20th century.' Chilling words indeed. Personally, I was delighted the USSR broke up and gave millions the chance to be free for the first time in decades. Ask the peoples of the Baltics if they would like to go back to it...

The USSR was a system that brutalised and destroyed the soul of millions. A system that sent untold numbers of its own people to gulags. A system that up until the mid-1980s was still locking up people as political prisoners.

The USSR was not only economically bust but also morally bankrupt. Today, a newer, more acceptable version of it seems to have been cleverly cultivated. The biggest link to the old USSR is the organised and professional whipping up of patriotism and nostalgia. Mr Putin has even recently been on an offensive to help rehabilitate Stalin. There is a gleaming new mosaic of Stalin in the Moscow Metro and Vladimir Putin in May 2015 said, 'The Stalin regime never aimed to exterminate entire ethnic groups.'

Try telling that to the Tatar people.

Putin is rewriting history and it seems to be working. And all this for a man who had millions of his own people enslaved and killed.

Russian history is presented to the people as a series of glorious victories over its enemies, while the crimes of the USSR are brushed away, not taught and not mentioned. To criticise or even question Russia is now seen as being 'anti-Russian'. Very clever indeed.

After what you have just read directly above, this next section may be confusing. Learning about it certainly confused me, initially. When I was in Russia in late 2015, I noticed a remarkable item on the news one morning (not Russian state TV, BBC online). The Russian authorities had just opened a new museum dedicated to the millions who died in the Soviet Gulags in the 1930s to the 1950s. I was astonished, because under

Putin's rule, Stalin's crimes have been downplayed repeatedly. I have thought long and hard about what to write regarding this (after initially thinking that it simply did not make any sense whatsoever).

Pictures of Stalin were banned under Khrushchev, but as I have already mentioned, we have seen Stalin's' rehabilitation by Russian authorities. So why have they officially allowed this museum to open? A friend in Moscow said to me, 'It's a ploy, a ploy to deflect attention away from our current problems and other Soviet crimes committed against ordinary people in the decades after Stalin.'

Now, that made me think.

Firstly, I salute the Russian authorities for opening this museum. But it's not enough. The buck does not stop with Stalin. They seem to want to make people feel that crimes against the Russian people only happened under Stalin. However, that is not true. Granted nothing happened from 1950 onwards on a 'Stalin scale', but people continued to be executed and held as political prisoners in fear of the KGB. They may not have been called Gulags anymore, but the USSR was locking up political prisoners even in the early 1980s.

What about the brutal put downs of pro-democracy protesters in Prague and Budapest in the '50s and '60s? These people wanted democracy, but were labelled as hooligans or fascists. They were gunned down in the streets. One only has to visit the House of Terror in Budapest or the KBG museum in Vilnius to see the terror that many people faced in their daily lives. A plaque in Vilnius states that during the Soviet occupation of Lithuania (which did not end until 1991) more than 300,000 Lithuanians were exiled, imprisoned, killed.

Stalin is controversial in Russia, but most people I have spoken with over the years do like him. They like him for making Russia a world power. They have told me that the sacrifices of those who died were worth it. I disagree. It's that, 'collectivism versus the individual' again. Others think he was wonderful and totally reject the mass killings, saying the West has grossly exaggerated them. Very few have ever told me that what he did to the Russian people was evil. In addition, very few Russians I have met (this being my real point) have any idea what was done to ordinary citizens by the Soviet authorities/KGB and their counterparts in other communist states.

I once took a Russian friend to visit the House of Terror in Budapest where people were tortured during the Nazi era and then in Soviet times.

She had previously told me that she had learned from her family that Russia had been very good to Hungary. She certainly did not know about 1956 and the slaughter. She walked with me through that well documented building in total shock. Later, outside, she sat down on a bench and cried.

Germany and its people know their dark history from the 1930s and 1940s. They do not deny Hitler and what he did. Why? Because they are taught about it. Many Russians do not know their real USSR history, they only know about the 'glorious victories'. That is why they claim most things I say as 'Western propaganda'. I even had a young Russian friend who was visiting me in Spain in 2013, tell me that Russia had saved all of Europe. She said that all peoples from the former republics and other eastern bloc countries should be grateful. I warned her that she should be extremely careful if she ever decided to voice these views in places such as Budapest, Prague, Vilnius, Tallinn, and Warsaw.

On another occasion, a Russian friend recently told me that Britain had started the Falklands War by invading and bombing the Argentinian women and children who lived on the islands. I didn't know whether to laugh or cry when I heard that, for it had to be the most brain-washed, ignorant and ridiculous statement I had ever heard.

This museum in Moscow will change nothing (even though those who love Stalin can now see that their own government admits millions perished). With all the recent rehabilitation of Stalin, and his face appearing in the metro and on posters, this museum seems to be a token gesture. Or as my friend said, 'A ploy, to deflect.'

Putin seems to have the majority of the Russian population supporting him. Some of my educated and open-minded Russian friends do not support him and do not believe the constant high poll ratings that Putin always gets. They say the figures are fudged. I cannot for the life of me understand why anyone thinks there is democracy in Russia. I just do not think it is possible that ex-KGB officers can run a country in a free democratic way. I said in a previous chapter that life has been far too cheap for far too long in Northern Ireland. As for Russia, the individual has been way down the list of priorities when it comes to building a 'strong state' for far too long.

I meet many Russians who support Putin and swallow all the anti-West bile. I have almost given up trying to get them to think for themselves. I constantly fail to get through. It saddens me immensely. I am on their side, but they can't see it. I will share a secret with you, I have been told by many Russian friends that what they cannot abide is Westerners criticising Russia. Even if I say something that they know to be true, it makes their blood boil. They themselves can voice said criticism, but they certainly do not like foreigners mentioning the criticism. Many seem to want to defend 'mother Russia' at all costs. It is the 'State versus the individual' again.

I do not think there is a nation on earth who has suffered so much for so long under their own leaders as the Russians have. For hundreds of years, the Tsars did precious little for ordinary Russians, with most of them living in terrible poverty. Then decades of communism killed millions and broke their spirit. If that was not enough, the car crash that was the 1990s of rampant crime and corruption left them even more demoralised. So, if the future doesn't look too bright, why not just look back? Look back with seriously rose-tinted spectacles, ignoring all the past bad bits, praying for a man who makes them feel strong again. Putin has done that in bucket loads, he has brought back a tremendous sense of pride. He has made Russians feel that Russia is great again. Putin is one very clever man indeed and he understands his people better than the rest of the world does. Like I said previously, individualism is not important, collectivism is. I would guess that the Kremlin's number one goal must be to keep it this way. If Russians in their millions started to think as individuals and not look to the state, the Kremlin's dream of control would crumble, just like the Berlin Wall did.

As a nation, many Russians may well think of their country as stronger these days. However, as individual human beings, they are suffering. That suffering is not because of anything the West has done to them; it is because of the system they live under and support. Unlike in the USSR, when they had no choice, they now have to take a large chunk of responsibility for the situation they find themselves in. They are allowing themselves to be held back by an increasingly repressive system. Only they and they alone can free themselves from this and join their rightful place, where they should be, alongside the peoples of Europe, living in democracy with free speech and accountable governments with effective opposition parties.

Will they take this stance? Many individuals will and do so now. Collectively though, I doubt it will happen. Russia is on the path it is on and I cannot see it changing direction any time soon. If ever. I genuinely feel for the Russian people at large. Russia today is not where it should be. It is spinning backwards.

With regard to helping someone out of the mess they are in: you can lead a horse to water, but you can't make it drink.

Despite clamping down on freedoms right across the board, Putin's personal poll ratings amongst Russians seem to always be over 80 per cent. Google the phrase 'Stockholm Syndrome' and make up your own mind. They want a strongman. They have him. 'If you don't stand up and be counted, you get the government you deserve.' I mentioned this to one of my more enlightened Russian friends and while he agreed with my statement about many of his fellow countrymen having Stockholm Syndrome, he told me that it's not as simple as just standing up to the system.

'The Russian system,' he told me, 'is absolutely rotten to the core. It is not just a case of getting rid of Putin. The whole system needs to go. Even if Putin were to somehow lose the next election and a guy who stood for democracy won it, nothing would change.'

'But that doesn't make sense,' I said. 'Sure it would take the new guy much time to turn things around, but if he truly believed in a new way of doing things then...'

My friend interrupted me and put me straight.

'George, he would be able to change nothing. Listen, the whole system is corrupt. It's a cancer that runs through all of Russian life. What needs to happen in Russia is change on a scale you can't imagine. Remember, that all through the Russian system every level of power and security and state business, is ran by people who are either ex KGB, ex-communists, or billion dollar businessmen. Everything and everyone is connected. Russia is a mafia state. None of them care about democracy, rule of law and such things. Everything in all levels would need to be thrown out with the thrash. Parliament, the judges and entire legal system, FSB, regional governors, and especially our police. Everything that is connected with how our country is run must go. Then we must start from scratch with people who have known and care about such things as real fair elections, true freedom of speech, and a system where government does not control the law and police. Just voting out Putin would solve nothing. Do you understand me?'

I did. I do. He is right.

Update March 2017

Many in the West were shocked by official reaction to Russian football fans fighting in France during Euro 2016. Sadly, I wasn't. Whilst the British press and politicians condemned the violence brought about by the usual minority drunken English fans, the Russians applauded their 'fans'. The establishment and press were proud and were actually praising them. Igor Lebedev, who is not only an MP but also the deputy of the Russian parliament and a member of the executive committee of the Russian football union, said; 'I don't see anything wrong with the fans fighting. Quite the opposite, well done lads, keep it up!'

Before this book went to print, I sent this chapter to a Russian friend who is not really into politics. I asked for her honest feedback and told her she could say anything she wanted. After taking much time to read the chapter, we talked on Skype. To be honest, I was nervous. Her opinion: with a sad somewhat heavy heart, she told me what I had written about her country was pretty much spot on. Another Russian who I have known for 23 years also read this chapter. She is the most open-minded Russian I know, yet she is very much in the minority. She told me the following:

'Nothing in your Russia chapter is offensive to me. As sad and depressing as it is, it's pretty much the truth. As much as I despise traditional show-off patriotism so popular in Russia these days, I still love my 'mother Russia' but the new free times haven't given us much to be proud about and a lot to be ashamed of. That might be one of the reasons people are turning to the past and elevating it in their minds. Too bad that instead of being inspired by the greats of the past, like writers and composers (who frequently had trouble with those who governed at the time), to do something worthy and inspiring themselves, people somehow glorify the system that existed at those times. That is just mind boggling to me. But that's how it is.

'And do not get me started on the rise of the bloody Russian

Orthodox Church, or I might explode. Thriving during the Tsars, oppressed and almost annihilated during the Soviet times, now we have a happily-ever-after union of the Church and the ex-KGB/ communist establishment happily ever after brainwashing people all the while enjoying their well-fed and generously funded union bliss. You just never know what's going to hit you next: pro-Kremlin propaganda or some religious bullshit or both. It pains me greatly to see this train wreck my country is experiencing and to know there's nothing I can do about it.'

Afterthought

I HAVE HAD MANY poignant experiences related to Russia over the years, and want to share three with you: May Day in Moscow, a visit to Volgograd, and in March 2014 – Kiev's Maidan.

Never could I have imagined from anytime between 1993 and even up to the middle of the 2000s that I would be witnessing what you are about to read. I would like to point out that I wrote the following when I was there on the ground and not while I was researching this book.

May Day in Moscow 2014

International Workers Day or, as I prefer to call it when in Moscow, the day of the un-dead red. I have attended numerous May Days in Moscow over the years and watched them change and evolve.

This is not an official government day, there are no vehicles with missiles or goose steeping soldiers stomping through Red Square – that's for Victory Day on 9 May. No, May Day was for when the humble people came out onto the streets to celebrate the day of the workers and the so-called glorious achievements of socialism.

For decades during the Soviet times, you had no choice, you took to the streets and waved your flag whether you believed in it or not. Staying at home listening (in secret) to the BBC World Service on short wave radio was certainly not a wise excuse to give for non-attendance.

Since 1991, you don't have to take part, it's only for those who want to. And that for me is the fascinating thing to observe, how the numbers involved and type of people involved plays along with the political comings and goings of the current year.

Forget about trying to find out just how many people take part in pro-communist marches, you will get a different answer from whichever side you listen to. In 1996, I witnessed the biggest one I ever saw in my life. Yeltsin's government claimed the number was as low as 10,000. The Communist Party said it was a quarter of a million. I do not know exactly how many, of course, but I guarantee to you it was nearer the Communist party figures than Yeltsin's. That was only weeks before the Communist leader Gennady Zyuganov almost caused a political earthquake when he ran Yeltsin a very close second for the presidency. He has never come close since.

In the 2000s, once Putin came to power and with Russia becoming increasingly more prosperous, the Communist Party looked old hat. During those years, the numbers on parade declined to the few thousands. May Day seemed to me to be turning into a sideshow, just a dwindling rump of dissatisfied old people who, through rose or red tinted specs, longed for an era that was over. However, today, Russian pride has never been stronger, and across all ages at that.

Watching young men and woman carrying pictures of Stalin in the second decade of the 21st century is unnerving. Stalin was one of the biggest mass murderers the world has ever seen, with millions of Russians dying. Yet few seem to blink an eye when Russians parade through the streets carrying pro-Stalin posters and claiming him a hero.

Can you image the international outcry if a German walked down the street in Munich carrying a poster in support of Hitler?

The march, as always, starts in front of the gigantic statue of Lenin, just outside the Oktyabrskaya metro station, a few kilometres from the city centre. Thousands upon thousands of men, women and children of all ages were kitted out in all things red and buoyed up, ready to show the world.

All streets have been cleared of traffic and the procession continues its slow march winding its way through the huge wide roads of the Russian capital. I am running around, darting in and out of the procession, taking photos left right and centre. The BBC are here, SKY, CNN and various other international channels and journalists. People hang huge Soviet flags out of dilapidated old apartment blocks from way up high. The crowd take notice and cheer. I climb a lamppost on the far side of the road from the Kremlin and get a stunning view as thousands of reds come marching over a bridge. The streets are full, it's a sea of red.

Eventually, as always, the demo ends in the same place every year, downtown Moscow, right in front of the statue of Karl Marx.

Sandwiched in the middle of the road, the Bolshoi Theatre behind me and the huge statue of Marx in front, I'm surrounded by thousands of comrades. Speeches are made by Zyuganov who bangs on about NATO and the West. I hear Ukraine mentioned and Crimea, which brings huge applause. I had not heard that in previous years.

The highlight of this day for me is at the very end when the crowd sings the old Soviet National Anthem. Written by Alexander Alexandrov, it is a stunning piece of music. As it blasts out from loudspeakers, I feel the hairs on the back of my neck stand up as the crowd in unison belt it out with a pride that is near indescribable.

Standing right next to me, is an old soldier in his late 80s, I would say. In full military uniform, his chest is covered in medals that I see include the Order of Lenin. He is simply bursting with pride. A tear rolls down his cheek as he sings.

The official Communist Party will never get back into power in Russia, but Putin's 'United Russia Party' is increasingly looking like a neo-communist party anyway.

The Russian bear has finally woken up after a long hibernation.

There is a buzz in Russia right now, and in my opinion, for all the wrong reasons.

Maidan, Kiev March 2014

I am writing this while still in Kiev, from an apartment, up a side street just off Independence Square. A square that now looks like a scene from a very realistic film set.

Only 48 hours before I arrived, government snipers from high up had been shooting to kill. Many picked off at random and shot dead.

Then, remarkably, the government fell, the President vanished and ranks of the armed to the teeth special police, simply melted away. Until they form a new government, the people run this city. Surprisingly there is no chaos, just a feeling of shock and a weird sense of calm.

The streets are black, caked in soot and the smell of burning is every-where, it gets into your skin and you cannot seem to wash it away. Burnt out cars and trucks are still visible. Buildings with smoke and gunfire damage evident. I look at the people's faces and right into their eyes. I see a mixture of elation, fear, resolve, shock, and exhaustion.

There are people walking around crying looking hopelessly lost. I am really struggling to write this. I feel choked.

Once the government fell, there could have so easily been a free for all orgy of theft, but no, there has been no looting. The self-restraint of the ordinary people I have seen will stand them in excellent stead in the eyes of the world. It certainly should.

Barricades of tyres, metal and barbed wire that stood as walls between people and the security forces are now shrines. Mountains of flowers lay where people were mown down. Individual shrines with photos and names. Utterly heart breaking. On more than one occasion this week I have had to go back to my apartment, I just couldn't take any more at that moment.

Back in my apartment, standing under a hot shower I rubbed hard to get the smoke grim and soot out of my skin. I sat down with a cold beer, clicked on YouTube on my laptop for I needed to watch something, anything that would take my mind off what I had just seen outside. The first episode of the classic British comedy 'Are You Being Served?' did the trick. However, half way through the second, I started to feel guilty. How could I sit in here with my clean clothes, cold beer and laugh at a TV programme? I felt ashamed. I put back on my dirty smoky clothes, and 15 minutes later was back out in Maidan standing with the people.

According to Russian news sites regarding Kiev, it's a 'fascist take over'. By email, a friend from Moscow tells me: 'What's happening to the Ukrainian people is terrible and it's all because America wants to take over the country.' I do not even bother replying to her, it is pointless.

I was in Kiev in 2004 after the Orange Revolution, but after the initial euphoria had died down, little changed as things went back to their corrupt old ways. Ten years on, we have just seen another revolution, but this time blood has been spilt.

No one, but no one can predict what will happen now this country. If we go by history, the omens are not good, and God only knows what Moscow's next move may be (NB the annexation of Crimea had not yet happened). The task for whoever comes into power will be to unite the Ukrainian people. In Kiev, doable, but six hours east of here in the pro-Russian cities, they are not pulling down statues of Lenin, they are protecting Lenin from being pulled down and are waving the hammer and sickle.

I was out wandering the soup kitchens that are supplying food and hot tea to the shattered protesters, when I noticed a man I had acknowledged a few times. Andrei and I got chatting and I asked him why they felt they still had to stay camped out like this.

'If we leave now, before a new government comes, then special police will come back.'

But good news came on Wednesday, when, to much applause, the infamous *Berkut* special police squad, responsible for the killings, were disbanded.

Millions of voters in Europe now wish to leave the EU. Countless regulations, bureaucracy, unaccountability and a wasting of taxpayer's money on huge bailouts disenchant them. However, in Kiev, Ukrainians have just shed their own blood on their own streets in order to move towards the EU.

I often get very despondent when I return to the UK, because I witness apathy and hear statements such as, 'Ah, I'm not voting in the next election, I can't be bothered.' I also hear comments about our 'terrible roads, failing schools, the NHS, the police, the UK political system.'

If there were an Olympic Games for whining, we Brits would win gold every time. I whole-heartedly admit, the UK is far from perfect, but next time you hear someone randomly slag off the workings of the UK, tell them to get some perspective and spare a thought for Ukraine and her people. In the UK, many of us do not even know we are living.

I have spent several hours writing this, but I sincerely doubt if what I have just written above will do any justice whatsoever to what I have witnessed in Kiev.

I have never experienced anything like it in my life. I feel numb and empty.

Stalingrad 2011

A concrete monolith, the hotel exterior was very unwelcoming, and inside not much more positive could be said about the middle age receptionist either. After 20 minutes of her company while filling in paperwork, I harboured no doubts she had graduated from the Soviet school of charm with an A+. This is *exactly* how Moscow felt back in the day.

My room was certainly rustic – dirty bathroom, electrical wires protruding from small holes, and the tiny balcony was crumbling away. Really not safe, and, since I was ten floors up, I decided not to venture out onto it again. Although officially going by the name of Volgograd since 1961, in the eyes of millions of Russians, this city I was stood in, will forever be known as Stalingrad.

It is always difficult in Russia at any time of the year to escape WWII, or as the Russians call it, 'The Great Patriotic War'. But here and especially right now, it's impossible, as Russia has recently celebrated the 70th anniversary of the battle of Stalingrad.

Often seen as a personal clash of hatred between Hitler and Stalin, the battle of Stalingrad saw Hitler determined to take the city that bore Stalin's name. Stalin, in return, demanded of his Marshal Zhukov 'Not a step backward'. The result was the surprising defeat of the mighty German Sixth Army and a major turning point in the war. It will never be known exactly how many died during the battle of Stalingrad, but it has been estimated to be around two million. What a waste of life, on both sides.

It is 2011 and I witness not just old museums stuffed with photos, but pro-Soviet victory posters prominently displayed on billboards, red flags, and streets named after Soviet heroes. In the UK we commemorate Remembrance Day. We do so by wearing poppies, standing in silence as the bugler plays the Last Post and we remember the fallen. In Russia, they celebrate victory day, many boisterously wave red flags as goose-stepping soldiers and tanks pass by to the blaring tunes of Soviet army songs. There is a difference.

In a city centre coffee shop, Anna, my young waitress, told me, 'The government is going to change the name of our city back to Stalingrad.' She beamed proudly as I smiled with respect while all the time feeling unnerved.

It was below zero with a wind chill of god only knows what when I hailed a taxi at 9.00pm. 'Mamayev Kurgan', I simply told the driver who needed no further instruction. Ten minutes later, he dropped me off outside the city and I began the long climb up the 200 steps. Each step chillingly representing a day in the famous battle of 1942–43.

I kept my head down as I wanted to count each step and wanted to leave it as long as possible before laying my eyes on my destination. Eventually I looked up, and up, and up... and took her in, in all her defiant glory, *Mamayev Kurgan*. Or as many simply call her, Mother Russia. A sculpture of a woman so gigantic that from her foot to the tip of her sword she stands at a colossal 269 feet.

To me, though, it was much more than just her height, it was the symbolism. I am certainly no apologist for the USSR, but I felt humbled being in her presence. I could hear music, haunting angelic sounds coming from the nearby eternal flame building.

Silently I stood in the freezing cold at the feet of Mother Russia, thinking of those who perished and were buried under her frozen earth.

I tried to imagine the horrors they had gone through at the battle of Stalingrad.

I could not.

Summary

Minds are like parachutes, they only function when open.

THE ABOVE IS A quote by the Scottish businessman Thomas Dewar (1864–1930) and it is my favourite quote of all time. I refer to it not just when I am working but also in my personal life when I find myself making decisions and judgments. It is such a powerful statement.

I make a real effort these days to try not to complain about life; well, not as much I used to anyway. However, when I do find myself back in the UK and moaning about something, I hear a little voice in my head reminding me of a divided country that I have recently been in. I picture the people and what they have to go through each and every day. It is a reality check and suddenly the road works on the drive to Edinburgh do not seem worth grumbling about anymore.

It seems that the more affluent we become, the more we complain, especially about everyday things. We in the West often do take our lives for granted. We moan about the NHS, the schools, the roads, the police and just about everything. We do like a good moan don't we?

But would we Brits really prefer to live under a repressive system like Belarus? Think our roads are bad? Come to Ukraine. Think our politicians are corrupt? I could take you to numerous countries and show you endemic corruption that runs through the heart of all echelons of society. Think the British police are corrupt? Don't make me laugh. Compared to large parts of the world they are a shining beacon of hope. Our police are there to protect us – the citizens. In some other countries they are there to protect the state and keep citizens suppressed. No comparison really.

Each divide I researched for this book has its own reasons for being. Religious divides, ethnic divides, political divides and some with all three. A small dose of patriotism is fine I guess, but rampant nationalism is becoming increasingly dangerous as it seems to create an 'us and them' mentality. Many define themselves simply by accident of birth. I feel it is often the same with religion, in the sense when say someone claims they are 'proud' to be a Protestant. Fair enough, but if they had been born in Iran, they would have been brought up under Islam and would therefore be proud to be a Muslim. Once again, I feel it is often an accident of birth that decides who is proud of what.

What have I learned from MGD? Apart from the obvious historical and current situation of each divide, I have learned mostly about human beings and what makes them tick. Unfortunately, what makes many tick is what their government or religion tells them makes them tick. There's too many sheep out there, in my view. People in divided countries must stop believing everything their side tells them, stop believing that they are always right and that the other side is wrong, for nothing is ever black or white. More people should also realise that those 'on the other side' are, at the end of the day, just like them. They may have a different flag, or belong to a different religion, but they are, when you get right down to it, just people. Ordinary people who want to earn money to provide for their families and live the best they can.

I could conclude that each divide needs its own unique set of requirements to resolve the issue at hand. To a certain extent, yes, but, there is one thing, one simple thing that would help to bring peace and stability to many divided and contested parts of the world. The magic solution? Talking to each other. Simply talking. At every level, official, diplomatic but especially at street level. Talking and mixing with the 'other side'. Easy? Definitely not, not as long as minds are closed and vested interests remain. Ultimately, only ordinary people on the ground can solve the mess, especially in areas where governments stoke up nationalism, suspicion and hatred of the other side. I will never forget when a Russian once said to me, 'If Russia doesn't have enemies, it will invent them.'

Peace is possible, if both sides talk and listen to each other. Naive? No, it is realistic, in my view anyway. Minds are like parachutes remember...

I accept that if people who live in one of these divides read this book, many will criticise me. They will say I am being naive and do not understand their problems because I don't live there and haven't been personally affected. Of course, I understand that point and to a certain degree, they are right, however I don't totally agree. Why? Well, I think not living there all the time and not having been brought up fed on a diet of one-sidedness does help me to understand the situation on the ground. It often takes someone from the outside who is looking in to be able to see the issues more clearly than those who are constantly inside the problem. That is why we have marriage guidance counsellors, or whatever they are called these days. Someone not directly involved, from the outside, looking in. Makes sense to me anyway.

We humans have created the divides; we have created the fear hatred and suspicion of the other side. We have put the walls up, both physical and mental, and only we can take them down again. The physical walls though are the easy bit; it is the mental walls that seem to be much harder to break down.

There is hatred and killings over religion and land, Muslims killing other Muslims, Greeks hating Turks they have never met, and Palestinian kids on children's TV saying that they want to kill Jews. What is wrong with the human race? Are we all suffering from a collective mental disease?

Revenge over past injustices are not worth killing over. Sure, you may finally have got the man who killed your friend ten years ago, but that man you just killed is also someone else's friend, and in turn they will come after you or another of your friends – and so it goes on and on and on...

We must move on from the past, we must stop carrying the hatred. What happened in and around each divide in question, happened, it cannot be undone, but it can be prevented from happening again.

I am not suggesting we all sit around the campfire, smile and sing 'Kumbaya'. I am not dreaming and hoping for a world of milk and honey where we all skip along holding hands. But things could be so much better in our world than they currently are.

Wherever we are from, whatever our backgrounds, history or personal beliefs, we are all human beings sharing one planet. All life is precious.

George R Mitchell

Luath Press Limited
committed to publishing well written books worth reading

LUATH PRESS takes its name from Robert Burns, whose little collie Luath (*Gael.,* swift or nimble) tripped up Jean Armour at a wedding and gave him the chance to speak to the woman who was to be his wife and the abiding love of his life. Burns called one of 'The Twa Dogs' Luath after Cuchullin's hunting dog in Ossian's *Fingal*. Luath Press was established in 1981 in the heart of Burns country, and now resides a few steps up the road from Burns' first lodgings on Edinburgh's Royal Mile. Luath offers you distinctive writing with a hint of unexpected pleasures.

Most bookshops in the UK, the US, Canada, Australia, New Zealand and parts of Europe either carry our books in stock or can order them for you. To order direct from us, please send a £sterling cheque, postal order, international money order or your credit card details (number, address of cardholder and expiry date) to us at the address below. Please add post and packing as follows: UK – £1.00 per delivery address; overseas surface mail – £2.50 per delivery address; overseas airmail – £3.50 for the first book to each delivery address, plus £1.00 for each additional book by airmail to the same address. If your order is a gift, we will happily enclose your card or message at no extra charge.

ILLUSTRATION: IAN KELLAS

Luath Press Limited
543/2 Castlehill
The Royal Mile
Edinburgh EH1 2ND
Scotland

Telephone: 0131 225 4326 (24 hours)
email: sales@luath.co.uk
Website: www.luath.co.uk